WITHDRAWN

J. WINEBRENNER.

John Winebrenner

John Winebrenner

Nineteenth Century Reformer

Richard Kern

Central Publishing House

Harrisburg, Pennsylvania

1974

JOHN WINEBRENNER: NINETEENTH CENTURY REFORMER

Published by

Central Publishing House

611 South Seventeenth Street

Harrisburg, Pa. 17105

Line drawings by

Marilyn Kern

Library of Congress Card No. 74—84501

Printed in U. S. A.

Dedication:

To Drs. Aletha Herwig, Gale Ritz, J. Russell Bucher, Sidney Mead—and all those gentle scholars who have taken their students seriously.

218098

PREFACE

To the extent that the name John Winebrenner is recognized at all, he is usually presented as the rather obscure founder of a small American church, today known as the Churches of God in North America. The following pages are an attempt to make Winebrenner less obscure and to place his work as a churchman in the general context of the reforming movements which were so much a part of America in the first half of the nineteenth century.

In presenting Winebrenner as I do, I trust I am not claiming more for him than history properly allows. No attempt is being made to present a man who is larger than life—one of the Great American Reformers. I doubt that Winebrenner himself would be happy cast in that mold. Rather, the following pages attempt to give Winebrenner his due. Long presented as a rather stern, uncompromising churchman whose primary function in life was destined to be the founding and early care of the Church of God, Winebrenner was in fact a multidimensional human being with an outstanding breadth of interest, whose reforming touch included, but was not limited to, ecclesiastical matters.

It would be impossible to list everyone who contributed to this work by sharing their time, ideas, and research with me. However, special appreciation is extended to the following for their generous assistance: Dr. W. T. Jackson, Acting President, Winebrenner Theological Seminary, Findlay, Ohio; Dr. William J. McBride, Vice President of Academic Affairs, Findlay College, Findlay, Ohio; Mr. Stuart Stiffler, Librarian, Findlay College; Mr. George Bricker, Librarian and Professor of Theology, Lancaster Theological Seminary, Lancaster, Pennsylvania; Mr. Charles Coleman Sellers, Librarian, Dickinson College, Carlisle, Pennsylvania; Mrs. Florence Steigerwalt, Reference Librarian, Pennsylvania State Library, Harrisburg, Pennsylvania; Pastor Jack Parthemore and Mr. Earl Reigel, Central Publishing House, Harrisburg, Pennsylvania; Ms. Mary Winebrenner, Hastings, Michigan; Ms. Gretta Spier, Ms. Laura Evison, Mr. Nicholas Smiar, and Mr. Melvyn Cornelius, Chicago, Illinois; Mr. Robert Grant Crist, Camp Hill, Pennsylvania; Dr. and Mrs. F. D. Rayle, Harrisburg, Pennsylvania; Ms. Constance Briner, Mr. Kenneth Kope, and the faculty, staff, and student body at Winebrenner

Theological Seminary; Ms. Ida Hickernell, Findlay, Ohio; Pastor James Moss, Finksburg, Maryland; Pastor Randall Bistline, York, Pennsylvania; and Ms. Marilyn Kern, Findlay—whose help has been inestimable.

Richard Kern
Findlay College
1973

INTRODUCTION

One disadvantage of the American denominational system is the fact that it is difficult for people to become familiar with religious leaders in different traditions. Anyone who goes to and fro among the churches, particularly an historian who visits archives and repositories or seminaries—any place where the bearded forefathers or bonneted grandmothers peer out from dusty paintings on the wall—knows that these figures tower over the traditions but are rarely heard of beyond them.

Too bad. We miss out on some lively company, as this study of John Winebrenner emphatically illustrates. The temptation may be for members of the Churches of God in North America alone to read this book. Let us hope they read it, for while it makes some demands upon the reader, it is particularly rewarding because of them. Richard Kern's book departs from the overused mold of denominational biography. Too many of these are exaggerated, pious, unrealistic if not untrue—and eminently forgettable. The heirs are happy that such a book exists; they keep it on a coffee table. But, reassured by its mere existence, they find no reason to read it.

This book takes Winebrenner seriously, and in effect honors the churches which regard him as a spiritual father by saying, "This is as straightforward and unbiased a story, as academically solid, as one would write were he or she dealing with Ralph Waldo Emerson or Theodore Roosevelt." This is not to say that it is a muckraking or debunking book, either. Winebrenner's faults are noticed, but not enlarged upon. Kern wears his tradition lightly but well.

Back to the point: it would be regrettable if only "Winebrennerians" of all sorts read the book. For its subject is an authentic American original, a major minor figure of the kind revered by other churches to whom the Churches of God have paid too little attention. I should confess that I went through bachelor, master's, and half-way into doctoral programs in the field of religious history before ever encountering him. The first encounter was pleasant but faintly negative. I used his version (1848) of I. D. Rupp's *History of all the Religious Denominations in the United States* and shared something of his antagonist John

Williamson Nevin's sentiment. Was it not arrogant for Winebrenner, the editor, to place a picture of himself alongside those of established fathers and founders in American religion? Since then I have come to note that his self-nomination was not so much an act of spiritual pride as a simple, natural, unself-conscious expression. It is almost as if he were saying, "Well, I have been leading a movement. It may not be big, but it's true. How will people learn the truth if we do not get equal time in this book about all the churches?"

What today would be an insufferable act of egotism was in his time such an expectable performance that it took a scather like Nevin to point out the problem. That expectability or naturalness is part of what was meant in my nomination of Winebrenner to the gallery of American originals. He was neither genius nor eccentric. He was what the times demanded, and did what they exacted from would-be leaders.

Winebrenner lived in a day we can hardly recover in imaginations, a time when wide open spaces beckoned, when the population stock symbolized almost nothing but promise. Anything could happen. "Wise men hoped." Religion was taken very seriously culturally. What one did in its sphere mattered greatly in a larger public. Men and women felt this, and it was true. The percentage of church members in the population was significantly smaller than it is now, but in matters of habit, custom, ethos, and outlook, they ran more of the show. Fairly conventional people could intervene in history, leave the stamp of their personalities on it, and have reason to believe that the world would be different.

In a time of crowding, apathy, and defeatism, it is refreshing to be reminded that there were such days and such people. While the age cannot be reborn and while simple nostalgia is uncreative, a revisiting of their times can inform us about the kinds of choices open today, in a different world. In those terms, the Winebrenners and others of his generation still determine part of the lives of people who never have heard of them or would rarely think about them.

Two features stand out particularly in this story of a life. First, Winebrenner was most painstaking about his attention to matters of the church. What would strike the reader as almost trivial items, taken by themselves, come to make quite a difference to a founder in a movement. Whoever has laid parquet on a floor knows that if there is the slightest misfit in the first row, it will exaggerate itself in subsequent rows and skew the whole pattern before long. Some instinct led Winebrenner to want to keep things in line at the beginning. Yet this attention to detail did not make him a constrictive type. He was free to be free-swinging, ecumenical, quite open on many issues.

The other element is his ability—shared with many other originals in his generation—to blend his churchmanship with extensive involvement in causes. Today we tend to divide church leaders into those who are institutionalists-bureaucrats-churchmen, turning all their gaze on the inward life of the church, *versus* activists, publicists, or celebrities, who trade on the church but keep their distance. Several chapters in this book, those on slavery, temperance, and peace, for example, show how his generation could not stay aloof from the day's great issues, even if they did not always know what to do in the face of them.

With the coming of the Civil War, a year after Winebrenner's death, the era came to a close. In the post-War era, as America industrialized, many of the ambiguous aspects of Winebrenner's types turned less attractive. Their revivalism became hucksterism or commercialism in the hands of urban mass evangelists. Their calling attention to themselves for the cause of Christ became a calling attention to one's self as a "prince of the pulpit" in the 1880s. Their involvement in social issues was left behind among self-seeking churchmen in a later age, when no one wanted to rock a boat, stain an image, or lead people to withhold consent from their church building efforts.

How Winebrenner would have acted in such an age, one cannot know. Perhaps fortunately for his reputation, he did not live into that time. Richard Kern has given us a last glimpse into his world and, through it, has provided a kind of window on the Protestant empire of an earlier day.

Martin E. Marty

The University of Chicago

TABLE OF CONTENTS

1

The Setting

John Winebrenner was born in 1797 and died in 1860. During the course of his life he witnessed a rapidly changing America engaged in a pursuit of national discovery and identity. But Winebrenner was more than a witness. As a reformer of society, he was fully a participant in the period. To a remarkable degree, he combined in his person, and in his various reformatory movements, the ideological patterns and national presuppositions of America in the Jacksonian Era and the years immediately preceding it.

Born a few weeks after John Adams was inaugurated the second president of the United States, and while George Washington was still living, Winebrenner died during the presidency of James Buchanan, just a few months before Lincoln's election and South Carolina's fateful secession from the Union. His *A Brief View of the Formation, Government, and Discipline of the Church of God,*[1] the theological rationale for the soon to be organized General Eldership of the Church of God, was printed in 1829, the year General Jackson became president.

Winebrenner's lifetime was the period of a growing, changing America. By every dimension the country was bigger in 1860 than in 1797. At his birth, the sixteen United States were largely confined to the Atlantic seaboard (the exceptions were Vermont, Tennessee, and Kentucky), the land beyond the Mississippi being not only unsettled but under nominal European control. In 1821 Missouri was admitted as a state, the first west of the Mississippi. By Winebrenner's death, there were thirty-two states in the Union, eight west of the Mississippi, two on the Pacific Coast, and the continental boundaries of the country had been rounded out (save Alaska). As the frontier moved continually westward, attitudes about the whole movement varied. The lore of the new west insisted that "the cowards never started and the weaklings fell by the way," whereas the skeptical easterner saw the west in continual danger of barbarism or, at best, Romanism. But whatever the attitude at the time, the frontier—with its individualism, localism, restlessness, and break with tradition—was in part responsible for shaping the American experience during this, the "national period" of the country's history.

Statistics likewise tell a story of growth, movement, and change. The population of the country was 5,308,483 in 1800; in 1860, it was 31,433,321—almost a six-fold increase. Around 8,000 immigrants entered the country in 1820. In 1860 the number had increased to 153,640. In 1800, the city of New York, with its suburbs, had a population of 63,000; in 1850, about 700,000. About five per cent of the American population was classed as urban in 1790; by 1860, almost twenty per cent. In 1829 the first American attempt was made to use a steam locomotive. On the eve of the Civil War, in 1860, there were about 30,000 miles of railroad track stretching across the country.

One of the essential attributes of this growing, moving, and changing America in the early and mid-nineteenth century was a native optimism. Jefferson had modestly suggested in 1801 that America was "the world's best hope," elaborating in his 1805 inaugural to the effect that the country was in the hands of that Being "who led our forefathers, as Israel of old."[2] The Puritan concept of God's elect was being expanded to cover the whole of the country. To be sure, shifting political winds, depressions, and antislavery agitation dampened the optimism for some; but still the country grew and prospered. Even the "barbarian" (according to John Quincy Adams), "ignorant, passionate, hypocritical, corrupt" (according to Henry Clay), General Andrew Jackson, proved a capable enough occupant of the White House. The editor of the *North American Review* undoubtedly reflected the feelings of a majority of Americans when he reported in 1829, the year of Jackson's inauguration, that the 1789 experiment had succeeded "beyond the expectations of the most sanguine." The "manifest destiny" or "mission" of America was a frequent assumption by the middle third of the nineteenth century. America as "The Great Nation of Futurity" is so described in *The United States Magazine and Democratic Review* of 1839:

> The far reaching, the boundless future will be the era of American greatness. In its magnificent domain of space and time, the nation of many nations is destined to manifest to mankind the excellence of divine principles; to establish on earth the noblest temple ever dedicated to the worship of the Most High—the Sacred and the True. Its floor shall be a

hemisphere—its roof the firmament of the star-studded heavens, and its congregation an Union of many Republics, comprising hundreds of happy millions, calling, owning no man master, but governed by God's natural and moral law of equality, the law of brother-hood—of "peace and good will amongst men."[3]

An extension of the optimism of the period was an assumption of the perfectibility of man and his institutions. John Adams could say in 1813, for example, that "our pure, virtuous, public-spirited, federative republic will last forever, govern the globe, and introduce the perfection of man . . ."[4]

Such optimism and perfectionism were reflected in the development of, and the increasing involvement by Americans in, a growing number of voluntary reform societies, especially in the middle third of the nineteenth century. Summing up the period in his *The Era of Reform, 1830-1860,* historian Henry Steele Commager has written that

it was a day of universal reform—a day when almost every man you met might draw a plan for a new society or a new government from his pocket; a day of infinite hope and infinite discontent. Every institution was called before the bar of reason, and of sentiment, too: the church, the state, the law, the army, the family property—and required to justify itself. Nothing was immune, nothing was sacred, nothing was taken for granted, nothing but the right of inquiry.

"If Man was divine, and mankind perfectible," continues Commager,

then it was unspeakably wicked that a man's body should be confined in slavery, his mind clouded by ignorance, his soul corrupted by superstition or by sin.[5]

This was the era that brought forth the utopianism of Bronson Alcott's Fruitlands and Noyes' Oneida Community; the pleas for women's rights of Catherine Beecher and Wendell Phillips; Horace Mann's activities on behalf of public education; Charles Sumner's pacifistic "The True Grandeur of Nations"; the efforts of Dorothea Dix for the insane and Charles Loring Brace for underprivileged children; and the heightened concern for the slave in men like William Lloyd Garrison and William Ellery Channing—to name but a few of the reforms and reformers.

Though somewhat isolated from the main streams of American reform by virtue of his residence in Harrisburg, in south-east central Pennsylvania, John Winebrenner became deeply involved in many of the reform movements of his time. The following

A

BRIEF VIEW,

OF THE

FORMATION,

GOVERNMENT AND DISCIPLINE,

OF THE

CHURCH OF GOD.

——◦◉◦——

BY JOHN WINEBRENNER,

An Elder of the Church of God.

Set in order the things that are wanting.   Titus I. 5.
And so ordain I in all Churches.   1 Cor. VII. 17.

HARRISBURG:

Montgomery and Dexter, *Printers.*

———

1829.

Title page from Winebrenner's *View of the Church,* first published in 1829.

chapters detail his efforts in behalf of the church, the slave, peace, and temperance.

A word about the church. In the late 1820's and early 1830's Winebrenner was in large part responsible for the organization of a new American denomination, the Church of God. In the context of early nineteenth century American church history, Winebrenner and the Church of God can be explained by reference to many of the characteristics of the American church during this period. Among these characteristics were: the emphasis on the part of many denominations on a return to the original church; an intense Biblicism, used to undercut ecclesiastical tradition and the authority of the established churches; an emphasis on "voluntaryism," and, frequently, its revivalistic excesses; missionary work; and "interdenominationalism" — an emphasis upon the actual or basic unity of all "converted" believers regardless of church affiliation.[6] The origin and development of the Church of God provide a good illustration of the above factors at work in the American church. Chapters 4 and 5 outline Winebrenner's role in the establishment of the Church of God and the theological presuppositions he expressed in it.

But while the Church of God unquestionably represents one result of changing ideas about the nature of the Christian Church and faith in early nineteenth century America, there is more to the story. In fact, we lack essential perspective on Winebrenner if we do not see the Church of God also as a natural product of his involvement in the American reforming impulse of the period. Certainly, it was as a reform movement that Winebrenner himself viewed the Church of God.

In his *A Brief View . . . of the Church of God,* Winebrenner presents a picture of desperate bewilderment on the part of churchmen because of the confusion surrounding the correct "formation, government, and discipline" of the church.[7] He writes further:

> These unhappy and deplorable circumstances, under which thousands are placed, should excite our tenderest sympathies, and prompt us to speedy and energetic efforts, to ameliorate their condition and bring about a salutary reformation in regard to these ecclesiastical matters, so manifestly wrong, and so much confused.[8]

It is in response to such "deplorable circumstances, under which thousands are placed" that Winebrenner offers his *A Brief View . . . of the Church of God* in order "to ameliorate their condition" much as he later would advocate abolitionism to ameliorate the slaves' condition and temperance programs to ameliorate the condition of the drunkard.

Winebrenner grants, of course, that such a reformation will not be an easy matter:

> The author, however, is not so sanguine in his expectations on this subject, as to believe that this publication will immediately correct and do away all the lamented evils before mentioned, and produce a *perfect reform* [emphasis mine] in ecclesiastical polity. He does not expect, in the *present imperfect state* [emphasis mine] of things, that all the different views entertained by men respecting these things, will be relinquished forthwith, and every body adopt what he conceives to be the best, or the scriptural view. To take the world is no easy matter. The work of reform is a work of time.

"Old forms and opinions though wrong," he adds,

> most men are loath to part with. This sentiment is beautifully expressed by the venerable framers of the American Declaration of Independence. "All experience," say they, "hath shown that mankind are more disposed to suffer, while evils are sufferable, than to right themselves by abolishing the forms to which they are accustomed."[9]

The optimism is obvious. Like many of his contemporary reformers, Winebrenner views the course of events as moving from a "present imperfect state" to future perfection. Time is needed of course. There is always the drag of "old forms and opinions" to contend with, as his forefathers in the American faith had experienced. But then, the framers of the American Declaration of Independence had been successful in their reform; and so would Winebrenner be in his. "To take the world is no easy matter," as he admits; but try to take it he would.

6

2

Early Years

We are not certain why Catherine Winebrenner, John Winebrenner's great-grandmother, left the Palatinate for Pennsylvania in 1753.

We have some ideas of course. The Palatinate, along the Rhine River in western Germany, was a war cursed state. Decimated by the 30 Years War (1618-1648), which possibly set back Germany 200 years, for the remainder of the seventeenth century the Palatinate was a much abused pawn in European politics. It was devastated by retreating French armies in 1689, an event which, coupled with the famine and pestilence which followed, led to the first sizeable overseas migration. The mainly Calvinist population was further burdened, after 1685, by the attempt of some of the Electors of the Palatinate to impose Roman Catholicism on their subjects. Little wonder when accounts of fabulous opportunities awaiting them in America were noised about that numbers of the Palatines packed or sold their belongings and left their homeland.

Leaving the Palatinate was one thing. Making it to the New World was quite another. For even the well prepared, the trip was risky at best. Travelling down the Rhine from the Palatinate to Rotterdam was both slow and expensive. Petty German principalities exacted tolls from the river traffic. (As late as 1804 there were at least 36 toll stations on the Rhine.) A five or six week trip to Rotterdam was to be expected. The voyage across the Atlantic held its own terrors. Overcrowding on the ships was general, disease common. Those crossing the ocean were frequently expected to bring their own food, which might not last the (at best) seven week trip, especially if the winds were bad. Water was eternally scarce, it seemed. In 1749, four years before Catherine Winebrenner left Rotterdam on the Rowand, under

Captain Arthur Tran, it is estimated that as many as 2,000 Germans died during the transatlantic crossing.[1]

Nor were problems necessarily at an end when a Palatinate immigrant landed in the New World. The poorer usually became indentured servants. Others found that, despite the obvious opportunities, Britain's North American colonies were not exactly what the over-zealous land agent had promised. Gold was not found in plentiful supply. The bison were not eager to be shot. The wolves were not easily tamed, and bears were not frequently seen herding peacefully with the swine. The land would flow with milk and honey, but only for those willing to work at it.

Still, for whatever her reasons, Catherine Winebrenner (Weinbrenner, Weybrenner) had decided to come to America in 1753 with her four children: Johann Christian, about 18; Johann Peter, just 12; Johann George, about 11; and, Katrina, just passed 8. There is no record of her husband. Probably Catherine was a widow when she left the Palatinate, although it remains a possibility that the husband and father died on the trip. It seems reasonable to suppose that he was named Johann, inasmuch as the three boys had it for their first name (apparently following a German custom of the time). The family landed at Philadelphia in September of 1753. On September 29, Johann Christian, the only Winebrenner male over 16, "qualified" (the signing of a pledge of allegiance to the British Crown and the Pennsylvania proprietors). The Winebrenners moved to the interior of Pennsylvania, settling near Hanover in York County, not far from the Maryland line. There is record of the Winebrenner name in the Monocacy River valley in Maryland, not far from Hanover, prior to 1750.[2] Possibly, therefore, the landing in America by a widow and her four children is to be explained by the existence of close relatives in a fertile Maryland river valley. Further research may someday give further answers.

Catherine Winebrenner died near Hanover, Pennsylvania, in 1755 at about 40 years of age. Her eldest son, Johann Christian, John Winebrenner's grandfather, in time purchased a farm of 162 acres near Hanover. In 1758 he married Christina, widow of Jacob Wyand of Dover Township. Selling the farm in 1772, the Winebrenners moved to Hagerstown. Johann Christian died there in 1815.

Philip Winebrenner, John's father, was born in 1759 in York County, Pennsylvania, the second of Johann Christian and Christina's seven children. As a young man he moved to the Woodsboro District of Frederick County, Maryland, where he acquired a farm of 200 acres. It would appear that he was a reasonably prosperous farmer. In 1810, he built a stone mansion replacing the log house in which all of his children were born. He died in 1841. Little is known about the background of John's mother, Eve Barrick. She was from Frederick County, was born in 1757 of Scotch-German ancestry, and died in 1831.

WINEBRENNER HOMESTEAD
FREDERICK COUNTY, MARYLAND

John Winebrenner was born on March 25, 1797. He was the fifth of six children born to Philip and Eve on the family farm in Frederick County. He was probably named for his grandfather, Johann Christian.[3] As a child and young man (he was 18 when Johann Christian died), he most likely absorbed his grandfather's account of the rigors associated with his trip from Europe to America. Conceivably, Johann Christian may have recounted also stories of princely political and religious oppression in the Palatinate. In his later reformist writings a recurring theme is his opposition to all forms of tyranny and his advocacy of American democratic forms. Winebrenner did not always like what "the people" decided (as when they voted against temperance legislation in Pennsylvania), but he never questioned their right to make the decision for themselves.

While there is conflicting testimony on the point, it appears that English was the language most generally spoken in the Philip Winebrenner household.[4] Later evidence suggests that Winebrenner was himself bilingual with a preference for English. English appears to have been the medium of instruction through most of his formal education, and in his seminary years it appears that he had to study German in order properly to preach in it.[5]

9

Winebrenner's collected letters are all in English. His publications are primarily in English, though a few are in German. The question of Winebrenner's native tongue is not altogether academic. The English speaking portion of the German Reformed Church in the first half of the nineteenth century was considered to be the "liberal" section, much more open to non-German Reformed influences, and especially amenable to Methodist theology and revivalistic extremes.

Both Philip and Eve Winebrenner were members of the Glades Reformed Church, located about a mile from their farm. It was in this church that John Winebrenner was presented for baptism at the age of two months. His early religious training was given him both by his parents and the pastors of the local church. His mother especially took to heart his spiritual instruction and guidance. Late in life (1858) he wrote:

> I was, parentally and providentially, restrained from the paths of vice and immorality. And as my mother trained me, from youth up, in the fear and admonition of the Lord, and instructed me in the great principles and duties of religion, I was graciously brought to feel my obligations to God at an early age, and my mind was deeply exercised on the subject of my soul's salvation.[6]

Winebrenner seems to have been inclined toward the ministry early in life. In his later years he recalled practicing the delivery of sermons in the wood near his home and attempting to preach to his comrades.[7] His mother was in favor of her son's entering the ministry, but his father was not similarly minded. According to Winebrenner, his father

> to divert my mind from this subject, and to induce me to abandon the idea of the ministry . . . made various propositions. One was, to send me to Baltimore, and to have me become a merchant. Another was, to send me to Frederick city, to read law, or study medicine. Anything, he seemed to think, would be preferable to that of becoming a preacher of the gospel.[8]

In time, however, his father yielded, giving both consent and financial assistance to son John for his ministerial education.

Dickinson College

Winebrenner had received his early education in a country school house across the road from the Glades German Reformed Church. He later attended an academy in Frederick, Maryland, about eight miles from his home. He then enrolled at Dickinson

College, Carlisle, Pennsylvania, as a member of the Class of 1818. The year of his matriculation is unknown, the matter being further complicated by the simultaneous existence of two, three, and four year programs at the college around that time. We do know that he did not graduate. The college closed for a few years following the fall, 1816, graduation. Apart from his listing in the alumni roll of the college, the only record we have of Winebrenner at Dickinson is his membership in the Union Philosophical Society in 1816.[9]

GLADES SCHOOL HOUSE

Winebrenner probably was directed to Dickinson by his pastor at the Glades Church, Jonathan Helffenstein, who was a trustee of the institution between 1807 and 1826. Apart from this connection, however, the college had much to recommend it. While Dickinson had lost some of the lustre given it by Principal Charles Nisbet, who had more or less shepherded the college from 1785 to his death in 1804, still, for all that, its reputation was a good one.[10] Influential families sent their sons there. Robert L. Madison, nephew of President James Madison, was a student at Dickinson in 1815, during his uncle's second term. Alfred Victor Du Pont

11

was an 1816 contemporary of Winebrenner's. Many of its alumni were men in high places, including Roger Brooke Taney, Class of 1795, one of the chief legal lights in Frederick. It had the advantage of being close to home, about fifty-five miles as the crow flies, although by reason of that day's roads, a not insignificant trip. The college was indirectly under Presbyterian control. Principal of Dickinson from 1809 to 1815 was Jeremiah Atwater, a protégé of Timothy Dwight, and former President of Middlebury College in Vermont. He was succeeded for a year by John McKnight, a Carlisle area Presbyterian minister. Both men had a reputation for piety and orthodoxy—a dossier scheduled to please most religiously inclined parents about to send their son away to college.

Whatever the reasons for his going there, Dickinson College must have had its interests for a Frederick County farmer's son. The somewhat less than 100 students at Dickinson when Winebrenner matriculated were developing a reputation for undisciplined activities. These included dueling, wreaking havoc in the college building, and, according to an 1811 letter of Principal Atwater, "lying in bed always till breakfast." [11] Not at all calculated to please the more conservative elements in the supporting church, faculty, Board of Trustees, or Carlisle community, was the instance of the Fourth of July celebration observed by a large group of Dickinson students in 1815. Twenty-one formal toasts, followed by a series less formal—considerably less formal, no doubt—excoriated the almost dead Federalist party and saluted Benjamin Franklin, Thomas Jefferson, Napoleon, and the student-oriented Dickinson faculty member, Thomas Cooper.

Cooper had come to Dickinson in 1811 as Professor of Chemistry and Natural Philosophy, succeeding a Dr. Frederick Aigster who voluntarily left town after interfering "in the marital affairs of two residents of Carlisle, claiming the young lady for himself." [12] Aigster, for his actions, was regarded by some as "deranged." Perhaps the question of sanity more properly is raised with regard to the action of the Board of Trustees which appointed Cooper to fill the vacancy left by Aigster. Cooper was at that time in the midst of a stormy career which took him from involvement in the French Revolution and friendship with expatriate Joseph Priestley to the presidency of the University of South Carolina and protagonist in the Nullification controversy. He came to Dickinson not long after his dismissal from the judgeship of Pennsylvania's Fourth District by the governor at the request of the State Legislature. His revolutionary and anti-clerical notoriety had preceded him, and his appointment to the

12

faculty was unsuccessfully opposed by Principal Atwater and a smaller, and probably more churchly inclined, portion of the Board of Trustees. Cooper sided with dueling students, drank freely, and was not overly respectful in his relations with the administration or faculty. Problems caused by his appointment were resolved only when he, Atwater, and most of the faculty resigned in September, 1815. Although Cooper did teach some in 1816, the college was all but dead. After a funereal year, aggravated by financial distress, Dickinson closed its doors in the fall of 1816.

We have no record of Winebrenner's feelings about his professors or college experience. It might be assumed that he found the theological position of Principal Atwater and/or Acting Principal McKnight generally congenial, and that he shared with the administration a concern that religion be respected on the campus.

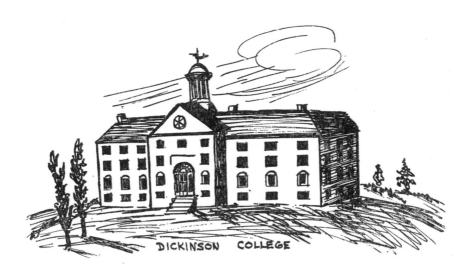
DICKINSON COLLEGE

But it is also possible that his teen-aged exposure to the iconoclastic and reform-minded Thomas Cooper had its later effect. Cooper's interest in law, medicine, and business (which would have pleased Winebrenner's father); his anti-slavery inclinations (at this time); and his crusade against privileged churches and clergy are all reflected to some degree in Winebrenner after 1825. His 1815-1816 year at Dickinson, with the college near collapse and the student body diminished, must have been depressing. Still, we surmise from his later efforts to establish a school for the Church of God that he left Carlisle with some appreciation for the time spent there.

Dr. Samuel Helffenstein

In 1817 Winebrenner went to Philadelphia to live with and receive his theological training under the Rev. Samuel Helffenstein, D.D., pastor of the Race Street Reformed Church and a brother to Jonathan Helffenstein at the Glades Church. The German Reformed Church at this time had not yet established a seminary, and this method of receiving a theological education was usual. While pastor in Philadelphia (1799-1831), Dr. Helffenstein himself trained twenty-seven men for the ministry.[13]

Samuel Helffenstein was one of the four minister sons of a most honored early minister of the German Reformed Church in America, the Rev. J. C. Albertus Helffenstein. The ministerial office in his family could be traced back to the Reformation. Orthodox in his theology, at least by nineteenth century American German Reformed standards, Dr. Helffenstein also had adopted to considerable extent the Pietistic-revivalistic methods of the day. He was an author of some note, and his general qualifications in the area of ministerial training were such that when the Reformed Church made an abortive attempt to establish a seminary in Harrisburg, Pennsylvania, in the early 1820's, Helffenstein was chosen as its professor. One of his students wrote the following with regard to the instruction received under Dr. Helffenstein in Philadelphia:

> The students were practiced by Helffenstein in the classic languages and all the branches of the theological sciences. Hebrew was Dr. Helffenstein's favorite Language. Each Sunday they had to take turns in delivering addresses at the almshouse and the hospital of the city.[14]

In 1817, when Winebrenner began his studies under Helffenstein, the final act of the German-English language controversy was being presented at the Race Street Church. As early as 1805, the English speaking members of the congregation had petitioned the synod for a service in English once a month. Their petition was unsuccessful, and this group consequently left the church. In 1816, the matter came up for discussion before the synod again. The German party urged the removal of Dr. Helffenstein who, having changed his previous views, favored the English party. The synod would not comply with the request for Helffenstein's removal. Therefore, in 1817, the German party, having elected a majority on the board of the congregation, dismissed their pastor.

Helffenstein did not leave immediately and the corporation closed the doors of the church against him. Thence the matter was taken to court and debated while Helffenstein and his friends went into the parochial school house and held services. The court ordered the board to open the church, and Helffenstein returned to his pulpit.[15]

These events, early in 1817, could not have helped but make an impression on young Winebrenner. When, six years later, Winebrenner himself became engaged in a controversy and was dismissed by the vestry of the Harrisburg Reformed Church, he probably thought back to his student days and Dr. Helffenstein's experience. Undoubtedly, also, Helffenstein's eventual vindication by the church and state courts would have been an essential ingredient of those thoughts.

The year 1817 was definitive for Winebrenner in another respect. Not long after the commencement of his theological training in Philadelphia, Winebrenner was converted. The experience occurred on Easter Sunday, April 6, 1817, in the Race Street Church under the preaching of his teacher, Dr. Helffenstein.[16] Winebrenner, recording the event at a later time, wrote:

Hence, I continued sinning and repenting for a number of years, till in the winter of 1817, when deep and pungent convictions laid hold of my guilty soul. Then, like Job, "I abhorred myself,"—like Ephraim, "I bemoaned myself,"— with the prodigal, I said, "I will arise, and go to my Father,"— and with the publican, I cried, "God, be merciful to me, a sinner." And after "chattering like the swallow," and "mourning as a dove," for three or four weary months, my poor woe-fraught soul found redemption in Immanuel's blood, even the forgiveness of sins. It was on Easter Sabbath, in the city of Philadelphia, in the presence of a large congregation of worshipers, that Jesus, the "Sun of Righteousness" arose, and shone upon my soul, "with healing in his wings." Truly, that was the happiest day of my life! My darkness was turned into day, and my sorrow into joy. Jesus became the joy of my heart, and the centre of my affections. His people became lovely and precious in my sight. His word was my delight. In it I beheld new beauties and beatitudes. Sin, that dreadful monster, became more odious and hateful to my soul. Zion's welfare lay near my heart. My bowels yearned for the salvation of sinners. I was in travail for my friends and kindred. I felt constrained to join with "the Spirit and the bride," and say to all, Come, O, come to Jesus![17]

Winebrenner's conversion under Samuel Helffenstein's preaching was not exceptional. An emphasis upon a personal experience of regeneration was very much a part of the Helffenstein family tradition. Samuel's father, the Rev. J. C. Albertus Helffenstein, died while conducting a revival service, and Samuel's sons—Samuel, Jr., Albert, and Jacob—were all revivalists.[18] When, in 1828, Charles

Grandison Finney brought his "new measure" revivalism to Philadelphia, he preached for months from Dr. Helffenstein's Race Street pulpit.

We get some idea of the theological bill of fare Winebrenner received in Philadelphia from *The Doctrines of Divine Revelation As Taught in the Holy Scriptures—Exhibited, Illustrated, and Vindicated*,[19] a Samuel Helffenstein and sons' [20] systematic theology printed in 1842. The expanded title explains its purpose: "Designed For The Use Of Christians Generally And For Young Men, Preparing For The Gospel Ministry In Particular." Within a general Reformed tradition,[21] and leaning heavily upon the Heidelberg Catechism, *The Doctrines* nonetheless accommodates itself here and there to prevailing concerns in the American church. Several pages are given over to proving the validity of baptism by other modes than immersion, and stressing the importance of infant baptism. Helffenstein of course disagreed with Roman Catholic and Lutheran teachings concerning the nature of Christ's presence in the Lord's Supper. But he also disagreed with both Calvin and Zwingli on the same subject, suggesting that "in opposition to all these errors, we believe that Christ . . . is spiritually present." [22] Whatever Helffenstein himself actually intended by his "spiritual presence," in the polemics later associated with the Mercersburg movement, the Helffenstein family position was considered "Zwinglian," and an American rejection of the verities of the Reformed tradition, by those connected with Mercersburg's high Calvinistic view.[23] As might be anticipated from the fact of Winebrenner's climactic conversion experience under Helffenstein, there is a recurring emphasis throughout the book on the necessity of the new birth. However, *The Doctrines* makes it quite clear that regeneration happens only in those so predestined. Man's role is entirely passive. There is no hint that Helffenstein sympathizes with revivalistic "techniques" and "measures," or man's active cooperation with God in attaining salvation.[24]

Winebrenner's father had stipulated, in the course of agreeing to his son's training for the ministry, that John preach his first sermon in German—perhaps a reflection of his displeasure with regard to the gradual Anglicizing of both church and home among the Germans in Maryland. These feelings were not unique. In the early 1820's, the strongly German section of the church east of the Susquehanna River decided to support the projected Reformed seminary only after it was agreed that instruction would be in German as well as English and that all students admitted to the institution must be able to understand and speak the German language.[25] His German copy book and German manuscript sermons from his seminary years indicate that Winebrenner spent considerable time preparing to fulfill his father's stipulation.[26]

In addition to his studies under Helffenstein, Winebrenner busied himself with the Sunday School associated with the Race Street Church, was trained in music by Henry Bibighaus (the Race Street Church organist), and spent some time with an otherwise unknown "Julia." He apparently became a close friend of his teacher and family, giving his name in 1818 to Samuel Helffenstein's youngest child, Benjamin Winebrenner Helffenstein.[27] A brotherly relationship developed between Winebrenner and his preceptor's older sons, Samuel, Jr., and Jacob. (In a September 5, 1822 letter to Winebrenner, Samuel, Jr., congratulates him on his forthcoming marriage, suggesting that after his ordination, in about a month, he would be able to perform the ceremony. He signs the letter, "Friend and Brother," and then adds in brotherly fashion, "Your former sweetheart Julia . . . remembers you with affection.") With Jacob, at least, this affection continued even after events surrounding Winebrenner's separation from the Reformed Church had alienated Winebrenner and Samuel, Sr.[28]

Winebrenner never evaluated his theological training for us. However without question he was deeply influenced by his years with Helffenstein. Although with the passage of time he gradually changed his views with regard to baptism, predestination and free will, and, to a degree, the nature of the church, his general theological orientation remained that of Helffenstein's *Doctrines*. Winebrenner made good use of the German language training received in Philadelphia, becoming an effective preacher in German and also publishing a number of books and tracts in that language. Winebrenner's later occasional use of Greek and Latin may derive at least in part from Helffenstein's teaching, though we have no way of knowing this with certainty.

However, Helffenstein's most enduring legacy to his young student was the stress placed by the former upon a personal experience of regeneration as the *sine qua non* of the Christian faith. Winebrenner learned from his teacher that to be "parentally and providentially restrained from the paths of vice and immorality," and to be trained "from youth up in the fear and admonition of the Lord . . . and instructed . . . in the great principles and duties of religion" [29] simply was not enough. A definite knowledge of one's own "new birth" was also required. Winebrenner was an intelligent sort of young man, and learned this lesson well.

Early in 1819, in the midst of his Philadelphia studies, Winebrenner was invited to fill the pulpit for a Sunday service at the

Salem Reformed Church in Harrisburg, Pennsylvania. Apparently anticipating a pastoral change,[30] the church had contacted Jonathan Helffenstein at the Glades Church for assistance in finding a replacement. He had been a supply pastor at Harrisburg prior to 1808. Helffenstein in turn had recommended his young parishioner, John Winebrenner. Accepting the invitation, Winebrenner delivered a sermon at the church on February 28. He was subsequently invited to preach two more sermons during the year at the Harrisburg Church, on May 21 and November 28. On December 16 Winebrenner was elected pastor of the Harrisburg charge, receiving forty-three out of forty-eight votes cast. Winebrenner's competitor was the Rev. Lewis Mayer, D.D., soon to become professor of the Reformed Seminary at Carlisle, and for several years a close friend and confidant.

The call to Winebrenner was made unanimous. There were four churches on the Harrisburg charge—the Harrisburg church itself and three country churches. On being advised of the decision of the Harrisburg charge, Winebrenner replied that he couldn't take up pastoral duties until he had completed his theological training and until after the next synod when he would present himself as a candidate for ordination. This was agreeable to the charge. His salary was a generous $1,000. a year: $425. for preaching in Harrisburg every two weeks; $150. for preaching at the Wenrick's Church, in Dauphin County, once every four weeks; $150. for preaching at the Shoop's Church, in Dauphin County, once every four weeks; and $275. for preaching at the Salem (Peace) Church, in Cumberland County near Shiremanstown, once every two weeks.[31] Winebrenner was ordained on September 24, 1820, at the Synod of the German Reformed Church meeting at Hagerstown, Maryland.[32] He sent his formal letter of acceptance to the Harrisburg charge on October 4, and preached his introductory sermon at Harrisburg on Sunday, October 22, 1820.

3

The New Measures

After three years in Philadelphia, still the largest city in the United States when he was there, Winebrenner must have found Harrisburg rather provincial. Its population of nearly 3,000, principally German and Scotch-Irish, almost could have been squeezed into Dr. Helffenstein's Race Street Church, the largest in Phila-

WINEBRENNER'S FIRST CHURCH IN HARRISBURG

delphia. The Harrisburg newspapers in the 1830's kept their readers informed on national and international news via clips from the larger seaboard cities. Rarely did an issue pass without rewards being offered for strays of every description—cows, horses, sheep, apprentices (including "German Redemptioners"), and, more ominously, slaves.[1]

Yet Harrisburg was a town with considerable promise. Located at the site of one of the best fords on the Susquehanna, and at the head of the Cumberland and Lebanon Valleys, the town had grown from its trading-post days to a center of inland transportation. Greatly stimulating this growth was the removal to Harrisburg, from Lancaster, of the state capital, in 1812—eight years before Winebrenner assumed his pastorate there. As capital of Pennsylvania, Harrisburg soon began to witness events of significance. In 1827 the National Tariff Convention met in Harrisburg. The Harrison-Tyler ticket was nominated by Whigs assembled in one of Harrisburg's churches in 1839. As might be expected, the capital was in on the beginnings of the Pennsylvania canal and railroad systems in the late 1820's and early 1830's.

Winebrenner slid into the tempo of Harrisburg's secular life with ease. In a journal which he kept briefly for the period January 1, 1826 to January 18, 1826,[2] he mentions "hearing the Legislature," and, over four evenings, being "highly pleased" with a Mr. Reynolds' lectures on "Capt. Symnse's [sic] new theory of the earth." Some idea of the good captain's theory may be gathered from *The Oracle of Dauphin County* for December 4, 1819. An article on "Approaching Winter" includes the following item:

> Captain Symmes of Ohio—who has made so much speculation on the passages at the poles into the inside of the earth—has predicted that the ensuing *Winter* will be mild, from the influence which the conjunctive situation of the *Sun, Jupiter* and *Saturn,* will have on the electric fluid, during the most part of it . . .

It would be interesting to know what part of Mr. Reynolds' lecture "highly pleased" Winebrenner the most.

Within a short time after his arrival in Harrisburg, Winebrenner was deeply immersed in the work of his ministry. He soon established a Sunday School at the Harrisburg Church, no doubt modelled after Dr. Helffenstein's in Philadelphia. According to the *Harrisburg Chronicle* for November 27, 1821, The Bible Association of Harrisburg, an organization geared to distributing Scriptures to the poor and overseeing an adult Negro Sunday School in town, elected him secretary. The local papers gave notice of his increasing number of weddings, inserting such vital statistics in columns which told also of discounts on bank note exchanges and the harvesting of an extraordinary carrot (4½ pounds, 24½ inches around) or apple (22 ounces, 15½ inches in circumference).[3]

Before his first year was out, Winebrenner pledged $100. out of his $1,000. annual salary toward the building of a new church in Harrisburg. In June of 1821, the cornerstone of the new church was laid, and a year later in August the edifice was dedicated. The construction of the church must have been a source of satisfaction to Winebrenner. Armed with a letter of endorsement from the Harrisburg vestry, and countersigned by Samuel Helffenstein, Sr., the young pastor had travelled many miles in securing out-of-town pledges and gifts for the church.[4]

In 1822, Winebrenner published *A Compendium of the Heidelberg Catechism: or, Method of Instruction in the Christian Religion, as the Same Is Taught in the German Reformed Church and Schools in North America*.[5] The *Compendium* is in good part traceable to Samuel Helffenstein's training. The only possible departure from his teacher's theology as later developed in *The Doctrines of Divine Revelation* [6] is the hint that Winebrenner is more amenable to the idea of baptism by immersion. According to Winebrenner, his new edition of the Heidelberg Catechism, "abridged," is "chiefly intended for the use of the Sunday School," and the "youthful part" of his ministerial care. Instruction in the "pure and perfect doctrines of salvation" is necessary, he continues,

> . . . in order that, there may be no schism, rent or division in the Church: but, that the whole body fitly joined together, may be kept in perfect love and harmony—and that we, by the grace of God, may constantly keep up the unity of the faith in the bonds of peace.[7]

The reference to "schism" was not accidental. Whatever success Winebrenner was having, there was trouble in the church.

Opposition

The first indication of this trouble, by Winebrenner's own account, was a disagreement between himself and his vestry at the Harrisburg Church. In a pamphlet published in 1824, *The Truth Made Known: or, A Fair and Correct Account of Facts, which Have Transpired in the German Reformed Congregation of Harrisburg, since the Fall of 1822*,[8] he wrote:

> The first aggrievance that was officially alleged against me since my settlement in Harrisburg, was the following:
>
> ["]The vestry of the German Reformed Salem Church at Harrisburg . . . having met on business relative to the church aforesaid, on Saturday the 8th of June, 1822, and it having been made known that the Rev. John Winebrenner read to the congregation, the result of the election held on the 27th

of May past—of one Trustee, one Elder, and four Deacons; and stated further, 'that he intended an ordination of that part of the vestry elected on the 27th of May past, on the 16th of June, 1822, if no objections were made against any.' That 'he particularly invited the congregation to examine into the fitness of said lately elected members, within the period above mentioned.'["]

The vestry resolved as follows:

["]That the election held on the 27th of May past pursuant to the 2d article of the provision of the articles of association of the charter of said church is valid and effectual and cannot be affected by, nor does it require any other subsequent ministerial proceeding or interference of the minister.

["]Signed on behalf of the vestry.

["]Jacob Bucher, Prest.["] [9]

In response to the charge of his "interference" Winebrenner went on to say that he was merely following "the uniform practice of the church, and the form of installation of church officers," which were required of him. The Reformed Church Constitution of 1748, prepared by John Philip Boehm and approved by Coetus after revision by the Classis of Amsterdam, contained the following Church Order Provision: "The persons elected to the consistory shall be announced . . . to ascertain whether any one has any lawful objection to offer, and if not they shall . . . be installed in office." [10] However,

. . . the gentlemen, who it would seem did not like to have their characters scrutinized, got offended at, and therefore sent me the above resolution; wherein they declare, what I had done from a sense of duty . . . "an unwarrantable interference." I was also informed, that they passed another resolution, declaring that the Elders and Deacons should not be ordained for the future.[11]

By the summer of 1822, then, Winebrenner and a majority of his vestry were alienated to a considerable degree. Worse was to come.

On September 29, 1822, not quite two years after Winebrenner had begun his ministry in Harrisburg, an application was made to the Synod of the German Reformed Church meeting in Harrisburg for an investigation of the causes of dissatisfaction between the Harrisburg congregation and its minister. With this application another document was presented to the Synod containing the complaints of *some* (primarily in the vestry) in the Harrisburg church against Winebrenner. With some abridgement, the complaints read as follows:

1. That he proceeds in the affairs of the church at Harrisburg as if there were no Vestry . . .

2. In his recommendation to attend strictly divine worship he mentioned the Methodist church particularly as a suitable place for his congregation, and on the same day after such recommendation he preached in the Methodist church. He further stated that if any members could not derive benefit by attending our church they should leave it, and that he himself would never have joined this Church if he had not devoted himself to the ministry. And at the time of the Quarterly Meeting of the Methodists, at Harrisburg, Pennsylvania, he attended there and took Love-feast with them, and kept his own congregation waiting till he returned from the Methodist meeting-house.

3. He held prayer-meetings denominated anxious meetings, where he divided the members into two classes—first, those who say they have experienced a change, and believe themselves to be Christians; and, secondly, the sinners, those who believe themselves to be mourning sinners. And during all prayer-meetings he encourages groaning, thereby disturbing others who might, if the groaning were omitted, receive some benefit. Allows during prayer certain persons to respond "Amen! Amen!" thereby drawing the attention of the gazing crowd which usually collect on the outside.

4. At a meeting held, which he called a conference meeting, on the last Monday of July, he allowed persons to converse, encouraged the Christians to speak to sinners, when Mr. Winebrenner, Mr. Jacob Helffenstein . . . and others at one and the same time exhorted, prayed and continued until James Officer commenced singing a lively tune, which produced a state of confusion among them. After that Mr. Winebrenner called out if any person wished to be prayed for they should come forward. That then numbers came forward, . . .

5. At a meeting held the last Monday in May, which he called an experience and conference meeting, which began at seven o'clock in the evening, he kept together all who would stay till four o'clock in the morning, at the breaking up of which he said, "This is the way to fan the chaff from the wheat."

6. His denunciation from the pulpit towards members and others has caused members to withdraw themselves from the church. And on one occasion, when he preached a funeral sermon, he said, "If I were to judge from Scripture, the majority buried in the neighboring graves must be in hell," from which expression he gave a general dissatisfaction to the bystanders on the burying ground. Afterward he said from the pulpit, he excepted the children from the expression given in the grave-yard, thereby evidencing the general displeasure his expressions have given to the people.

7. He is now making, or has already made, arrangements to give up two of the congregations which form a part of our connection.

8. He has given such general dissatisfaction that on several late occasions where there were funerals in families of his members they passed him by; would not have him attend their funerals, and obtained ministers of other denominations.

9. He has admitted persons (who on account of misconduct in the church they previously belonged to were expelled from membership) to become members of our church without consulting the Vestry.

10. He is very remiss in visiting members of our congregation, especially at such times when any are sick; and he absents himself from his residence that he can not pay the necessary visits to his members, and he has refused to baptize children of the members when he had been particularly requested.[12]

The Synod appointed a committee of seven to investigate the charges, hear Winebrenner's rebuttal, and arrange a compromise if at all possible. The committee met with Winebrenner and his accusers on October 2, 1822, during the Synod meetings, at the home of vestryman Kelker, between 7 P.M. and 2 A.M.[13] The charges were read to Winebrenner. He prefaced his reply to them with the following:

I am brought to the disagreeable necessity of declaring a great portion of them [the complaints] incorrect and devoid of truth. There are, however, I admit, some facts contained in the paper; which, when freed from error and misrepresentations, I am not ashamed to confess.[14]

In the course of his rebuttal, Winebrenner admitted that he had not always consulted the vestry because there was no chance for cooperation. Consistently the vestry refused to attend his prayer meetings held in private homes. They would not conduct such meetings or pray at them, even should Winebrenner accede to their request to move them into the church. At any rate, according to Winebrenner, the vestry was continually holding meetings to which he was never invited.

Winebrenner admitted that he preached for the Methodists, who had established a permanent congregation in Harrisburg around 1820, and he was not ashamed of it. However, the point that he kept his congregation waiting while he took Love Feast with the Methodists was incorrect. He had once invited his people to hear him preach at the Methodist Church, to be sure, and he did not see anything wrong with it. (By way of context it might be well to point out here that during the preceding year someone had blown up the Methodist Meeting House pulpit in Harrisburg, and burned down a Methodist church in Cumberland County across the river from Harrisburg.)[15]

Anxious meetings had been held in order to discover who were awakened and who were not. But as for separating the saints and sinners, he left that up to each individual to decide. No, he did not encourage groaning, although when a sinner groaned for redemption, he was naturally glad to hear it. Winebrenner's concept of the *via media* in the matter of unnecessary noise in his meetings is interesting:

> That there has sometimes been an unnecessary noise, I am willing to admit; and yet, it would be hard to say which have sinned the most; those who attend meetings and groan too much, or those who never attend, unless it be with the "gazing crowd." The plain fact is this, there is danger on both sides.—On the one hand we may become too noisy, and on the other too silent or formal. The Lord save us from both extremes.[16]

Winebrenner admitted that he had held a conference meeting and that the charges were true "with the exception of a few mistakes which are generally committed when persons undertake to relate something they have from hearsay . . ."[17] He further admitted that he had kept his "experience and conference" meeting until four o'clock in the morning. However, it was untrue that he had said, "This is the way to fan the chaff from the wheat."

He did not deny denouncing members from the pulpit, suggesting that "If men will become my enemies; yea, withdraw themselves from the church, because I tell them the truth, I can not help it. But I know of none save perhaps the few men who have lodged these complaints against me."[18] With regard to the probable state of the dead mentioned in his funeral sermon, Winebrenner referred his accusers to several Scripture references.

The two country churches would not be left without preaching. But if arrangements could be made for them, he would like to serve two Reformed churches, formerly with the Harrisburg charge, that were now without the services of a minister. Regarding the fact that he had been by-passed when it came to funerals in his own church, Winebrenner merely replied, "I do rejoice to say, that, so far as I know, the pious and serious part of the congregation have always been my warm and affectionate friends."[19]

Winebrenner admitted fellowshipping the excommunicated member of another church, but claimed that the said person had professed true religion at the time. In fact, continued Winebrenner, "he manifested, to all appearance, as much sincerity, and in my opinion gave far stronger evidence of it, than many who ignorantly gloried in the enjoyment of such privileges." [20]

Finally, Winebrenner said that if he had known of anyone in the congregation being sick, he would not have been remiss about visiting him. In the course of dealing with this accusation he was interrupted by one of the elders present

> . . . who declared "that he had been sick for two weeks, and that during the whole time of his sickness, I had not once visited him." To this I replied, that I had told him before, I was not aware of his being sick at the time,—and if I had, I was not certain but what I would have hesitated to visit him. For I had reason to believe he was not very fond of hearing prayer when in health, (because he seldom went to church) and therefore might have doubted whether he would relish such exercises on a sick bed. And besides, said I, you, as an Elder of the church of Christ, are also in duty bound, and most sacredly bound, to visit the sick. Now, pray tell us, how many sick have you ever visited and prayed for? Why said he, "I can't pray." And what is the reason, said I? An Elder of the church and cannot pray? Astonishing! [21]

After this interchange, scarcely calculated to improve the Harrisburg pastor's relationship with his vestry, Winebrenner concluded by saying that it was true that he had refused to baptize the children of unbelieving parents, and furthermore, that this would continue to be his position.

Having heard Winebrenner through, the committee advised forgiving and forgetting. Winebrenner was agreeable, but the vestry balked. If Pastor Winebrenner would agree to cease holding his social prayer meetings in homes and deliver instead a lecture in the church during the week, reconciliation would be possible. Winebrenner agreed to instituting the lecture but would not abandon his prayer meetings, regardless of the vestry's attitude. The committee subsequently dissolved without reaching a solution.

Whatever Winebrenner's feelings in the matter were, they did not stop him from getting married six days later, on October 8, to Miss Charlotte Reutter of Harrisburg. Immediately following the marriage, John introduced Charlotte to his family and friends in Philadelphia and Maryland through the course of a combination wedding trip and preaching-exhorting mission, lasting at least through the rest of the month.[22]

Throughout the winter of 1822-1823 there was apparently little improvement in the difficulties which beset the Reformed

HARRISBURG REFORMED CHURCH

BUILT DURING WINEBRENNER'S PASTORATE
NOW SALEM UNITED CHURCH OF CHRIST

Church and its pastor. Winebrenner continued holding experience meetings [23] and the vestry continued in its resolute opposition. Then on Sunday morning, March 23, 1823,[24] Winebrenner announced from the pulpit of the Harrisburg Church that, due to a funeral in the country, he had engaged a Mr. Brown to preach in his stead for the afternoon service. Mr. Brown was not a minister in the German Reformed Synod, and on that account vestryman Zinn prohibited the sexton from ringing the bell or unlocking the doors of the church. Having been informed of Mr. Zinn's action, at the close of the evening service Winebrenner told his congregation that he did not know if he could be the pastor of the church any longer. At least a part of the congregation understood him to say further that if he preached the next Friday evening (March 28, Good Friday) he would preach the following Sunday—a stipulation Winebrenner apparently did not recall making.[25] Whatever was actually said from the Harrisburg pulpit on Sunday evening, March 23, Winebrenner did not preach on the following Friday, and a majority of the vestry eventually took this as his resignation from the church. However, inasmuch as Winebrenner did not seem to regard his failure to preach on Friday as tantamount to a resignation, confusion followed.

At some time during the week following his Sunday evening announcement, a committee of two from the vestry called on Winebrenner, asking for an explanation.[26] Winebrenner, in turn, asked the committee whether Mr. Zinn had the authority to countermand the pastor's appointments for the Harrisburg pulpit. Further, he asked whether it were true, as Mr. Zinn had earlier told Winebrenner, that the vestry could no longer make up Winebrenner's salary. (After almost two and one-half years of preaching at the Harrisburg Church, Winebrenner had received only $550.—about one-half of what originally had been subscribed.) In response to Winebrenner's queries, the vestry met with him on a weekday evening and informed their pastor that his salary had been collected, and if he would observe certain rules, he would be retained.[27] These rules included Winebrenner's preaching only for their church, the exclusion of unordained preachers from the pulpit, and the limitation of prayer meetings per week to one, to be adjourned before nine o'clock at night. Winebrenner refused to accept the vestry's regulation. He countered with a statement to the effect that he was a free man, preached a free gospel, and would go where the Lord called him.

The Sunday following Winebrenner's conference with the vestry, he found the church door locked and a crowd gathered outside on the street. With approximately half of the congregation, Pastor Winebrenner adjourned to the banks of the Susquehanna River two blocks away, where he had the morning service.[28] The date of the lockout is unknown. It could not have been on Easter, March 30. Harrisburg had the biggest blizzard of the season then, according to the *Harrisburg Intelligencer* of April 11, 1823. April 6 or 13 are the best possibilities. A part of the congregation subsequently met and absolved itself of all relationships with Winebrenner as of March 23, 1823. Another meeting, on April 18, of all the male members of the congregation voted unanimously not to retain Winebrenner as pastor. However, only twenty-one votes were cast. Winebrenner's friends had withdrawn before the election. Meetings on April 23 and May 19 likewise resulted in victories for the anti-Winebrenner faction.

There were those who tried to find a compromise. In July, some "propositions" to restore harmony were drawn up by sixteen members of the Harrisburg congregation, identified at the time with neither the vestry or Winebrenner. The propositions give a good idea of how that part of the congregation viewed the issues. The propositions (abridged) were:

1. While we regard it to be the duty of Christians to love the image of Christ . . . we deem it expedient that every denomination should adhere to the views and modes common among them in both social and public worship . . .

2. While we would not impeach the religious character or standing of any Minister of the gospel, yet in inviting Ministers of other denominations to preach in our pulpit, a regard should be had to the views and sentiments he entertains on religious subjects . . . none shall be invited but with the advice and by the consent of the vestry of this church.

3. We esteem it the duty and privilege of Christians to meet often . . . for the purpose of social conference and prayer . . . Yet we think it cannot be the duty of anyone to attend these meetings . . . that these meetings should not be held to such an unreasonable hour . . . and that they should be conducted with that order and solemnity which ever becomes the spiritual and rational worship of the Great Jehovah.

4. We deem it the duty of all christians to cherish and cultivate prayer. . . . Yet we do not consider it the duty of all to pray in public. . . .

5. While we consider it to be the imperative duty of Ministers of the gospel to be plain and faithful in declaring the whole counsel of God. . . . Yet we think the sacred desk ought never to be made the place for indulging in personal remarks. . . .

6. That a minister may be free from worldly cares and avocations . . . we consider it a duty of a congregation to give him competent support.

7. Mutual forgiveness and forbearance, we regard to be a christian duty, . . . we regard it our duty to implore the forgiveness of God . . . and also forgive one another.[29]

Five of the seven propositions carry implicit criticism of Winebrenner and his past actions. Yet, in the context of their appearance in *The Truth Made Known,* it appears that Winebrenner was prepared to accept them. The vestry, however, would not relent. They obviously did not want back in the pulpit a man who had openly criticized the lack of true Christian faith on the part of at least some of the vestrymen. Thereupon, the originators of the propositions called for another congregational meeting to discuss them. The vestry, alone responsible for calling such meetings, refused.

Actually, the vestry's adamant stand worked in Winebrenner's favor, gaining him the sympathy of a growing number of the congregation. A petition, circulated by those who had drawn up the propositions, was signed by 134 members (not all of whom were *voting* members) who desired "that Mr. John Winebrenner should be continued and supported by the congregation." [30] Winebrenner offered an interesting analysis of the petition in *The Truth Made Known,* reflecting, it would seem, some underlying economic tensions which existed in his congregation:

> From this document the reader may learn, that there is a large majority of the congregation in my favor; yet this vast majority must yield to, and be governed by a few men, merely because they have a little more "of this world's goods." For, no doubt, if they were poor men, they would have been silenced long ago. . . . It has often, if not always been so, and therefore, the children of the kingdom must learn to be "patient in tribulation, and in patience to possess their souls." [31]

Winebrenner may have been able to enlist the sympathy of a greater part of the congregation. However, the wealth of the church, and therefore his salary, was in an alienated vestry. One ministerial "child of the kingdom" was in the process of learning certain economic facts of church life. But "patient in tribulation" he was not to be.

Matters, bad enough as they were, were complicated still further by the desire of the German Reformed Church to establish a seminary in the early 1820's. Harrisburg first had been suggested as the site for the school during the Synod of 1822—meeting at Harrisburg—with the seminary professor to become pastor of the Harrisburg Church. A committee, appointed by the Synod on Friday morning, October 4, to meet with the consistory of the church, reported that:

1. The Consistory is convinced that Harrisburg would be an appropriate place for the establishment of the Seminary.

2. It [the consistory] is willing and prepared to take the elected Professor as their Pastor with the stipulation that Mr. Weinbrenner give his consent, in order that everything takes place peaceably.

3. It [the consistory] promises to pay the Professor the sum of $500 in wages; but it is also of the opinion that more could be given.[32]

Winebrenner, whose salary of (at most) $425. a year from the Harrisburg Church even then was in arrears, and who had stayed up until two in the morning on Thursday answering charges (extravagant, by his thinking) brought against him by some of the consistory members,[33] undoubtedly was not as convinced as the consistory that "Harrisburg would be an appropriate place for the Seminary." His consent was withheld. He asked for permission first to consult his congregations, possibly to raise the issue of his salary, and the Synod postponed further action.

A committee appointed by the Synod at Baltimore in 1823 to meet with the Harrisburg representatives, reported that the Harrisburg Church was without a pastor, and that the church continued to offer $500. toward the salary of the professor, provided the seminary were located there.[34] Even though Winebrenner occupied considerable time on the Synod floor relating his position concerning the unresolved issues between him and the church,[35] the Synod nonetheless officially chose Harrisburg as the site for the seminary,[36] and elected as its first professor (and hence as pastor of the Harrisburg Church) none other than Dr. Samuel Helffenstein. Winebrenner thereupon was asked if he would stop preaching in town (apparently to that part of the congregation loyal to him), and give over his congregation to his former theological teacher.[37] Winebrenner said he was agreeable, providing the vestry paid him his back salary and a majority of the congregation would accept Samuel Helffenstein. The Synod wrote to the vestry requesting them to settle their affairs with Winebrenner. The vestry refused and invited Helffenstein to come anyway. Helffenstein turned down the dubious opportunity.

What happened between the Synods of 1823 and 1824 is obscure, although certain facts stand out. The seminary of the German Reformed Church was not established at Harrisburg, almost certainly because of the dissension there. The vestry of the Harrisburg Church, representing a minority of the members, secured a new pastor, Albert Helffenstein (Samuel, Sr.'s son), who assumed his duties on March 24, 1824.[38] Possibly he was invited as a sort of interim pastor, to be succeeded by his father when the difficulties with Winebrenner were cleared up. Shortly after Winebrenner's lockout from the Harrisburg Church, Samuel Helffenstein had sent him a letter offering to present him as a candidate for the German Reformed Church in New York City, with a salary of $800. for the first year.[39]

Finally, conditions between Winebrenner and his now former vestry had deteriorated to such a point that the church complained officially to the Synod of 1824 at Bedford, Pennsylvania:

> The congregation at Harrisburg complains about the conduct of the Rev. J. Winebrenner; hopes the Shoop's and Wenrich's congregations will soon connect themselves with the Harrisburg congregation, and refers to Judge Bucher for an explanation of the matter.[40]

The response was a resolution, presumably offered by Winebrenner's friends, which must have startled the vestry:

> *Resolved,* That the Harrisburg, Shoop's, Wenrich's, and Peace (Salem) Congregations hold an election whether Mr. Winebrenner shall be their pastor or not.[41]

Upon returning home from the Synod of 1824, Winebrenner notified the Harrisburg vestry of the Synod's decision. The vestry once again ignored their former pastor. Winebrenner's friends then printed ballots and held an election. It accomplished nothing inasmuch as the anti-Winebrenner group did not attend. Frustrated, Winebrenner for a time considered legal action.[42]

The resolution of the Synod of 1824 ordering an election for the Harrisburg charge was a cause of concern not only to the Harrisburg vestry, but also to the Lebanon Classis to which the Harrisburg Church had belonged since 1822. At its meeting on April 27, 1823, following Winebrenner's lockout, the Classis had sided with the vestry and in effect declared the Harrisburg pulpit vacant.[43] Winebrenner, however, had appealed to the Susquehanna Classis, using for his reason that in 1822 the Synod had transferred the Harrisburg Church but not himself from the Susquehanna to the Lebanon Classis.[44] The Susquehanna Classis supported Winebrenner. Hence, at the Synod of 1825 in Philadelphia, the Lebanon and Susquehanna Classes were arraigned against one another in a jurisdictional dispute. After "much debate" the Synod sustained the Lebanon Classis by a majority vote.[45] The issues between Winebrenner and the Harrisburg Church vestry were once and for all settled.

Winebrenner took the action of the Synod in supporting the Lebanon Classis as a personal rebuke. The Synod of 1825 was the last he attended. Over the next year he began to cut his ties with the German Reformed Church, becoming something of an "independent" minister in the Harrisburg area. The Synod of 1826 meeting at Frederick, Maryland, received charges of "the disorderly conduct of the Rev. John Weinbrenner" and others.[46] Similar charges were brought before the Synod of 1827 at York by both the Lebanon and Susquehanna Classes.[47] The charges included Winebrenner's "throwing away" infant baptism and holding camp meetings.[48] A committee was appointed to try the charges. Its report to the Synod of 1828 is contained in the following minute:

> The committee which had been appointed by the Synod at a meeting held at York, Pa., to investigate the case of the Rev. Messrs. Winebrenner and Habliston, and to report at this meeting, reported that Mr. Winebrenner had not obeyed their citation, and he did not appear before them; and that, in their opinion, he ought not to be any longer considered a member of this body.[49]

The report was accepted and Winebrenner's connections with the German Reformed Church were now officially severed.

The Issue

What was the basic issue, insofar as we can reduce the conflict to any one issue, involved in John Winebrenner's separation from the Harrisburg, and, eventually, the entire German Reformed Church?

Professor James I. Good, the Reformed Church historian, has suggested that the ultimate issue in Winebrenner's defection from the Reformed Church was his "insubordination." The roots of the matter, Good conjectured, were to be found in Winebrenner's disappointment over his not being appointed professor of the projected seminary at Harrisburg. He explained:

> Winebrenner had not at first opposed the seminary project, but had been quite sanguine in it, for in 1821 he pledged $200 a year toward it. It has been suggested that later, when he found that Harrisburg would be its location, he conceived the notion that, as he was pastor there, he might be elected professor. But he was as yet too young a man for such a position, having been only two years in the ministry. . . . It has been said that he was driven out of our church because he was a revivalist. That is not true, for at that time there were other men in the synod as full of revival zeal as he. It was his continued insubordination that drove him out.[50]

Good does not offer documentation for his hypothesis that Winebrenner had his eye on the seminary post at Harrisburg. The statement, "It has been suggested that . . ." is, at best, vague. There is, moreover, another side to the story.

A study of German Reformed sources available could easily suggest that the placing of the seminary in Harrisburg was, in fact, a convenient pretext used by the vestry of the Harrisburg congregation to rid themselves of a pastor with whom they previously had been in conflict. Good, oddly enough, says as much. In noting that the Synod of 1822 planned to establish a seminary at Harrisburg with the consent of the Harrisburg vestry he writes:

> But there was a difficulty in the way. The pastor of the Harrisburg congregation at that time was Rev. John Winebrenner. An influential party in the congregation were seeking to get rid of him and thought this a good method of doing so.[51]

It should be noted further that the attempt of the Synod to place the seminary at Harrisburg caused some dissension within the Synod itself. At the Synod of 1822 there were "serious difficulties" following the report of the committee which had conferred with the Harrisburg consistory and, consequently, it was resolved that "the decision of the matter be postponed until the next meeting of the Synod."[52] It may have been that some of Winebrenner's friends in the Synod resented the way in which the Harrisburg vestry was using the seminary issue to rid itself of its pastor. There can be but little doubt that Winebrenner did.

Church of God writers from Winebrenner on have maintained that the primary factor in Winebrenner's expulsion from the German Reformed Church was the opposition in that church to his intense evangelistic fervor and revivalism. Forney notes in referring to Winebrenner and the Harrisburg church: "Soon after his settlement in his charge a work of grace commenced among the people. . . . This developed great and bitter opposition. . . ."[53] Yahn adds more explicitly:

> He [Winebrenner] was pre-eminently an evangelistic preacher, and God honored his preaching with "glorious revivals of religion." But it also aroused, as he says, "vehement opposition" on the part of those who were unwilling to yield to his pleas for a genuine Christian life. This was the primary and fundamental cause of the cleavage which, about five years after he assumed the responsibilities of the pastorate, resulted in his separation from the German Reformed denomination.[54]

In support of their thesis, Church of God writers have quoted John Williamson Nevin of the German Reformed Church who had

34

characterized the state of religion in his church in the early nineteenth century as follows:

> To be confirmed and then to take the sacrament occasionally was counted by the multitude all that was necessary to make one a good Christian, if only a tolerable decency of outward life were maintained besides, without any regard at all to the religion of the heart. True, serious piety was indeed often treated with open and marked scorn. In the bosom of the church itself it was stigmatized as miserable, driveling Methodism. The idea of the new birth was treated as a pietistic whimsey. Experimental religion, in all its forms was eschewed as a new fangled invention of cunning imposters, brought in to turn the heads of the weak, and to lead captive silly women. Prayer-meetings were held to be a spiritual abomination. Family worship was a species of saintly affectation, barely tolerable in the case of ministers (though many of them gloried in having no altar in their houses), but absolutely disgraceful for common Christians. To show an awakened concern on the subject of religion, a disposition to call on God in daily secret prayer, was to incur certain reproach. . . . The picture, it must be acknowledged, is dark, but not more so than the truth of history would seem to require.[55]

This passage would seem to indicate that Winebrenner's evangelistic efforts could not help but raise some determined opposition.

Another statement quoted by a Church of God writer in order to show the religious climate in which Winebrenner worked is the following from the pen of the Rev. R. Weiser, in the *Lutheran Observer* for August 17, 1877:

> The first revival of religion of which I have any personal knowledge, was in York, Pa., in the winter of 1825-26. This work started in the German Reformed Church. Rev. James R. Reily was pastor of that church, and he had Rev. John Winebrenner, to assist at a communion. Mr. Winebrenner was then in his prime, and was a powerful and effective preacher, especially in German. The interest commenced in the Reformed Church, but soon spread over the whole community.[56]

However, the history of the German Reformed Church in the United States simply does not support the Church of God contention that revivalism was the basic issue in Winebrenner's leaving the German Reformed Church. The quotes from Nevin and Weiser above to the contrary, there had been a long tradition of a pietistic-revivalistic type of religion in the German Reformed Church ever since its establishment in the United States.[57] Winebrenner apparently grew up in this tradition. His childhood pastors at the Glades German Reformed Church, J. W. Runkel and Daniel Wagner, are described as "eminently good, active in the ministry, and aiming, as much as possible, at immediate effect."[58] Jonathan Helffenstein, pastor at the Glades Church from 1811 to 1828, was pleased to observe a religious awakening among the young in his Frederick Church (on the same charge with Glades) in 1828, during which "upwards of eighty professors . . . passed from death unto life. . . ."[59]

Samuel Helffenstein, Sr., Winebrenner's teacher at Philadelphia, inherited the same pietistic-revivalistic tradition as brother Jonathan, passing it on to his sons and students, including Winebrenner. Lewis Mayer, first president of the Reformed Seminary at Carlisle and a close friend of Winebrenner's, had been soundly converted as a young man in the Frederick, Maryland, Reformed Church, and continued to speak of the importance of "vital religion" later in life.[60] At least some of Mayer's students at the seminary were revivalistically oriented. For example, J. G. Fritchey, a student at the time, rejoices in the conversion of his sister under Winebrenner, adding, "but more especially too I rejoice that you have been made the happy instrument in the hands of King Immanuel in stirring up a revival in that second sodom [sic] I mean Linglestown."[61] Of more than passing interest is the fact that shortly after the Synod of 1825 had backed the Harrisburg vestry, Albert Helffenstein, and the Lebanon Classis against Winebrenner, the students at the seminary displayed their respect for the former Harrisburg pastor by electing him an honorary member of the seminary's Adelphimanian Society.[62] That revivalism as such was not the issue at hand in the dispute between Winebrenner and the Harrisburg vestry is further suggested by the fact that Samuel Helffenstein, the very man responsible for Winebrenner's conversion, was elected president of the seminary-to-be in Harrisburg, and consequently, pastor of the Harrisburg Church. The vestry, as we have seen, was pleased with the arrangement.

An examination of Winebrenner's initial difficulty with the Harrisburg vestry, the complaints made against him at the Synod of 1822, and the attempts at reconciliation in 1823,[63] strongly suggest that the opposition to Winebrenner found its origin not in his revivalism, but rather in his extreme revivalistic methods. The revivalistic measures employed by Winebrenner (as reported in the charges of his church against him) bear close resemblance to the "new measures" which were to become a subject of considerable acrimonious debate in the American church from the late 1820's on. Thus, in July of 1827, a group of ministers met at New Lebanon, New York, "to see in what respects there is agreement between brethren from different sections of the country, in regard to principles and measures in conduction and promoting revivals of religion." [64] Among the measures which these ministers discussed at that time were:

1. Women praying in assemblies where men are present.

2. Praying for a person by name in a public meeting.

3. The intrusion of evangelists in the parish of a settled minister without that minister's consent.

4. Holding meetings until an unusually late hour at night.[65]

The measures which, in a book published in 1835, revivalist Charles Finney noted as having "chiefly attracted remark" are:

1. The "Anxious meeting," i.e., a meeting especially for those concerned about their soul's salvation.

2. The "Anxious seat," i.e., a particular place in a church or meeting house where those seeking the conversion experience could go for special prayer and assistance.

3. The "protracted meeting," i.e., a meeting held over a period of days or weeks in the same meeting place in order to stimulate a religious response.[66]

Besides those already named, there was a plethora of additional techniques identified with the "new measures" and "new measure" ministers, especially by opponents of the measures. There is, for example, the reported practice of whipping children in order to persuade them to "submit to God." The Oneida Presbytery in New York investigated this reputed "new measure." However, "all they could ascertain was that one good mother in her chamber did once whip a child to induce it to submit to God; but immediately after she was convinced of her mistake and bitterly bemoaned it." [67]

The similarities between the measures mentioned above—measures which were at that time causing no little friction in the American Church—and the revivalistic measures employed by Winebrenner are obvious. Those in the Harrisburg Church who were in opposition to Winebrenner opposed him, not for his emphasis on regeneration, but rather for the techniques he was using in getting his message across. They simply did not want personal references made in the pulpit or unordained non-German Reformed men preaching debatable things to them in their own church. Their experience with revivalism or "conversionism," whatever it had been in the past, did not include "anxious," "experience and conference," or "protracted" meetings—especially when such meetings were liable to last until four o'clock in the morning and were attended with an unchurchly clamor. Alienation was inevitable after attempts at compromise failed.

Illustrating Winebrenner's "new measure" approach are entries in the diary of one Levi Merkel, a seventeen year old parishioner of Winebrenner's at his Salem Church in the country. Hav-

PEACE CHURCH
near SHIREMANSTOWN

ing attended an anticipatory "day of fasting and prayer" called by Pastor Winebrenner for Saturday, April 17, 1824, Merkel records his experiences on Sunday, April 18, as follows:

> At 10 o'clock public preaching commenced. For God so loved the world that he gave his only begotten son etc.—was the text which appeared to be attended with power and the energy of the Spirit of God. At last he [Winebrenner] went upon his knees in the pulpit and prayed and entreated the careless sinners to turn, which had great influence on the whole congregation. Brother Winebrenner became so full at last that he could not speak to them. For sometime there was nothing heard but weaping [sic], lamenting, and groaning [in] every direction, and Winebrenner every now and then calling from the pulpit, ["]Brethren pray on, Sisters pray on, the grace of God is working.["] Some were on their knees— and the most kept their seats. Through this shower I received a great Blessing to my soul. . . .

After a short English discourse and administration of the ordinance of baptism,

> Winebrenner expressed the dificulty [sic] he was having in
> the administration of this Holy ordinance [the Lord's Supper],
> in consequence of so many offering themselves for communion
> who by appearance were in an unrenewed and carnal state
> . . . .[68]

In August of 1826, Winebrenner was also dismissed from the Salem Church, apparently by the locked door route.

It should be noted that Winebrenner was not the only "new measure" man in the Reformed Church of his time. As the complaints brought against Winebrenner at the Synod of 1822 indicate, Jacob Helffenstein, Samuel, Sr.'s son, was among those exhorting at one of Winebrenner's conference meetings.[69] Henry Habliston, a minister in Zion's Classis, also assisted Winebrenner at his meetings. Jacob Helffenstein later had a stormy career as a minister, leaving the German Reformed Church for a while and then returning. Henry Habliston was exscinded from the Reformed Church with Winebrenner at the Synod of 1828.

Other pastors, contemporaries of Winebrenner who remained in the Reformed Church, were influenced to a certain degree by "new measurism." However, the lack of consensus as to what constituted a "new measure" has clouded the issue historically. (Prayer meetings were considered by some as a "new measure." However the use of prayer meetings extended far back into the American German Reformed Church heritage. The eighteenth century pastors, many of whom had a Halle or Halle-related background, used them frequently.) Some of the Helffensteins, other than Jacob, were claimed to be "new measure" ministers, although their histories indicate a more cautious and moderate approach than Winebrenner's. Albert Helffenstein, who succeeded Winebrenner at Harrisburg's Reformed Church, was later said to be a "new measure" minister even though it is apparent from what happened at the Harrisburg Church that he did not represent the same revivalistic method as Winebrenner. Indeed, Lewis Mayer found Albert Helffenstein "too unacquainted with vital religion" to successfully fill the Harrisburg Reformed Church pulpit.[70] Too, it should be mentioned that the degree of receptivity to "new measures" varied from church to church and classis to classis in the German Reformed Synod. What was acceptable in one area was not necessarily acceptable in others.

Finally, while focusing attention on "new measures" as the cause of Winebrenner's separation from the Reformed Church, some allowance should be made for the intrusion into the basic issue of problems related to the seminary establishment in Harrisburg, the background of the Harrisburg Church vestry and congregation, and Winebrenner's own personality. Secondary priorities here are difficult to establish and, given the lack of additional data, conjectural. However, on the basis of information available, it would seem that it was Winebrenner's whole-hearted adoption of "new measures," probably under the influence of the local Methodists, which led to his eventual separation from the German Reformed Church. After some experimentation, the Synod decided that it did not have room for such measures or John Winebrenner.

4

A New Church

In the *Weekly Messenger* of the German Reformed Church for November 15, 1843, one "L. S." wrote a letter to the editor in connection with the Winebrenner-John Williamson Nevin correspondence controversy then being carried in the *Messenger* and the Church of God periodical, the *Gospel Publisher*.[1] In the course of reviewing the history of Winebrenner's relationship with the Reformed Church, "L. S.," who called himself a "former friend" of Winebrenner's, offered the following letter he was supposed to have received from his former friend not long after the Synod of 1825 at Philadelphia:

Nov. 2d 1825

Permit me here to inform you what a number of our ministers have in contemplation, namely, to form a new denomination. When I was at the Synod in Philadelphia it was strongly talked of; and it is thought by some, that we would have a meeting on the subject some time next Spring. Some of the brethren are very anxious for it, and so am I. I really believe that it would be much to the interest of the Redeemer's Kingdom were we to form a connexion of such a character as the church under its first formation was, and God designed it should be, "pure and undefiled," at least as much so as the present state and condition of the world would admit of. You know my friend, that our church is awfully corrupted, and I despair of seeing a better state of things, until a separation takes place, and those whom God has enlightened unite with each other in building up a holy and Christian Society. If we do have a meeting in the Spring, I hope that God will incline your heart, and the hearts of all our experienced brethren to meet together, and aid in forming such a connexion.

I remain your Brother, etc.,

John Winebrenner

"L. S." then commented: "This pretended move in the church was new to me, and I could not persuade myself that it existed anywhere but in the disappointed bosom of Mr. Winebrenner. . . ."

Such letters are, of course, generally suspect. Especially is this so when they have lain preserved quietly for eighteen years and then are suddenly resurrected for insertion into a heated, polemical debate. Still, there are reasons for giving it more than casual examination. Apart from the letter, "L. S." is accurate in reporting to the editor of the *Messenger* details connected with Winebrenner's separation from the Reformed Church. When the "L. S." letter was brought to Winebrenner's attention, he did not automatically deny the truth of its contents, although he did request the privilege of responding to it in the pages of the *Messenger*.[2]

Then too, the situation in the Synod of the German Reformed Church in the early 1820's should be taken into account. Schism, threatened or otherwise, was in the air. In 1821, several prominent pastors declared their intention to secede with their churches to the Dutch Reformed Church if the plan for the projected seminary were defeated at the Synod that year.[3] The so-called "Free Synod," made up of a considerable number of more conservative, German-speaking Reformed churches, was organized in 1822. A significant separation, it was due in part to the seminary issue and in part to personal differences.[4] In 1824, the Ohio Classis left the Synod forming a Synod of its own which later the West Pennsylvania Classis joined. This being the situation, it is not beyond the realm of possibility that a "number of . . . ministers" may have contemplated the formation of a new denomination following the Synod of 1825. It was a Synod, after all, at which two Classes were in dispute. Only after "much debate" was the issue settled, and then only by a majority vote.[5] Very possibly after the vote Winebrenner and his friends in the minority would have become convinced that "our church is awfully corrupted" and that the only remedy was a "connexion of such a character as the church under its first formation was . . . 'pure and undefiled,' . . ." In his later writings, Winebrenner always regarded 1825 as his year of separation from the Reformed Church.

Whatever the truth of the matter is with regard to "L. S." 's letter, Winebrenner appeared to have maintained at least a peripheral relationship to the Reformed Church for a while following the Synod of 1825. He continued serving two of his country churches formerly on the Harrisburg charge into 1826. The German Reformed churches at Hagerstown, Maryland, and York, Pennsylvania, expressed an interest in having Winebrenner as their pastor in December of 1825.[6] The Hagerstown Church issued him a call in January, 1826.[7] (Hagerstown was in the revivalistically oriented Maryland Classis. Winebrenner had been recommended to the Hagerstown charge in March, 1825, by one of the pastors on the charge, and a friend of Winebrenner's, James Ross Reily. Reily was shortly to leave for Europe to raise money for the Reformed Seminary at Carlisle. Winebrenner probably preached a "trial sermon" at Hagerstown in the late spring of 1825.[8] At the church election, Winebrenner received thirty-one out of fifty-two votes cast, suggesting significant opposition.) He later declined their invitation, although not without giving it some serious thought.[9] In a letter addressed in March of 1826 to Rev. James R. Reily in Amsterdam, Holland, Winebrenner tells his close friend of various occurrences within the German Reformed Church, expressing the hope that "our infant seminary will grow and flourish." [10] Yet, while some of the old ties remained, Winebrenner was following an increasingly independent course. The situation with regard to his Harrisburg congregation seemed to leave him with little choice.

The Church of God

Up until the Synod of 1825, Winebrenner and his followers in Harrisburg could still lay claim to being the legitimate Reformed Church in Harrisburg, unlawfully excluded from the church property by the action of the vestry. The majority ruling of the Synod of 1825 had changed all that. What then were Winebrenner and his congregation to do? Dissolution was not the answer; it was an active, growing congregation. In his letter of March 18, 1826, to Reily, Winebrenner reported an extensive revival chiefly confined to his own congregation, in which upwards of fifty had "already been soundly converted to God." [11] The answer seemed to be the erection of a church building to house Winebrenner and his "new measure" group. Accordingly, at a meeting of Winebrenner's congregation on May 9, 1826, the following actions were agreed upon unanimously:

1. That whereas J. Winebrenner and his congregation has no suitable place of worship at present, we immediately proceed (God willing) to build a Church, provided a sufficient sum, in money, materials and work can be raised for that purpose.

2. That the Church be and remain free for the use of all Christian Denominations when it is not occupied by the Congregation.[12]

The record does not indicate any denominational affiliation, but suggests, rather, that these are actions of a completely independent congregation. When the cornerstone of the church building was laid a year later on May 12, 1827, a local newspaper called the church the "Union Bethel." [13]

MULBERRY STREET "UNION BETHEL"

Events similar to those in Harrisburg began to happen elsewhere as well. An account of John Winebrenner and his ministerial efforts in and around the Harrisburg area about this time comes to us in a letter written by John Seybert, later to become the first bishop of the Evangelical Association. Seybert, in the letter dated March 2, 1826, asked one of his friends:

You also know something of the Reformed minister, John Winebrenner, do you not? The same is earnestly engaged in the Lord's work, labors with great success and God is with him. This can not be denied, but the ungodly and even all the Egyptian sorcerers can not gain say it. Winebrenner preaches in a certain locality, in Cumberland county, where the people are boundlessly wicked. But since he is preaching there, a work of grace has broken out, and it is asserted that the people of Lisbon and vicinity are nearly all awakened and converted. This man manifests great zeal, and is no respecter of persons or station. He preaches to the wicked and the good, among the high and the low, the rich and the poor, Methodists, white or black. He is loved by the good, and by the false teachers he is hated and persecuted.[14]

As the letter indicates, Winebrenner (still thought of as a German Reformed minister) and his "new measures" were finding a considerable following in the Harrisburg area. When locked out of the country churches on the Harrisburg Reformed charge, many of his parishioners removed themselves from these Reformed congregations and worshipped with their pastor in such places as could be obtained.[15] Likewise, converts from an increasing number of Winebrenner's revivals and camp meetings in and around Harrisburg began to look to Winebrenner as their pastor, worshipping with him and others of like mind rather than associating themselves with the established churches in the area. The formation of independent churches made up of "converted" Christians only was a natural step.

Winebrenner himself later (in 1844) telescoped the story of events in 1825 and after as follows:

> About this time (1825) more extensive and glorious revivals of religion commenced in different towns and neighbourhoods, to wit: New Cumberland, Linglestown, Middletown, Millerstown, Lebanon, Lancaster, Shippensburg, Elizabethtown, Mount Joy, Marietta, and various other places. In these glorious revivals there were hundreds and multitudes happily converted to God. The conversion of these scores and multitudes in different places led to the organization of churches. And, as the writer's views had by this time materially changed, as to the true nature of a scriptural organization of churches, he adopted the apostolic plan, as taught in the New Testament, and established spiritual, free, and independent churches, consisting of believers or Christians only, without any human name, or creed, or ordinances, or laws, etc.[16]

For Winebrenner then, the underlying or motivating principle in the establishment of these independent churches soon came to be thought of as the restoration of primitive or Biblical Christianity, i.e., what Winebrenner and his followers conceived of as being "the apostolic plan, as taught in the New Testament;" hence, eventually, the concept of the local "church of God."

The church, Winebrenner reasoned, is a Biblical institution (although Winebrenner confined its origins to the New Testament). It therefore should have a Biblical name, *viz.* "Church of God," and not a human one. Winebrenner explained:

> The name or title, Church of God, is undeniably the true and proper appellation by which the New Testament church

ought to be designated. This is her scriptural and appropriate name. This and no other title, is given her by divine authority. This name or title, therefore, ought to be adopted and worn to the exclusion of all others.

There are those, who have pleaded for the use, and for the exclusive use, of some other appellations: such as the name of Christian; others for that of Disciples; and others, again, for the name Brethren, etc. But it ought to be recollected, that not one of those is a proper noun, or a patronymic, and, therefore, none of them is ever used in Scripture as an appellation for the church. The individual members of the church are, and may be, very properly so called; but not so with regard to the church herself. We nowhere read of the "Christian Church," or of the "Disciples' Church," nor of the "Brethren's Church," etc.[17]

This emphasis on a Biblical name and Scriptural foundation for the church enabled Winebrenner and his friends to argue against the charge that the "Church of God" or "churches of God" was the beginning of a new denomination. The "Church of God" was merely the "re-emergence," as it were, of the apostolic church and hence should be considered *The* Church rather than *a* church. To be sure, there were Christians, or "converted persons," in church organizations other than the churches of God, but only in the churches of God had Christians re-discovered or restored the apostolic plan of the church. Hence, the "Church of God" so conceived was a reform, and, to some extent, unity movement within the American church as a whole.

Polity, Ordinances, and Teachings

In 1829, Winebrenner published his *A Brief View of the Formation, Government and Discipline of the Church of God.* As Forney notes, "The only departure from the German Reformed faith indicated in this book relates to church name, and church formation and government." [18] In the above publication, Winebrenner held the only proper name for a church was "church of God" and that each church possessed "sufficient power to perform all acts of religious worship, and everything relating to ecclesiastic government and discipline." [19] The officers of each church so constituted were, Winebrenner found in the New Testament, elders (or presbyters) and deacons. Hence, Winebrenner declared that the presbyterian form of government on the local church level was scriptural, but at this time he had no idea of a presbyterian system outside the local church (i.e. a presbytery or synod). Winebrenner insisted that "every individual church is strictly independent of all others, as it respects religious worship and the general government of its own affairs." [20] (This probably reflected his former situation in the Reformed Church. As far as Winebrenner was concerned, it was the Synod which had ultimately deprived him of his position at the Harrisburg Church, even though his supporters represented a majority of the congregation.) Cooperation between various local churches was left up to each congregation. Winebrenner's views on this last point soon were to change.

By 1830 local churches of God had been established at several points in the Harrisburg area (primarily at those places where Winebrenner and other "new measure" ministers had held revival meetings) and the movement was spreading. The summer of 1830 saw an effort in the direction of a system of cooperation between these local churches. In spite of some determined opposition, in October of 1830 an "eldership" was organized, consisting of six "teaching elders" (ministers) from several, but not all, of the churches of God. (Winebrenner, in his *A Brief View . . . of the Church of God,* had made provision for the ordination of teaching elders by the local church.) [21] The story of the formation of the first eldership was related by Winebrenner as follows:

> From among the young converts, in these newly planted churches, it pleased God to raise up several able men, to take upon them the solemn and responsible office of the gospel ministry. These ministering brethren, with a few other great and good men with similar views and kindred spirits, labored and co-operated with each other but, finally they agreed to hold a meeting for the purpose of adopting a regular system of co-operation.

> Accordingly, they met together for this purpose, pursuant to public notice, in the Union Bethel, at Harrisburg, in the month of October 1830, and organized the meeting by appointing John Winebrenner, of Harrisburg, speaker; and John Elliott, of Lancaster, clerk.

Winebrenner concluded: "Thus originated the Church of God, properly so called, in the United States of America; and thus, also, originated the first eldership." [22]

Just as Winebrenner's views on church polity changed, so also did his views on the sacraments or "ordinances" of the church. The prevailing German Reformed conception of the Lord's Supper apparently occasioned no difficulty with Winebrenner, but baptism was another matter. He had been immersing converts as early as 1826, if the converts so desired, but had reached no personal conclusions on the matter until 1830. In that year, after "reading the Bible on his knees," Winebrenner concluded that the only scriptural baptism is the immersion of believers. Having made this decision, Winebrenner preached a locally famous "Sermon on Baptism" and was immersed by Jacob Erb, a United Brethren minister.[23]

The practice of feet-washing was common to several religious bodies in Pennsylvania in Winebrenner's time, including the German Baptists, Mennonites, and United Brethren. Winebrenner had not reached a decision on the validity of the practice as late as 1828. When asked at a camp meeting during this year to participate with some United Brethren ministers in a feet-washing service, Winebrenner replied, "Do not bind your brother's conscience. You believe that it is a positive command, and I do not."[24] However, by 1829, just a year later, Winebrenner was participating in the ordinance and accepting it as a "positive command."

Winebrenner's religious opinions, general theological position, and the emphases of the Church of God in the 1830's and early 1840's were summed up in twenty-seven points given by Winebrenner himself in 1844 as "the avowed principles of the Church of God in the United States." (The scripture proof-texts accompanying each point are omitted.)

1. She believes the Bible, or the canonical books of the Old and New Testament to be the word of God, a revelation from God to man, and the only authoritative rule of faith and practice.

2. She believes in one Supreme God, consisting of Father, Son, and Holy Spirit, and that these three are co-equal and co-eternal.

3. She believes in the fall and depravity of man; that is to say, that man by nature is destitute of the favor and image of God.

4. She believes in the redemption of man through the atonement, or vicarious sacrifice of Jesus Christ.

5. She believes in the gift and office-work of the Holy Spirit; that is, in the enlightening, regenerating, and sanctifying influence and power of the Spirit.

6. She believes in the free, moral agency of man; that he has moral ability, because commanded to repent and believe, in order to be saved; and that the doctrine of unconditional election and reprobation, has no foundation in the oracles of God.

A

PRAYER MEETING

AND

REVIVAL HYMN BOOK,

OR

A Selection

OF THE BEST

"PSALMS & HYMNS & SPIRI-TUAL SONGS."

FROM VARIOUS AUTHORS, FOR THE USE OF

SOCIAL PRAYER MEETINGS,

AND

REVIVALS OF RELIGION

BY JOHN WINEBRENNER, V. D. M

" Let the word of Christ dwell in you richly in all
wisdom, teaching and admonishing one another t.
Psalms and Hymns and Spiritual Songs, singing with
grace in your hearts unto the Lord."—Col. III. 16.

HARRISBURG:

PRINTED BY J. & M. W. M'KINLEY,

Office of the Religious Visiter.

1825.

Title page from Winebrenner's *Revival Hymn Book*, first published in 1825.

7. She believes that man is justified by faith in Christ, and not by the works of the law, or by works of his own righteousness.

8. She believes in the necessity of regeneration or the new birth; or, in the change of man's moral nature, after the image of God, by the influence and power of the word and spirit of God, through faith in Christ Jesus.

9. She believes in three positive ordinances of perpetual standing in the church, viz., *Baptism, Feet-washing,* and the *Lord's Supper.*

10. She believes two things essential to the validity of baptism, viz., *faith* and *immersion*: that faith should always precede immersion; and that where either is wanting, there can be no scriptural baptism.

11. She believes that the ordinance of *feet-washing,* that is, the literal washing of the saints' feet, according to the words and example of Christ, is obligatory upon all Christians, and ought to be observed by all the churches of God.

12. She believes that the *Lord's Supper* should be often administered, and, to be consistent, to Christians only, in a sitting posture, and always in the evening.

13. She believes in the institution of the Lord's day, or Christian Sabbath, as a day of rest and religious worship.

14. She believes that the reading and preaching of God's word, the singing of psalms and hymns, and spiritual songs, and the offering up of prayers, are ordained of God, and ought to be regularly and devoutly observed by all the people and churches of God.

15. She believes in the propriety and utility of holding fast-days, experience meetings, anxious meetings, camp meetings, and other special meetings of united and protracted efforts for the edification of the church and the conversion of sinners.

16. She believes that the gospel ministry, sabbath schools, education, the religious press, the Bible, missionary, temperance, and all other benevolent causes, ought to be heartily and liberally supported.

17. She believes that the church ought to relieve and take care of her own poor saints, superannuated ministers, widows and orphans.

18. She believes that the manufacture, traffic, and use of ardent spirits, as a beverage or common drink, is injurious and immoral, and ought to be abandoned.

19. She believes the system or institution of involuntary slavery to be impolitic or unchristian.

50

20. She believes that all civil wars are unholy and sinful, and in which the saints of the Most High ought never to participate.

21. She believes that civil governments are ordained of God for the general good; that Christians ought to be subject to the same in all things, except what is manifestly unscriputral; and that appeals to the law, out of the church, for justice, and the adjustments of civil rights, are not inconsistent with the principles and duties of the Christian religion.

22. She believes in the necessity of a virtuous and holy life, and that Christ will save those only who obey him.

23. She believes in the visibility, unity, sanctity, universality, and perpetuity of the church of God.

24. She believes in the personal coming and reign of Jesus Christ.

25. She believes in the resurrection of the dead, "both of the just and the unjust"; that the resurrection of the just will precede the resurrection of the unjust; that the first will take place at the beginning, and the second at the end of the millenium.

26. She believes in the creation of new heavens and a new earth.

27. She believes in the immortality of the soul; in a universal and eternal judgment; and in future and everlasting rewards and punishments.[25]

The points generally reflect a nineteenth century American Protestant orthodoxy which Winebrenner would have inherited from Samuel Helffenstein. Winebrenner's relationship with the Methodists or Methodist-related church organizations like the United Brethren, and the Anabaptist oriented groups in the Harrisburg area would be sufficient to explain references to the "free, moral agency of man," believer's baptism by immersion, and feet-washing as a perpetual ordinance. "New measures" are explicitly defended (points fourteen and fifteen). Winebrenner's interest in the reform of what he and many of his contemporary "evangelical" churchmen considered were immoral social and political structures is also apparent. His allowance of a Christian appeal to the civil law "out of the church" is possibly a reaction to Harrisburg area Mennonite or German Anabaptist teachings on the subject. His eschatology is not unique, although it should be mentioned that his other writings do not indicate a preoccupation with "last things," even during the Millerite excitement.

The obvious influence of other church groups on Winebrenner and the development of the Church of God led to some interesting descriptions of the Church in the various compendia of religion appearing in America in the middle and late nineteenth century. Baird, in his *Religion in America,* made the Church of God "a sect of German Baptists."[26] Belcher, however, listed the Church of God with "miscellaneous churches" and then told why:

> Their confession of faith is of the Arminian character; their views of Baptism correspond with those of the Baptist body; their church government is generally that of the Presbyterians, except that, like the Methodists, they frequently remove their pastors to other localities; and they entirely approve of the methods usually adopted to extend the gospel of Christ at home and abroad.[27]

In other words, the Church of God could not be catalogued with any one of the major streams of American Protestant Christianity.

Finally, there is the matter of Winebrenner's use of the name "church of God" to apply first to a local church congregation, and then as "Church of God" to refer to an organization of churches. (As far as I have been able to determine, the "Church of God" as organized in 1830 under Winebrenner's leadership was the first of many American denominations to use the name.) The emphasis on Biblical literalism, restorationism, and repristination in the early nineteenth century American Church brought forth a number of movements similar to the Church of God, like the "Church of Christ," the "Christian Church," and the "Disciples of Christ." The use of the term "Church of God" as applying to groups of Christians spiritually united enjoyed wide currency among the Germans in eastern Pennsylvania in Winebrenner's time. Count Zinzendorf's "Congregation of God in the Spirit" formed in the 1740's to foster unity among the German churches may well have left some early nineteenth century residuum. "The True Church of God and Its Origin" and "The Ungodly and False Church of God" are subjects of extensive discussion in *Der Blutige Schau-Platz oder Martyrer Spiegel,* published in its first German edition in America in 1748.[28] Winebrenner was familiar with this work, which was especially popular among German Anabaptist groups, and advertised the prospectus for the first English edition in the *Gospel Publisher* in 1835.[29]

Moreover, there were in existence in eastern Pennsylvania a number of independent local "churches of God," not related to each other, prior to Winebrenner's assumption of the name. One of these was organized in Lancaster, Pennsylvania, in 1816,[30] one year after the second American edition (in German, again) of *Der Blutige Schau-Platz* was published in the same place. The pastor of the Church of God in Lancaster was a John Elliott, an Englishman with some education, about whom, unfortunately, we know very little.[31] What we do know suggests that if any one person was responsible for Winebrenner's use of the name "Church of God" it was John Elliott. Winebrenner was on close terms with Elliott by 1822, three years before the climactic German Reformed Synod of 1825. It appears that Elliott and Winebrenner were exchanging pulpits in revival oriented services.[32] According to the *Harrisburg Chronicle* for May 7, 1827, when the Harrisburg "Union Bethel" (literally, "Union House of God") was dedicated on May 12, 1827, Elliott was the speaker for the occasion. (The same issue of the *Chronicle* carried a notice of a camp meeting near Mt. Joy, Pennsylvania, to be held under the direction of "J. Winebrenner and others." It is the first notice of a camp meeting in the Harrisburg or Dauphin County papers I have been able to find.) Later, the Lancaster pastor was elected clerk of the first eldership of the Church of God in 1830. While we do not know exactly when Winebrenner first began to use the appellation "church of God" in referring to his Harrisburg congregation, sometime in 1826 seems most likely.

Further ramifications of Winebrenner's concept of the Church of God are pointed up in the course of his controversy with John Williamson Nevin of the Reformed Church. It is to this controversy that we now turn.

5

The Winebrenner-Nevin Controversy

John Winebrenner's "new measures" and "Church of God" brought forth a number of opponents. What Winebrenner considered church reform, they considered rank and unholy schism. By far the most capable of these opponents was John Williamson Nevin of the Reformed Church. The controversy between Winebrenner and Nevin, extending over an eight year period, pointed up the basic presuppositions of both men—representing entirely different styles of churchmanship—as they viewed the state of the American Church in the 1840's. In the course of defending himself and the Church of God against Nevin, Winebrenner was forced to spell out *in detail* how he interpreted the nature of the church and the relationship between Christ, man, and the church—something he did nowhere else in his writings. The controversy is also valuable for the light it throws on the character of Winebrenner, and especially his concerns in the early 1840's—the period between his editorships of the *Gospel Publisher* and the *Church Advocate*.

John Williamson Nevin

John Williamson Nevin was born of Presbyterian Scotch-Irish ancestry on February 20, 1803, at Herron's Branch, Pennsylvania. His parents were farmers in the fertile Cumberland Valley.

In 1821 he graduated from Union College in Schenectady, New York, the youngest in his class. From Union, after a period at home to recover his health, he went on to Princeton Seminary, where he graduated in 1826. Between 1826 and 1828 he taught at Princeton. In 1830 he began teaching at Western Theological Seminary at Allegheny City, Pennsylvania. At Western he became a valuable member of the faculty and also a controversial one because of his views on slavery, temperance, church fairs, and the like. In 1840 he transferred to the German Reformed Church and its theological seminary at Mercersburg, Pennsylvania. Together with Dr. Philip Schaff, Nevin was responsible for the development of the "Mercersburg Theology"—a theology emphasizing the "churchly" and sacramental side of the Christian faith.

Between 1840 and 1851, Nevin served the German Reformed Church as professor in its seminary. From 1841 to 1853, he was also acting president of Marshall College in Mercersburg. In addition to his heavy duties as administrator, teacher, author, and preacher, he was for most of this time a controversialist through the columns of the German Reformed *Weekly Messenger* and (from 1849 on) the *Mercersburg Review*.

In the early 1850's, Nevin gave serious consideration to joining the Roman Catholic Church. For this reason, and because of poor health, he was in partial retirement from 1853 to 1861. From 1861 to 1866 he was Professor of Aesthetics and History at Franklin and Marshall College in Lancaster, Pennsylvania. He served as president of Franklin and Marshall from 1866 to 1876, most of which time he was also Professor of Mental and Moral Philosophy (1868-1876). He died in 1886.[1]

In many respects, Nevin and Winebrenner were similar. They were born within fifty miles and about six years of each other. Their parents were moderately well-to-do farmers who generously supported their children. Living close to each other for most of their lives, they had several friends (and detractors) in common. While each used English as his native tongue, Winebrenner was fluent in German from his early years and Nevin read German well by the late 1830's.

Both Winebrenner and Nevin went to college and seminary (although Winebrenner's educational background hardly could be regarded as equal to Nevin's) at a time when it was not especially common. They studied many of the same authors. Both were converted while away at school—Nevin at college, Winebrenner while studying theology. Each man strongly supported the temperance, Bible, and missionary societies of the day. Both were strong antislavery men in the 1830's and both tempered their position in later years.

As both assumed positions of authority in the church, they devoted much time to combating sectarianism, and emphasizing a visible, normative church. Both disseminated their views through church papers and books.

Yet, while similar, there were differences between the two men—significant differences. The remainder of the chapter is devoted to these.

The Controversy: 1842 and 1843

In the spring of 1840 John Williamson Nevin left Western Theological Seminary at Allegheny City, Pennsylvania, for the German Reformed Seminary at Mercersburg, Pennsylvania, where he assumed the chair of theology. In December of that year he began a series of articles on the Heidelberg Catechism in the German Reformed paper, the *Weekly Messenger*. Extending to August, 1842, the series was not only a history of the catechism, but also a history of the German Reformed Church from its beginnings in Europe to its present situation in the United States. In the course of the series, in the issue of August 10, 1842, Nevin made the following evaluation of John Winebrenner's separation from the German Reformed Church:

> More recently still, and as is generally supposed with less purity of intention, Winebrenner, of Harrisburg (A. D. 1829) has had dexterity enough to put in motion a similar ball [sect], which continues rolling to this hour, not without abundance of sound. This latter sect especially glory in being the patrons of ignorance, rail at hireling ministers, encourage all sorts of fanatical unscriptural disorder in their worship, institute their own fancies and feelings in religion, for the calm deep power of faith. In doctrine they are of course pelagianistic.[2]

The result of this statement was a series of ten letters between Winebrenner and Nevin, extending from August, 1842 to July, 1843. The letters were later published in the *Gospel Publisher*, the Church of God paper, beginning with the issue of October 18, 1843.

Winebrenner's first letter to Nevin, dated August 11, 1842,[3] from Shippensburg, Pennsylvania, informed Nevin that Winebrenner's attention was called to Nevin's article in the *Messenger* by one of Nevin's "brother ministers" in the German Reformed Church.[4] He suggested that Nevin had misrepresented the Church of God and himself with uncharitable words and closed as follows:

> After thus referring and submitting this matter to your cool and deliberate reflection, may I not hope, that you will be prepared to answer, with all candor and meekness, the following questions, viz:
>
> 1. Whether you have made these assertions, for want of better knowledge, or whether you profess to know the things

you have alledged, to be facts, and have endorsed the same upon your own responsibility?

2. Whether you feel willing to disabuse the public mind by retracting the allegations you have made, provided I can furnish sufficient evidence of their falsity?

Your answer, Sir, to these few plain interrogatories, will be anxiously awaited and will very much oblige,

Yours in the kingdom and patience of Jesus Christ

John Winebrenner

Nevin's reply, dated "August, 1842," [5] from Mercersburg, Pennsylvania, stated that his estimation of the Church of God was based upon general information or *"fama clamosa"*—public fame. (Both writers have a penchant for throwing a little Latin into the correspondence.) "We differ," he suggested, "as to what constitutes fanaticism, disorder, rant, etc. in the worship of God. What I consider to be of this character, you perhaps regard as true Christian zeal." [6] In the event Winebrenner could show to Nevin's satisfaction that Nevin had misrepresented the "Winebrennerians," he agreed to "retract or modify" what he had written. Indeed, he continued, "even if I should not be convinced that I have been in error, I am willing to let it be known that you hold the representation to be incorrect—provided I can be informed precisely in what respects you consider it to be so." He then asked Winebrenner about the nature of Church of God meetings, indicating his identification of the Church of God and Winebrenner with the "new measure" revivalism then current. [7]

Are women suffered to pray in your meetings, where men are present, or are they not suffered? And do you, or do you not, approve of this unscriptural practice?

Is loud groaning, crying, and shouting, clapping of hands, jumping, falling down, etc. tolerated in your meetings, or not? And do you approve of such wild and disorderly doings, or do you not?

Is it, or is it not, with your people, customary to take it for granted that all who come to the anxious seat, and there declare they have found peace, in the midst of all animal excitement around them, are truly converted, etc.? Do you, or do you not, consider such *getting through*, as they call it, the great business of religion, instead of discouraging it as dangerous to souls?

Winebrenner's reply to Nevin, dated September 30, 1842, [8] from Harrisburg, Pennsylvania, is the third and longest letter in the series. Taking up eleven and one-half columns in the *Gospel*

Publisher, it is Winebrenner's defense of the "new measures" revivalistic system, and illustrates many of the theological presuppositions basic to John Winebrenner and the American pietistic-revivalistic conception of Christianity in the first half of the nineteenth century.[9]

After suggesting that Nevin in the future refer to the Church of God as the Church of God and not as the "Winebrennerians"— a suggestion that Nevin was reluctant to accept—Winebrenner undertook to show Nevin how the Mercersburg professor had misrepresented (1) Winebrenner, and (2) the Church of God.

First, with reference to Nevin's misrepresentation of Winebrenner and the "purity of intentions" inherent in the latter's leaving the German Reformed Church, Winebrenner told Nevin that he left that church in 1825 (not, as Nevin stated, in 1829) and for good reasons. The church was spiritually corrupt. It was a "Synagogue of Satan," the ministers and people of which persecuted Winebrenner. To support his contention, Winebrenner quoted generously from Nevin's own low estimation of the spiritual character of the German Reformed Church in the early nineteenth century presented in Nevin's series of articles on the Heidelberg Catechism in the *Messenger.* In the issue of August 10, 1842 he had written that

> True serious piety indeed was too often treated with open and marked scorn. . . . The idea of the new birth was considered a pietistic whimry. Experimental religion, in all its forms, was eschewed as a new fangled invention of cunning impostors brought in to turn the heads of the weak and to lead captive silly women. . . . To show an awakened concern on the subject of religion, a disposition to call upon God in daily secret prayer, was to incur certain reproach.[10]

Winebrenner then added to the above quotation:

> Such then is the dark, but true picture which you have drawn with your own hand, of the German Reformed Church. I am glad that you concur with me in my opinion. . . . Now when such a spirit once becomes generally prevalent in a Church, is it not high time to come out of her? . . . He doubtless, is the greater sinner who will not dissolve his connection, but jeopardize his soul and his eternal all in the communion of such a fallen and corrupt Church.

The temper of the times, with its Bibliocentric and anti-sectarian emphases, was presented in another "main reason" Winebrenner gave for leaving Nevin's church. He left

> . . . because she [the German Reformed Church] is . . . a sect— and withal a mal-practicing sect. Her mal-practices are, such

as, Confirmation, Infant Baptism, etc. These and other things, although unsupported by either precept or example in the Bible, are nevertheless rigidly upheld and practiced by her, whilst other things, founded on the authority of both, are discarded and opposed.

To Nevin's charge that Winebrenner, "has had dexterity to put in motion a similar ball [sect], which continues rolling to this hour, not without abundance of sound," [11] Winebrenner responded by appealing once again to the anti-sectarian spirit of the times, adding the note of repristination frequently found with Winebrenner. Picking up Nevin's analogy of the ball, and probably carrying it much farther than it should go, he wrote:

But, sir, I did not retire for the ignoble purpose, as you have intimated, of putting another sectarian ball in motion, that should roll on with abundance of sound. No, not at all. I had seen through mercy, the great evil of these rolling balls— put in motion, and kept in motion, by the cunning craftiness of men and devils—and how, by their repeated and unhappy collisions, they hindred [sic] and marred the work of God in the earth; and therefore, I resolved to fall back upon original grounds—to stand aloof from all these sectarian balls, and to do the work of an Evangelist and Minister of Christ by building up the *Church of God*,—(the only true Church) according to the plan and pattern as shown us in the New Testament. This is the high and firm ground we take. Our ball therefore, is not like your ball, nor similar to other human balls. Ours is the Lord's ball. It was not cut out of the Romish Church, by the hands of Calvin and others, as was yours. But it was "cut out of the mountain without hands." The ball commenced rolling upwards of eighteen hundred years ago, and it continues rolling to this hour—yea, and it will never cease rolling till every other man-made ball shall be either crushed or rolled up by it, . . .

If Nevin is even slightly amused by reference to "the Lord's ball," he does not let on. "Rolling balls" were popular about this time. The Harrison-Tyler campaign of 1840 featured the rolling of large balls (up to fifteen feet in diameter) city to city to the accompaniment of such rousing ditties as:

With heart and soul
This ball we roll;
May time improve
As on we move.

and

This Democratic ball
Set rolling first by Benton
Is on another track
From that it first was sent on.[12]

Next Winebrenner turned to what he considered was Nevin's misrepresentation of the Church of God. Here he dealt with Nevin's original evaluation of the Church of God as a sect which "glory in being the patrons of ignorance, rail at hireling ministers, encourage all sorts of fanatical unscriptural disorder . . . , and substitute their own . . . feelings in religion for the calm deep power of faith" and, further, are "pelagianistic" in doctrine.[13] It is at this point that he endeavored to answer explicitly the questions posed by Nevin in his previous letter.

The people of the Church of God were not "patrons of ignorance" as Nevin supposed; rather, its ministers and people appreciated learning. He pleaded that while the Church of God had no colleges and theological seminaries as yet, the preachers, especially, "are wise and well informed—not in classic lore, but in biblical which is better." The Church of God ministers were men of the Bible, not of the catechism. "They are *verbum Dei Studiosi*, [students of the Word of God], and graduates of the school of Christ. In this school, the best education is acquired." Winebrenner emphasized that he personally always had regarded learning as a "necessary and useful qualification in a minister of the Gospel." Illustrating this point were his writings and support of ministerial education while still a member of the German Reformed Church. (In fairness to Winebrenner, it should be said that throughout his life he did display an interest in college and seminary education. In addition to his own college and "seminary" [studying with Samuel Helffenstein, Sr.] background, he strongly supported the initial movements of the German Reformed Church to found a theological seminary. Later, as an elder in the Church of God, he was continually urging the development of educational ventures.)

Going one step further, he asserted that it is the German Reformed Church which had patronized ignorance. Once again he was able to call upon Nevin himself for substantiation:

This character is more applicable to your own party, according to your own showing. For of the *Church* you say, "It delighted in fine farms more than in thriving churches. It made more account of well fed stock, than of well educated children. It took more pride in building big barns, than founding schools and colleges." And of the Ministers you say, "In many cases men appeared in office, who were as little fitted to edify by their example as to instruct by their sermons." [14]

Winebrenner further denied that the Church of God railed at "hireling ministers." "This charge," he wrote,

61

likewise is without foundation. The church, in no case, is opposed to ministers receiving a fair and competent support for themselves and families. . . This fact is well known to all the readers of the *Gospel Publisher,* and to all who have any knowledge of her internal economy.

Howbeit, there may be those in the Church, who are opposed to "mere hireling ministers." That is to say, to those who are "greedy of filthy lucre," and who can be called any *way* and every *where* for a high station and a big salary. . . . Yet I know not, that any in the Church of God would even "rail" at these, because they are rather objects of pity than of scorn or raillery.

Winebrenner, of course, held Nevin to be wrong in asserting that the Church of God encouraged "all sorts of fanatical unscriptural disorder in their worship." It was true that women prayed in meetings where men were present. But Winebrenner did not see this as either wild or disorderly and certainly did not consider it unscriptural, as Nevin did. (He challenged Nevin to prove it unscriptural.) Relative to "noise in meetings," Winebrenner, admitting its existence, suggested that such noise should not be regarded necessarily as "fanatical unscriptural disorder." So he wrote:

> . . . This is the wisdom of the Church. She tolerates and approves of "loud groaning, crying, shouting, clapping of hands, jumping, falling down, etc.," so far, and so far only, as it is the effect produced by a divine influence. And who can deny but that the divine power does sometimes so operate as to cause a *noise,* but such as are ignorant of "the Scriptures and the power of God."

After supporting noise in meetings by the Scriptures, he continued:

> I have not inclination however, to justify all sorts of noise and bodily exercises. I admit, there may sometimes be much animal excitement and great deal of noise, when at the same time, there is little or no operation of the Spirit. . . . Yet notwithstanding, these things are sometimes so, there is still no part of the Bible that will warrant a man to denounce all kinds of noise and bodily exercise indiscriminately, as "fanaticism, disorder, and rant in the worship of God."

Once again, the Scriptures (so interpreted) are appealed to as a criterion for action. Winebrenner gives evidence of feeling somewhat uncomfortable here. While a "new measure" man, Winebrenner was not unaware of potential problems arising from an extremely individualistic interpretation of the Christian faith. Individualism leading to a lack of unity in the Church of God was a source of continuing concern to him and many of his friends, who, with Winebrenner, also emphasized the unity, visibility, sanctity, universality, and perpetuity of the Church of God. Further, in later years he tended to emphasize the importance of "commonly accepted" beliefs in the Church. Yet his reliance upon the Bible as a self-evident source of truth for the serious investigator never wavered.

To the charge that the Church of God substituted "our fancies and feelings in religion for the calm deep power of faith," Winebrenner replied:

> It is customary with the ministers and people of the Church of God, to insist on *immediate, implicit, and unconditional submission to God,* on the part of sinners; and whether this submission is yielded to, "in the midst of all animal excitement around," or in the midst of a still solemn calm, and whether it be on the anxious seat, at the altar, or in the pew— and whether in time of preaching singing or praying, it mattes [*sic*] not. . . . This true conversion of the soul, is what the people of God look for. . . . You may call it *getting through,* or what you please . . .

There follows an exposition centering around "true piety, or experimental religion," during which he again quoted from Nevin's series on the Heidelberg Catechism for support. Winebrenner suggested, moreover, that his own background had prepared him to better evaluate the nature of the German Reformed Church than had Nevin's. With a hint of paternalism (Winebrenner is forty-five; Nevin thirty-nine), he explained that

> To mix with the people, is the way to learn to understand their morals. And to labour in revivals of religion is the way to become acquainted with men's true moral nature and character. Had the German Reformed Church called you to the office of an evangelist—instead of calling you to the Presidency of Marshall college and the Professorship of the Theological Seminary—and had you itinerated in the Church as an evangelist, half the days of years that I have done, you would have understood the true complexion of that Church much better than what you can possibly learn to understand it in your present situation. This knowledge can alone be acquired in the school of experience. It is not to be gained, in the Theological Seminary at Princeton in New Jersey—nor in the Western Theological Seminary at Pittsburg—neither in the Marshal [*sic*] college and Theological Seminary at Mercersburg.

Finally, Winebrenner addressed himself to Nevin's appraisal of the Church of God as "Pelagianistic." This was a frequent charge levelled against those churches emphasizing freedom of the will. It was especially directed against those churches which emphasized the necessity of man taking the initial steps (assumedly apart from divine grace) toward his own salvation. (Giving a heretic's label to opposition religious movements would seem to have been a nineteenth century pastime in the American Church.) "Mere hear say," said Winebrenner. Prove it or it must remain "a false charge and misrepresentation." Once again he emphasized the anti-sectarian nature of the Church of God:

> At any rate, we are no more Pelagianistic, than Calvinistic or Nevinistic. So far as Pelagius held the truth, we may be called (by those who choose,) Pelagianistic.—So far as John Calvin held the truth, we may be called Calvinistic—and so far as John W. Nevin holds the truth we may be called Nevinistic, but no further. We, the Ministers and people of the Church of God, repudiate all those istics and isms, with all other human distinctions and inventions.

In closing, Winebrenner submitted it to Nevin's judgment "as a gentleman and as a Christian" whether he has shown the latter's representation of the Church of God to be "incorrect and fallacious" and whether or not Nevin owes Winebrenner an apology.

If Winebrenner actually expected an apology (and the nature of nineteenth century polemical correspondence does not make it altogether certain that he did), he was disappointed. Nevin's response, dated October 17, 1842,[15] from Mercersburg, made it clear that his opinion with regard to Winebrenner and the Church of God generally remained unchanged. It is a short letter, to the point, and is quoted here in its entirety.

Rev. and Dear Sir:

> Your communication intended to vindicate your person and cause from what you conceive to be an aspersion on my part, has been received and carefully read. It turns out much as I expected. I am willing to give you the full benefit of your own statements, but am by no means convinced by them that my general representation of the spirit and character of your body are incorrect. We differ not so much with regard to facts, as with regard to the light in which they should be viewed. What I hold to be sheer fanaticism, you consider the life of religion itself. What I am not afraid to denounce as spiritual quackery, you cry up as the "great power of God"— It would be useless to embark in a controversy, on the merits of the main question. I should despair of showing you that *you* are wrong; and I am very sure you would not convert *me* soon to views of piety, which seem to me so shallow and dangerous to souls, as those which prevail practically among your people.—I am not prepared of course to retract, so far as any material point contained in my statement is concerned—Still,

as I have already said, I am willing to publish a card, stating
that you deny and contradict the applicability of my censure
to yourself and your body if you desire it.—Or would you
wish to have your whole article published in the *Messenger*?
If the editor would allow it, I should be perfectly agreed.—
only, I would accompany it with remarks, not in the way of
controversy, but in the way of general religious discussion.
And with this the matter would be closed; as I have no idea
of going into a regular controversy with you on the general
question.

I remain yours in the gospel, J. W. Nevin

Winebrenner's reply to the above letter is dated "Harrisburg,
October 27, 1842."[16] A portion of it, however, was written on
December 30 of the same year. The tone was different from his
two earlier letters. Nevin had refused to modify substantially his
earlier charges against Winebrenner (whose "purity of intention," therefore, was still open to question) or the Church of God.
Nevin's reply to his long vindicatory letter was negative, extremely
short, and more or less charged Winebrenner with "sheer fanaticism" and "spiritual quackery." Winebrenner answered with
acerbity. This letter, more than any of his others, is noteworthy
for its attack on Nevin's character. He wrote:

> . . . I was by no means sanguine of success, in satisfying your
> mind, that you were in error. Nevertheless what I essayed,
> I believe, I have fully accomplished, viz:—the refutation of
> your statement. Therefore, I want no sculking and dodging
> about the matter. Either acknowledge your wrong or sustain
> your position. If the latter, then meet the whole subject in
> manly argument. Let us have something tangible—something
> more than mere assertions, founded on public rumor.

In the event the professor would neither retract or modify what
he had published about Winebrenner and the Church of God,

> . . . then as another way of settling the matter, I invite you
> to the bar of public opinion, in the way you propose:—Let the
> whole correspondence, on the subject between us hitherto, be
> laid before the public, through the *Messenger,* and let each of
> us have the privilege, to follow with such remarks and ex-
> planations, as we severally, may see proper to make; and so, let
> the whole matter be closed.[17]

At this point, Winebrenner gave his own construction of the differences between himself and Nevin:

> But, Not withstanding, these remarks strongly savor the
> speech of one that is par blind in the things of God; yet, I
> cannot bring my mind to believe that there exists such a wide

difference to our views of true religion, as what you imagine. I am rather disposed to think, that you do not understand our principles, nor our practice.[18]

Our difference, is perhaps,[19] more about *measures* than anything else. Yet if it really be so, that "what we consider the life of religion, you hold to be sheer fanaticism," and "What we regard as the power of God, you are not afraid to denounce as spiritual quackery," then may the Lord help you!

The next section of the letter is dated "Dec. 30th." Winebrenner noted he had been out of town and "found it inconvenient to give this subject any further attention, until now." (He had been engaged in a series of successful revival services—lasting over a year, by the way—at the Lancaster Church of God. His success at Lancaster must have made Nevin's position all the more untenable to Winebrenner.) In the meantime, he had secured a copy of the *Messenger* containing Nevin's twenty-ninth and last article on the Catechism. This article, like the previous ones, he found abounding "with mere fancy work, and moonshine statements."

Winebrenner quoted extensively from the article, especially those sections which analyzed negatively the spiritual state of the German Reformed Church. He then attempted to turn the article against Nevin, in what may have been an appeal to the church (or at least some of its members) to repudiate their theological professor and college president at Mercersburg.

This [Nevin's] estimate of the spiritual character of the German Reformed Church agrees with what I said before, with regard to the present state of religion in your denomination. Had thus much been written by myself or some one else not in connexion with your body, it would have been repudiated as a slanderous statement. And I am not quite sure, as it is, that it will not prove offensive to many of your people. . . . You have a ticklish people to deal with; and I wonder very much whether they will acquiesce in having so much truth told, the great quantum of flattery in-corporated with it to the contrary notwithstanding. Yet I would put it to your conscience, whether this way of writing and preaching is not ten fold more dangerous and hurtful to souls, than all that fanaticism and spiritual quackery against which you so bitterly inveigh. Yes, it is doubtless vastly more so—it is voluntary homicidal quackery.

In closing the letter, Winebrenner once again appealed to both Scripture and Latin.

Dear Sir, you will remember it is written, in the Book of books, "Judge not, that ye be not judged." "Be not high minded, but fear." I counsel thee, therefore, to stay thy hand

and put up thy sword, lest, *Contra Stimulum calces.* ["You kick against the prick."]

> Yours with esteem, etc.
>
> John Winebrenner

Nevin did not reply to Winebrenner. Winebrenner, however, would not be put off. On May 2, 1843,[20] four months from his last letter, he reopened the correspondence by dropping Nevin a line from Harrisburg. He reviewed their previous correspondence and requested satisfaction in the following terms:

> But as you have gone on to trifle with us, by adding worse to bad, and treated the whole subject finely with silent contempt; I would now, therefore, say, and I want you distinctly to understand, that the time has fully come for something definite to be done by yourself, to bring this matter to a just and honorable issue; or else, I shall pursue my own course for the attainment of this object. [Probably the publication of the entire correspondence, which Winebrenner did later anyway.]
>
> I would therefore, in conclusion request, please let me hear from you without delay, and let me know what you are willing to do—whether you have seen your error, and are willing to recall what you have unjustly said about us—or, whether you will have the correspondence, as proposed, published in the *Messenger,* or not.
>
> I remain yours, as heretofore, in gospel bonds.
>
> John Winebrenner

Nevin did reply to the above letter—as courteously as possible, considering the circumstances. His letter was sent from Mercersburg, dated May 30, 1843.[21] He summed up his understanding of the situation, suggesting the reason he had not written sooner was because he had said all he could say about the matter. (In terms of their previous correspondence, Nevin's is the correct construction of the case.) He felt satisfied that his original evaluation of the Church of God was correct. He would not retract what he had written. He was willing to present Winebrenner's letter of "vindication" (number three in the series) to the editor of the *Weekly Messenger* for publication; but he would not accede to Winebrenner's proposition to have the entire correspondence published. He concluded, in a post-script:

> Should you prefer it, I am willing myself to state in the *Messenger,* that you consider yourself wronged, mentioning such particulars as you may be pleased to point out. But probably you would like best, to present your statement over your own name, and so far as I myself am concerned this will be allowed cheerfully to go, without reply, for all it may be

worth. The public can then judge for itself whether I have been guilty of misrepresentation or not, and this will, I trust, be satisfactory. Into a public controversy, I have neither time nor inclination to enter.

FIRST CHURCH OF GOD, HARRISBURG

Nevin did not want controversy. He had enough of it in his own church, as well as being burdened with his duties as theological professor and acting president of Marshall College. Yet, Winebrenner was insistent—probably because Nevin occupied the honored position in the German Reformed Church that he did. Winebrenner's letter of June 14, 1843,[22] again reviewed the previous correspondence, concluding with what can only be conceived of as an arrogant tone:

Now then, you have the whole plan and terms of reconciliation before you. Out of these, you can make your choice. The Editors of the *Messenger* will, I hope, give you leave to do any one of the three. My explanatory letter is long, I acknowledge; but if it be objectionable on account of its great length, as you have alledged, you must content yourself to bear that blame, for you caused it. I cannot agree to abridge it.

In conclusion I would say, what thou doest, do quickly. Do not let this matter lie over three or four months longer . . .

With due respect, I remain Yours, etc., John Winebrenner

Nevin's answer is dated June 29, 1843,[23] and, as all of his previous letters, was sent from Mercersburg. Because of the sidelights it throws on Nevin's character, it is quoted in full.

Rev. and Dear Sir:—

Yours of the 16th came regularly to hand.—In compliance with your wish, I have inclosed your *Vindicatory Letter* as a communication for the *Weekly Messenger,* accompanied with a request that it may be published. I have been waiting only for a private opportunity to send it over to Chambersburg, which will present itself shortly; not wishing to tax the establishment with quadruple postage in the case. I trust no objection will be made to publishing the letter. You may rest assured that I am personally perfectly willing to have it appear in this way; and your insinuation that I wish to equivocate in the matter is wholly gratuitous:—like a good many more of your insinuations thrown out in this correspondence, more vulgar, to say the least, than genteel, and not savoring much of that divine charity, better than all gifts, for the want of which you have been pleased to take me to task.

I wish you to understand distinctly too, that in declining your proposition to publish the whole correpondence, I have not been influenced by any wish to keep it out of sight. You are at perfect liberty, if you please, to publish all in any form you choose, and to handle me as unmercifully as you can with your pen besides. I do not deprecate at all any castigation of this sort you may be inclined to lay upon my shoulders. I have become somewhat accustomed to such treatment, and try to take it patiently. It may be a gratification to you perhaps to know, that quite recently a German paper in the West has poured upon me two columns of abuse for representing the want of spiritual religion to be so great among the emigration from Germany.

Controversy had begun to gather about Nevin and Mercersburg. Nevin, with a bit of the martyr touch, seemed to be resigned to mistreatment from any quarter—including Winebrenner's. He concluded on a surprisingly irenic note:

You must not think that I cherish towards you any personal ill will. I think honestly, you erred in breaking away from the German Ref. Church when you did. Your acknowledged system of religion, practically considered, is to my mind, whether in your hands or in the hands of others, (for under different names it abounds in the country) radically defective and full of danger. In the fire and whirlwind system of converting sinners, I have less confidence the longer I live; I believe four are deceived by it, for every one that is saved, if it be overruled, to the salvation of any. Such are my views. I do not utter them in the way of railing—and it is not necessary at all that in holding them I should hate those who like yourself think differently.

Yours in the Gospel, J. W. Nevin

The "fire and whirlwind system" referred, of course, to Winebrenner's "new measures." With his estimation of the odds against salvation through Winebrenner's "system of religion" standing at four to one, at best, it is little wonder his *Anxious Bench* [24] came to be written within the next few months.

Winebrenner had the last word. The tenth and final letter was sent from Harrisburg on July 6, 1843.[25] As would be expected, Winebrenner took exception to what he considered Nevin's undignified language. His conclusion obviously was intended for dramatic effect:

As to your opinion, about my breaking away from the German Reformed Church, I shall let that pass with this single remark; that whereas you think honestly,

I erred in breaking away from that church, I think no less honestly, I trust, that you erred *in breaking into her* pale not only, but even into her theological professorship—and besides, I candidly think, that all the converted ministers and members of that denomination, err, and err greatly in not "breaking away from her," immediately; because God has said, "be not unequally yoked together with unbelievers."

Yours with due respect, John Winebrenner

Once again Winebrenner's final appeal was to the Scriptures as Winebrenner interpreted them.

Winebrenner's letter of "Vindication" was published in the *Weekly Messenger* for July 12, 1843, with an introduction by Nevin. Nevin's introduction to the "Vindication" explained the reason for Winebrenner's letter. With a caustic turn, he informed the reader that not only had he sought a place for the letter in the columns of the *Messenger*, but was now asking that the letter be read, in that "it will operate . . . with sensible people as an antidote to the views for which it is intended to be an apology." As a closing item he stated that he "may hereafter take up that subject, in some different form, without particular reference to Mr. Winebrenner or 'THE Church' that glories in his name." The "different form" turned out to be Nevin's epic pamphlet, the *Anxious Bench*.

On August 9, 1843, the *Gospel Publisher* reprinted Winebrenner's "Vindication" and Nevin's introduction to it together with an introduction and post-script relating to Nevin's introduction by J. F. Weishampel, editor of the *Publisher*. In the course of dissecting Nevin's introduction he suggested, among many other things, that Nevin became willing to have Winebrenner's vindicatory letter printed in the *Messenger*, only after Winebrenner "threatened to publish the whole matter, letters and all, in pamphlet form . . ."

Weishampel's remarks were brought to the attention of Nevin who responded in an article entitled, "Winebrenner Again," in the *Weekly Messenger* for September 13, 1843. He noted that Weishampel was incorrect in stating that he solicited publication for Winebrenner's "Vindication" in the *Messenger* only after Winebrenner had threatened to publish their entire correspondence, intimating that it was probably Winebrenner who gave Weishampel the false information. After giving the "Vindication" (noting that the "publication of the letter followed, without the change of a syllable, except to rectify occasionally its mistakes in spelling"), he informed his readers:

> Altogether this is rather a little business; and I have balanced a good deal between the *fourth* and *fifth* verses of the 26th chapter of Proverbs, before making up my mind to notice it at all. [Prov. 26:4: "Answer not a fool according to his folly, lest thou also be like unto him." Prov. 26:5: "Answer a fool according to his folly, lest he be wise in his own conceit." Both quotations from KJV.] But it seems right, to hold the thing up to view. It may help still farther to illustrate the spirit of the system to which it belongs.

It was then that he announced a forthcoming work on the "new measures."

> I mentioned before that I might take up the whole subject of "New Measures," in a separate publication, without direct reference to Mr. Winebrenner, or "THE CHURCH," commonly distinguished by his name.[26] I may now add that I have prepared a tract according to this intimation which may be expected to appear under the title of the ANXIOUS BENCH, in the course of a few days. J. W. N.
>
> Sept. 9th 1843

71

When Winebrenner's attention was directed to Nevin's "Winebrenner Again" in the *Messenger,* he wrote a letter, dated October 4, 1843,[27] to Weishampel, taking proper offense at Nevin's article. In the letter he especially resented the insinuation that he had supplied Weishampel with false information relative to the publication of his "Vindication," and suggested that Weishampel had "inadvertently made a mistake" in the matter. He then offered to send Weishampel a copy of the correspondence in question for inclusion in the *Publisher.*

In the October 11, 1843 issue of the *Publisher,* Weishampel printed Winebrenner's letter of October 4, 1843; Nevin's "Winebrenner Again" as it appeared in the September 13, 1843 *Messenger;* and a few comments of his own on Nevin's article. He exonerated Winebrenner of threatening to have the letters published if Nevin did not have Winebrenner's "Vindication" printed.[28] However, the argument was academic. Weishampel had decided to publish the correspondence anyway, and informed his readers of the fact. The first two letters appeared in the October 18, 1843 *Publisher.*

In closing this section it should be noted that the Winebrenner-Nevin correspondence was ultimately responsible for a number of other letters displaying partisan sentiments in both the *Weekly Messenger,* and *Gospel Publisher.* Some of these are particularly important in that they shed additional light on Winebrenner's character and his original difficulties with the German Reformed Church.

On August 2, 1843, the *Weekly Messenger* carried a letter from "A Friend to the German Reformed Church." The anonymous "Friend" had read Winebrenner's "Vindication" in the *Messenger* on July 12 of that year and wrote to take issue with several of Winebrenner's assertions. The letter was reprinted in the *Gospel Publisher* for October 18, 1843, with an answering letter from "A Friend to Truth," who wrote suspiciously like John Winebrenner.

The *Weekly Messenger* for November 15, 1843 printed a letter from "L. S." who described himself as a former friend of Winebrenner's.[29] He gave a detailed resume of events leading up to Winebrenner's separation from the German Reformed Church. He also quoted a letter purported to be from Winebrenner and addressed to "L. S." dated November 2, 1825, in which Winebrenner stated that he had in mind the formation of a new denomination. "L. S." 's letter, perhaps significantly, was not reprinted in the *Publisher.* However in the *Gospel Publisher* for December 6, 1843, there was reprinted the copy of a note sent by

Winebrenner to the editors of the *Weekly Messenger* requesting the real names of "A Friend to the German Reformed Church" and S. L." (presumably "L. S.") and the privilege of replying to their letters in the *Messenger*. To my knowledge the privilege was never granted.

The Controversy: 1848-1850

In 1848 Nevin's *Anti-Christ; Or the Spirit of Sect and Schism* was published.[30] It contained his analysis of sectarianism in the United States.

The Nevin who now wrote of the "Marks of the Antichrist" was quite different from the Nevin who, six years earlier in 1842, had entangled himself over revivalistic "new measures" in his correspondence with John Winebrenner. Between the time of his correspondence with Winebrenner and the publication of his *Anti-Christ,* Nevin had put aside his individualistic evangelicalism with any rationalistic-subjectivistic tendencies therein involved. He had begun to stress "organic" union with Christ and the corporate, objective, "given" nature of the Christian Church.[31] In *Anti-Christ* he explained his theological presuppositions.

First, the person of Christ is made to be the ultimate fact of Christianity, rather than his doctrine merely, or work; secondly, the supernatural life which this included, is represented as coming through him into organic union with the life of nature, for the redemption of the world.[32]

"Sectarianism," on the other hand,

is ever inclined to place Christ wholly in the clouds, or turn him into an ideal phantom, that it may be left the more free in the exercise of its own subjectivity. . . . In this way, however, it is carried over, by a sort of inward necessity, to the sphere of theoretic Rationalism. As a spirit of heresy and schism [sect spirit], we pronounce it to be emphatically the Anti-christ of the Church in our own time.[33]

This "Antichrist," moreover,

is both rational and schismatic . . . in his very nature. . . . In the name of Protestantism, a large part of the Christian world has come to be rationalistic and schismatic now, on principle . . . making no question of its power and right to shape theology and fashion the structure of the Church, as in its own eyes the case may seem to require.[34]

Nevin then noted the "marks of Antichrist"—sect spirit, the "spirit of heresy and schism . . . in our own time." [35] These included: subjective salvation and the lack of real mediation between God and Man; an undervaluation of the mystery of Christ's person; no faith in the Church as "a real supernatural constitution always present in the world"; a low view of the ministry, sacraments, and worship generally; a contempt for history and authority; an affectation of individual freedom; a tendency to hyperspiritualism; a "hopeless, helpless, *dualism*" with "no faith in organic grace"; fanaticism; a spirit of "endless division"; a tendency to "end in flesh"; and a false theology.

Stamped with one or more of these marks, to a greater or lesser extent, were most of the Protestant churches in Nevin's time. Of course, the "Winebrennerians" were included. Noting that the remedy for sectarianism was not to be found in a new church or a *"non-sect* Sect," he wrote:

> Witness the sect of the Christians . . . and the "Church of God," as founded a few years since by John Winebrenner etc. . . . these agree, in casting off creeds and tradition, and going back to the Bible. That is, they are absolutely unhistorical; and for this very reason their pretended catholicity has no contents or substance whatever.[36]

It was with this general approach to sectarianism in the United States that Nevin reviewed Rupp's and Winebrenner's *History of all the Religious Denominations in the United States* [37] in the *Mercersburg Review* [*Reformed Church Review*] in 1849.[38] One of his longer book reviews (forty-two pages), appearing in both the September and November issues, it afforded Nevin the opportunity of applying his attitude on sectarianism to what was becoming a standard work on American denominations. The book was the epitome of everything Nevin was struggling against on the American church scene. In passing, he had mentioned Rupp's edition of 1844, negatively, in his *Anti-Christ*.[39] Since then, however, Winebrenner (who had become Nevin's *bete noire*) had published the second edition. Nevin's review dripped with sarcasm.

He wrote by way of introduction:

> As a business interest, at all events, the importance of the work is fully established. We have it, accordingly, stereotyped now, and done up in holiday style, as a second improved edition, under the auspices of Mr. Winebrenner, V. D. M., (by interpretation, Minister of the Word of God); who himself figures conspicuously in the book, both as the founder and historiographer of one of its sects, (one among the "fifty-three eminent authors" mentioned on its title-page) with the honor of a portrait to signalize such double distinction.[40]

74

"We had no ambition to have it in our library"; Nevin continued,

> and, to speak the plain truth, when called upon by a strenuous agent, not long since, who insisted on making us buy a copy of this second improved edition, with pictures, gilt backs and embossed sides, we took it finally, more to get rid of the application . . . than for the sake of any comfort or satisfaction we expected to find in its ownership.

> But we were wrong. That first judgment was quite too hasty and sweeping; and we have been brought to entertain since, a much more favorable feeling towards the work thus forced into our hands. Allowing it to be as valueless as now represented, for the purposes of a scientific text-book, or dictionary, of the widely extended sphere it proposes to fill, are there not other sides and aspects under which it may still deserve to challenge our careful regard? . . . Our prejudice is fairly converted into a sort of fond partiality. We positively like the book, and would not consent to part with it easily. Though no History of Religious Denominations, exactly in the sense of an Ullmann or a Neander, it is, in its own way, a most interesting and valuable Commentary on the Sect System, which both Ullman and Neander would read, no doubt, with no small amount of instruction and profit. In this view, the conception of the work is such as to do credit to the mind from which it sprang. It was well, aside from all bibliopolistical ends, to give this moral Babel an opportunity of speaking for itself; and now that it has thus spoken, it is well to lend an ear to the cataract of discordant sounds that is poured forth from its tongue.[41]

The book obviously made a deep impression!

Nevin, however, reserved his most caustic comments for Winebrenner himself. In speaking of the lithographed pictures of "distinguished men in the different denominations" which accompanied this particular edition of the book, he wrote:

> Last, though of course not least, deserves to be mentioned the full bust and particularly speaking face of John Winebrenner, V. D. M., the present publisher of this book himself; to whom we are indebted for the idea of these "splendid portraits of distinguished men," and who has the honor besides, as we here learn, of being the originator of a sect styling itself the "Church of God," (about the year 1825), one of the heroes thus of his own book; to say nothing of the distinction which belongs to him as the historiographer of his sect, one of the "fifty-three eminent authors," as before noticed, to whose united paternity the book before us refers itself on the title page. Mr. Winebrenner's portrait may be said to go beyond all the rest, in a certain self-consciousness of its own historical significance and interest. It has an attitude, studied for dramatic effect; an air of independence; an

The "particularly speaking face of John Winebrenner," according to John Williamson Nevin, which appears in the second and improved edition of Winebrenner's *History of All the Religious Denominations in the United States* in 1848.

open Bible in the hands; in token, we presume, that Wine-brennerism makes more of this blessed volume than any other sect, and that it was never much understood till Mr. Wine-brenner was raised up at Harrisburg, in these last days, to set all right, and give the "Church of God" a fresh start, by means of it, out of his own mind.[42]

Throughout the remainder of the review, Nevin again and again used Winebrenner and the Church of God (among others) to illustrate what was wrong with the sect system in America. For instance, after noting that the emphasis the sects placed upon the Bible as the only authoritative rule of faith and practice really meant an emphasis on the Bible as interpreted by the leader of the sect, he pointed to Winebrenner and his church as an example. Although the Church of God claimed no creed but the Bible, it also had a list of twenty-seven articles, showing the church's view on leading matters of faith.

. . . so we have a regular confession of 27 articles, (p. 176-181,) all ostensibly supported by proof from the Bible as understood by Mr. Winebrenner, fencing in thus her "scriptural and apostolical" communion, and of course fencing out all who, in the exercise of their private judgment, may be so unfortunate as not to see things in precisely the same way.[43]

In like manner he attacked the Church of God and Winebrenner for their rationalistic approach to the Lord's Supper and the sacramental system in general; running the concept of justification by faith into revivalistic extremes; and presenting a false picture of the role of private judgment and authority of the Bible in Christianity.

Where, finally, Nevin had a word of commendation for the teachings of Winebrenner and the Church of God, he placed it in such a highly critical context that its only value became one of negative illustration. Relative to the concept of the universal Church in the sects, Nevin noted:

In some cases, we have surprising confessions in favor of the true idea of the Church, where they might seem to be wholly out of place. Mr. Winebrenner (p. 175), insists on visibility, unity, sanctity, universality and perpetuity, as the necessary attributes of the church. "An invisible church that some divines speak of," he tells us, "is altogether an anomaly in christian theology." So again: "The union of sects, into one general evangelical alliance, or into one human organization diverse in character, faith and practice, from the one true church of God, as characterized in the Bible, we have no belief in nor sympathy for." [44]

It sounds like a point for Winebrenner. But not so, really. Nevin had introduced the paragraph from which the above quotation was taken as follows:

> It is encouraging however, as well as curious, to see how the sect system is made to lend testimony throughout, against itself, to the idea of the Holy Catholic Church; not unlike the devils in the New Testament, who were forced to acknowledge Christ, while fighting against him or fleeing from his presence.[45]

That there be no mistake, he added later in the same paragraph:

> . . . every sect, so far as it can be called a church at all, becomes necessarily a caricature of the catholicity with which it pretends to make war, and so, like every other caricature, bears witness to the truth, which is thus distorted by it and brought into contempt.[46]

For Nevin then, Winebrenner and the Church of God incorporated all of the worst features of the sect system, at least as Nevin conceived the system. The marks of the Antichrist, "the spirit of sect and schism," were everywhere apparent. The Church of God had no redeeming features. Indeed, he hinted, its very existence was diabolical.

Winebrenner was unhappy with the review, to understate the case. The proliferation of denominations in America had been as much a source of concern to Winebrenner as it was to Nevin. Years before Nevin, Winebrenner had been preaching the evils of sectarianism. (Both Winebrenner and Nevin frequently, but not exclusively, used "sect" for "denomination" because both assumed a normative Church which alone was correct in essential doctrines and practices. The assumption was that "denomination" implied only one of many names for—or aspects of—the true Church. A "sect" carried the connotation of a religious body dissenting from the established or true Church.) Now to find Nevin emphasizing the sectarian nature of both the Church of God and himself was more than he could take.

Nevin's review came to the attention of Winebrenner not long after the appearance of the September, 1849 issue of the *Mercersburg Review*. Not waiting for the conclusion of the professor's remarks in the November issue, he used the columns of the *Church Advocate* (successor to the *Gospel Publisher*), which he was now editing, to express his sentiments. In the issue of October 15, 1849, in an article entitled "Nevin on the Sect Spirit," he had this to say:

Not content with the troubles he [Nevin] has made at home—in the church which adopted him—he every now and then walks abroad, and trys to pick a quarrel with his neighbors. In the article under consideration, he repeatedly sounds the *"war-hoop"* and makes saucy and impudent attacks on various Denominations: such as the Congregationalists, the New School Presbyterians, Lutherans, Baptists, Disciples, etc., etc. [For some reason Winebrenner did not mention Nevin's attack on him personally or on the Church of God.] The fact is, he is full of the war spirit, and if we mistake not, is laboring for a warrior's crown. . . .

On the whole, would it not be more befitting for that learned sage, as a professed minister of Christ and Professor of theology, to study to be quiet, to mind his own business, to cast the beams out of his own eye, and to meddle less with other people's matters. We make this suggestion for his particular benefit and consideration.

At this point Winebrenner denounced Nevin with the sharpest words in the history of their relationship.

We have neither time nor inclination to review his article at present, (we may hereafter correct some of his blunders,) nor, in any way, to come in contact with him. Not because we fear him, but because he is a coward, a railer, and a bitter Sectarian. Heretofore we have proved him, and found him to be such. [Presumably with reference to their previous correspondence.] Hence we seek no controversy with him.

As in their previous correspondence, Winebrenner expressed concern for his former brethren in the German Reformed Church.

But we cordially sympathize with the people of the German Reformed Denomination, that they have been so unfortunate as to get such a Puseyistic distractor at the head of their literary and theological institutions.[47] . . . But time, by and by, will show whether it was good policy in them,—whether for their weal or wo [sic], that they went abroad, to buy up their Professors in Germany or among the Presbyterians.

Winebrenner concluded his review of Nevin's review by quoting him out of context. Nevin's sarcastic approval of the *History of Denominations* (because it illustrated so well the futility of the American sect system) was converted by Winebrenner into enthusiastic approbation. "Howbeit," Winebrenner explained,

Dr. Nevin has said and written some good things. Even in this fulsome article, on the sect spirit, etc., there are some excellent sayings. For the present we shall only notice what he has been pleased to say in commendation of the book in question.

Then, by omitting the negative sentiments (without indication), he went on to make Nevin say:

> We are willing to acknowledge, that we made very small account of this book when it first came in our way. But we were wrong. That first judgment was quite too hasty and sweeping; and we have been brought to entertain since, a much more favorable feeling towards the work. Our prejudice is fairly converted into a sort of fond partiality. We positively like the book, and would not consent to part with it easily. There is much to be learned from it for a seriously thoughtful mind; something directly; and a good deal more in the way of suggestion and silent circuitous meditation.[48]

In terms of mid-nineteenth century polemical churchmanship, it would be called making the best out of a bad thing.[49]

If Winebrenner was not looking for a controversy with Nevin in October of 1849, he was about five months later after hearing Nevin preach a sermon on the name "Christian." (As far as is known, this was the closest Winebrenner and Nevin came to meeting one another.) Winebrenner's report of the sermon in the *Church Advocate* for April 1, 1850, was considerably more irenic than his evaluation of Nevin's review of the *History of Denominations*. He wrote:

> A few Sabbaths ago, we heard **Dr. J. W. Nevin** preach a sermon on the origin and import of the name Christian.
>
> . . . .
>
> His remarks on the official character of the Messiah, in the exercise of these functions, were highly interesting and evangelical. But, when he came to the elucidation of these functional duties, as involved in the name and character of the Christian and of the Christian Church, he rather overstepped the teachings of the New Testament. At any rate, we were at a loss to see the consistency of his doctrine and practice. If the name Christian is so sacred, so highly important, involves so much official dignity, and imposes such weighty responsibilities, as the Professor intimated, then I should like to see his answers to the following questions.
>
> 1st. Why is it that Paul never uses the name Christian in any of his 14 epistles, seeing he knew the importance of this name, and wrote all his epistles subsequent to the time that the disciples received the designation?
>
> 2d. Why does not the Professor quit wearing human names and assume Scriptural ones? Why does he go by that unseemly misnomer, "German Reformed Church?"—And why indulge so frequently in the hateful practice of nicknaming others, who would go by the name that the mouth of the Lord has given? [An obvious reference to Nevin's use of "Wine-

brennerians" for the "Church of God."] Let him answer
these questions if he can.

The quotation illustrates Winebrenner's continuing emphasis
on the authority of the Scriptures. Nevin was "highly interesting
and evangelical" until he "overstepped the teaching of the New
Testament."

Winebrenner's statement that he failed "to see the consistency
of his doctrine and practice" probably was rhetorical. However,
seen in another light, it is also possible that Winebrenner really did
not understand Nevin's basic theological approach. At any rate
neither in this passage nor in his response to Nevin's review of the
History of Denominations did Winebrenner seem to address himself to the issues.

At the conclusion of his short review of Nevin's sermon,
Winebrenner challenged the professor to answer two questions.
Nevin, as far as is known, did not take the gauntlet. Winebrenner
carried one further item regarding Nevin in the *Church Advocate*.
As far as Winebrenner was concerned, it probably served as a
fitting climax to their past relationship. In the issue of November
15, 1851, Winebrenner quoted the following from the *New York
Observer,* under the heading "Resignation of Professor Nevin":

> Professor Nevin, who for some years has filled one of
> the Professorships in the Theological Seminary of the German
> Reformed Church, situated at Mercersburg, Pa., has tendered
> his resignation to the Board of Directors, who have referred
> it to Synod. This event is to be referred to the increasing
> spirit of dissatisfaction in the German Church, on account of
> the peculiar doctrines broached by the Professor on the sub-
> jects of Church and sacraments, which are supposed to border
> strongly on Popery.

Winebrenner did not comment on the item. He did not have to.

Theological Considerations

The conflict between John Nevin and John Winebrenner was
focused on two areas. The first was the "new measure" controversy during the first half of the nineteenth century; the second, the
issue of sectarianism and, by inference, the nature of the church.

As we have seen, Winebrenner's "new measures" were an
important factor in his separation from the German Reformed
Church in the mid-1820's. There is no indication that he seriously
modified his advocacy of them throughout the remainder of his

ministry. We have, for example, an account of a Church of God camp meeting given us by the Rev. A. D. Williams in the *Church Advocate* for March 1, 1849.[50] Mr. Williams was a Free Will Baptist pastor engaged in acquainting himself with the Church of God. (A merger between the two groups was discussed in the middle and late nineteenth century.) He spoke of the camp meeting favorably and in fact, with Winebrenner, participated in it.

> The general order of the services at the Camp Meeting (which the writer attended, held on the Cumberland road near Harrisburg), was, prayer meeting in the morning; preaching at ten, followed by an exhortation from some other minister, nearly as long as the sermon; preaching again at two with another exhortation, frequently followed by a call for mourners; preaching in the evening with an exhortation and call for penitents; ending with an excited and exciting scene of prayer, singing and shouting, which usually lasted until after midnight, and sometimes till near dawn of day. Shouting was frequent with both men and women, though more frequent with the latter; while some would commence jumping up and down and alternately swinging their arms back and striking them together in front, moderately at first, but increasing in rapidity and force until long after it would seem that they must be utterly exhausted, and uttering at the same time, a sort of half shout, half groan. Others would lose their strength and remain for some time rigid; and, as they afterwards affirmed, in a state of exalted happiness. The two latter classes were not large.

For his part, Nevin was constitutionally and theologically (and in 1842-1843 perhaps that is the correct order) opposed to the "new measure" system. It had not been a part of his background in the Presbyterian Church. He did not care to see it extend its influence any further in the German Reformed Church. Both Winebrenner and Nevin would agree that the state of the German Reformed Zion was deplorable in the early nineteenth century. Their correspondence made that quite clear. But for Nevin "new measure" revivalism was not the way to cure deadening formalism or spiritual lethargy. In exchange for "new measures," he proposed the following standards:

> A ministry apt to teach; sermons full of unction and light; faithful, systematic instruction; zeal for the interests of holiness; pastoral visitation; catechetical training; due attention to order and discipline; patient perseverance in the details of the ministerial work: . . .[51]

He then added:

> Where these are fully employed, there will be revivals; but they will be only as it were the natural fruit of the general

culture going before, without that spasmodic, meteoric character, which too often distinguishes excitements under this name; while the life of religion will show itself abidingly at work, in the reigning temper of the Church, at all other times.[52]

"For distinction sake," Nevin termed his system "the system of the Catechism." It was a system which could not live in harmony with the system of "new measures" and its "anxious bench." Indeed, "the spirit of the Anxious Bench is at war with the spirit of the Catechism." [53]

It is clear that Winebrenner was, to some extent, responsible for Nevin's *Anxious Bench,* first printed in the fall of 1843. Nevin certainly was disturbed when W. Ramsay, his Princeton classmate and a returned missionary from China, produced an "anxious bench" in the Old Stone Church at Mercersburg late in 1842.[54] This eventually led to a series of lectures on the new measures in his class on pastoral practice which he probably revised for the *Anxious Bench.* Nevin similarly was disturbed by the support of "new measures" on the part of the *Lutheran Observer.* He would have expected better things of the Lutheran Church. The Lutherans and German Reformed—churches of the Protestant Reformation—both should have been interested in maintaining their Reformation heritage against the fanaticism of "new measure" sectarianism. He frequently quoted from the *Observer* in the *Anxious Bench.* Yet Nevin's statement, at the conclusion of his correspondence with Winebrenner, that he would take up the matter of "new measures" in a separate publication, without referring directly to Winebrenner or the Church of God, also indicates that both Winebrenner and the Church of God were on his mind when he wrote it.

This is substantiated by Nevin's use of Winebrenner in the *Anxious Bench.* The fact of the matter is that in the *Anxious Bench* Nevin did specifically mention and refer not too obliquely to Winebrenner and the Church of God in a number of places. A few quotations will help give the picture.

All wild and fanatical sects employ it [the anxious bench], with equal success. Campellites [*sic*], Winebrennerians, and Universalists, show the same power, when necessary, in producing revivals under this form.[55]

. . . .

The measure of the danger will vary of course, with the extent to which the characteristic spirit of the system is allowed to work. A Winebrennerian camp meeting ... will carry with it a more disastrous operation than the simple Anxious Bench in a respectable and orderly church.[56]

Referring to what he considered a highly contrived apology for the "anxious bench" system given by the editor of the *Lutheran Observer*, Nevin declared:

> The most franctic [*sic*] disciple of Winebrenner could ask no more, to justify his greatest outrages on decency and common sense.[57]

Then a few lines later he quoted from his correspondence with Winebrenner:

> Even Mr. Winebrenner himself, when interrogated on the subject of noise, only answers, "What is from heaven I approve of, but what is from men I disapprove of:" though he goes on immediately to sanction "loud groaning, crying, shouting, clapping of hands, jumping, falling down, etc." as forms in which a divine influence may be expected at times to work.[58]

The conflict between Winebrenner and Nevin concerning sectarianism carried with it some confusion related to Winebrenner's concept of the church. The name of the church was important for Winebrenner. He wrote:

> The name or title, Church of God, is undeniably the true and proper appellation by which the New Testament church ought to be designated. This is her scriptural and appropriate name. This, and no other title, is given her by divine authority. This name or title, therefore, ought to be adopted and worn to the exclusion of all others.[59]

The nature of the relationship of this Church of God to other churches was implied in his discussion of its origin.

> As to the origin of the Church of God, we maintain, and truth compels us to say, that she justly claims priority to all evangelical churches. Her illustrious and adorable founder is the Lord Jesus Christ. He bought her with his blood. He founded her on the Rock.[60]

The term "church" could be regarded in either a "general" or a "local" sense. He wrote:

> Accordingly, the saints, or body of believers, in any given place, constitute the Church of God in that place; whilst those different, local and individual churches, collectively taken, constitute the one, holy, general church of God, spread abroad throughout the world.[61]

The criteria for membership in the church were "Christian experience and Church covenanting."

Now, if neither subscription to orthodoxy, nor Christian character, nor baptism, are properly Scriptural terms of Church membership, what then are the true ones? We answer . . . Christian experience and Church covenanting. Christian experience, or salvation from sin, brings men into the general Church, and Church covenanting introduces them into a particular or local Church.[62]

Finally, the essential attributes of this Church of God composed of experiential Christians were visibility, unity, sanctity, universality, and perpetuity.[63]

Winebrenner assumed, with most of his contemporaries, that the early church was a pure church and provided a norm by which nineteenth century churches should be judged. "The first christians," he wrote,

were chiefly all converted and organized into churches under the ministry of the inspired apostle. Consequently their order and practice may be regarded as infallibly correct, and their faith and worship as a perfect model for all the churches in after ages.[64]

He further assumed that the Church of God with which he was associated perfectly reflected the early church pattern and was, therefore, the nineteenth century equivalent of the apostolic church, including the name. About the year 1825, Winebrenner had

united with others in adopting the apostolic plan, as taught in the New Testament, and established free, and independent churches, consisting of believers or Christians only, without any human name, or creed, or laws, etc.[65]

The Church of God was, therefore, not one among many. The Church of God was the true, apostolic church.

Some problems immediately presented themselves. What was to be done, for instance, with the matter of the existence of the church between the close of the apostolic period and the year 1825? Winebrenner had stated clearly that "the true Church of God never ceased to exist" and yet "that the Roman Catholic Church never was the true Church of God." [66] The usual nineteenth century options at this point were either to declare for an invisible church or to trace a "true" church through various early heresies to the Waldensians and thence to the Reformation. Winebrenner did neither. He declared explicit, "An invisible church . . . that some divines speak of, is altogether an anomaly in Christian theology." [67] Nor did he make an effort (as far as I know) to trace a visible continuity from the apostolic period to the present. The reason is fairly obvious. It was only with Wine-brenner that the "true" church once again received its true pattern, including its true name. Only then could the apostolic church be precisely duplicated in the nineteenth century.

What then are we to make of his statement that "the true church never ceased to exist"? The only answer that seems to make sense is that in Winebrenner's writings we should read "invisible" for "general." A Christian experience of salvation from sin through Christ brings an individual into the general church which is the "true" church in any age. Then, through a church covenant, the Christian joins a local church.

This leads us to the matter of sectarianism. For Winebrenner any church other than the Church of God was a sect. Other churches *had* to be sects—not "denominations" or "names" for the "true" church—because only Winebrenner's Church of God was "true" and therefore normative. It was the true church by virtue of its being the only truly Scriptural Church up to, and including, the name. Thus Winebrenner could write: ". . . the Church of God is emphatically the true church; the church of the Bible. To her communion it becomes every child of God to be-long." [68] To his nineteenth century detractors, Winebrenner's view of the church was regarded as being not only unnecessarily stringent but certainly presumptuous.

Yet it is important to realize that, in the last analysis, Winebrenner really shared the feelings characteristic of most American theologians of his time in making the church one thing, and Christianity quite another. Winebrenner's continuing emphasis was on the conversion experience. It was this experience which qualified an individual for the name "Christian," not church membership. The converted Christian automatically became a member of the general Church of God. Then he had an option as to which local church to join. If he joined a United Brethren or German Reformed Church he became a member of the Church of God wearing a sectarian label. If he instead covenanted with a Church of God (the group associated with Winebrenner) he joined the Church of God which had dropped all sectarian labels. Given this position, Winebrenner was able to write:

> So we disallow sectarianism, and yet admit there are sectarian Christians. If there are no saints in Babylon, the call for such to come out of her would be useless.[69]

For Winebrenner then, to be a sectarian was to be anti-true (local) church. But it did not necessarily imply that a person was not a true Christian. The result was to make the (local) church a sort of adiaphoristic appendage to the Christian's experience of new life in Christ.

The importance of Winebrenner's emphasis on experience as the real *sine qua non* of Christianity comes through most clearly in his consideration of the sacraments. As for many of his contemporaries, the sacraments of the church were actually only ordinances for the Christian—duties commanded or ordered by Christ through an infallible New Testament. Winebrenner found three ordinances in the New Testament: the Lord's Supper, baptism, and feet-washing. He emphasized these, especially feet-washing, a great deal. Yet, when it was all said and done, participation in the ordinances became a personal matter—a personal response to Christ's command—and not something upon which church membership depended. To this day baptism is not a requirement for membership in the Churches of God.

Underlying Winebrenner's theology was a type of pietistic rationalism which was fairly characteristic of the age. Also, especially in his early years, he frequently called attention to a natural law upon which the principles of sound religion were based.

Winebrenner argued for the necessity of "being born again," first from the Bible, and then from the "nature of things." Under the "nature of things" he wrote:

Reason, experience, and observation, go to show . . . that the happiness of all living beings . . . depends upon the congeniality and suitableness between their natures and the things to be enjoyed.[70]

In his *A Brief View . . . of the Church of God* Winebrenner carefully carried through his emphasis upon reason and dependence upon natural law. He quoted approvingly from Dr. Watts' *Rational Foundation of a Christian Church:*

The principles on which christian churches are built and governed, are so plain, so natural, and easy, and so much the same with those which give rise, vigour, and stability to all the well founded societies in the world, that one would think there could not be such matter of debate and controversy among christians, upon these subjects, as we have unhappily found.[71]

A church established on these principles allowed, according to Winebrenner, "the most perfect liberty of men and christians."

Its Elders, or Rulers, have no power and authority to command any thing but what is found in the Bible, and what reason and common prudence will dictate.[72]

As would be assumed, this emphasis on reason was much in evidence in his approach to the ordinances of the church:

The words, This is my body, and, This is my blood, are to be understood in a figurative and not in a literal sense. To understand them literally is contrary to reason, and is contradicted by the evidence of our senses.[73]

There are certain surface similarities between Nevin's and Winebrenner's views of the church. Both assumed a visible, normative church. Both could agree that the marks of this church were visibility, unity, sanctity, universality, and perpetuity. Both particularly emphasized visibility and unity in their writings. Neither could find an invisible church. Both were oppressed with the way in which the sects destroyed the unity of the church. However, the similarities were primarily verbal. When Nevin and Winebrenner spoke of the church and the sects, the substance behind their verbal forms was quite different.

As indicated earlier,[74] by the time Nevin reviewed the Rupp-Winebrenner *History of Denominations* in 1849, his concept of the church was one which emphasized its objective, "given" nature. He summarized in his preface to *The Mystical Presence:*

If the fact of the incarnation be indeed the principle and source of a new supernatural order of life for humanity itself, the Church, of course, is no abstraction. It must be a true, living, divine-human constitution in the world; strictly organic in its nature—not a device or contrivance ingeniously fitted to serve certain purposes beyond itself—but the necessary, essential form of Christianity, in whose presence only it is possible to conceive intelligently of piety in its individual manifestations. The life of the single Christian can be real and healthful only as it is born from the general life of the Church, and carried by it onward to the end. We are Christians singly, by partaking (having part) in the general life-revelation, which is already at hand organically in the Church, the living and life-giving body of Jesus Christ.[75]

The church was not something "tacked-on" to a conversion experience; it was the "necessary, essential form of Christianity." For Nevin, unlike Winebrenner, the individual was subordinate to the church.

Nor could the church be historically static and limited to one (apostolic) form. The church was a growing, developing, existence. So Nevin wrote: "Surely to be historical at all, Christianity must be in the world under the forms of history, which itself implies organic life and growth . . ." [76] In any case, "It is not from the infancy of the Church . . . , that we are to look for clear and satisfactory statements of theological truth. The fathers form no binding authority for the faith of later times. . . ." [77] Winebrenner would not have been able to agree.

Again, Nevin spoke of the "visible" church in terms inadmissible to Winebrenner. According to Nevin, "the visible Church may be imperfect, corrupt, false to its own conception and calling . . . ." [78] For Winebrenner, with his concept of a church constituted by believers, such a statement would have been, theoretically at least, impossible. If the church were imperfect and corrupt, it would not be composed of regenerated Christians; and if the church were not composed of regenerated Christians, it would no longer be the church.

Nevin granted the normative value of the Bible. However he related the Bible to the Christian faith in a way which would have seemed strange to Winebrenner in that, for Nevin, the Bible did not fix the limits of the Christian faith. Nevin wrote:

> Christianity, it is true, has its "fixed standard" in the Bible. But the standard is not itself Christianity, the thing it is to try and measure. *That* is a divine fact, from Christ onward, out of the Bible and beyond it. [79]

Nevin was especially critical of the emphasis by Winebrenner and many of his contemporaries of "justification by faith alone," as opposed to "justification by works." "Justification by faith" tended to mean, for the "new measure" revivalist, that if only a man *willed* to be saved, he could be. Nevin's approach, with its emphasis on the necessity of divine grace and God's election, led him to charge Winebrenner with "Pelagianism," or, roughly, self-salvation. For Nevin, the sinner could not repent and believe of his own free will. Therefore, the "new measure" appeal to the emotions in order to get a sinner to "accept Christ" was not only useless, it was also a perversion of true religion. Nevin made this emphasis on "justification by faith" into one of the marks of an unchurchly sect spirit.

> It is well to note how generally the sect system adheres to the article of *justification by faith,* and how prone it is to run this side of Christianity out to a false extreme. . . . With many persons . . . the test of all soundness in religion is made to stand in the idea of salvation by grace as opposed to works, Christ's righteousness set over to our account in an

outward way, and a corresponding experience more or less magical in the case of those who receive it, which goes under the name of evangelical conversion. But now it falls in precisely with the abstract mechanism of the sect mind, to throw itself mainly on this view of religion, to the exclusion or at least vast undervaluation of all that is comprised in the mystery of christianity as the power of a new creation historically at hand in the church.[80]

At this point especially, the "new measures" controversy between Winebrenner and Nevin and their conflict over the nature of the church came together.

Nevin's "marks of the Antichrist," or sect spirit, have already been noted.[81] Sects were more or less subjectivistic and rationalistic entities which denied the divine fact of the church. The tendency of both Winebrenner and Nevin was to make the "sectarian" a person who did not agree with them theologically. In 1849, at the Classis of Mercersburg, the matter of re-ordaining a pastor from the Evangelical Association (Albright Brethren) was discussed. For Nevin this was a highly important question. On it hinged the practical application of his concept of the authenticity of the German Reformed Church and the sectarian nature of those churches with which he most violently disagreed. It was eventually decided, almost unanimously, that the Albright Brethren ordination was invalid. Nevin's statement with relation to this action is most interesting:

> On this broad principle, we justify the Reformation; It was a product of the old Catholic Church itself; . . . it was in the end, the organic outburst plainly of the life of Christianity, as an objective historical whole, which simply laid hold of the Reformers, and brought itself to pass by them as its organs, without any calculation of its own . . . on this principle, accordingly, we find no difficulty in distinguishing between it and all minor religious revolutions [like the Albright Brethren] that seek to shelter and excuse themselves under its shadow. [The brotherhood of Jacob Albright] rose in a corner; it had no historical necessity. . . . There is no room for any rational comparison here with the Reformation. . . . Luther was the organ of the Church; Jacob Albright was the subject of mere private fancy and caprice.[82]

Nevin still placed his confidence in the normative values of the Reformation. (A few years later his confidence began to waver.) A summary statement (in 1849) of Nevin's concept of the church and the role of the sects in relation to it, is the following:

> If the Church be of any force at all outwardly, as an object of faith and trust, and if schism in the old ecclesiastical sense

is to be regarded as still possible . . . it must be plain that such self-constituted upstart bodies as the Albright Brethren, the followers of John Winebrenner, etc., have no right or title whatever to be recognized as any part of the heavenly corporation.[83]

Nevin's reaction to what he considered was the rampant rationalism of Winebrenner and the general age has been illustrated by several previous quotations. A tendency toward "theoretic Rationalism" was characteristic of Sectarianism.[84] The Protestantism of his era was both "rationalistic and schismatic . . . in principle."[85] It shaped theology and fashioned the church "as in its own eyes the case" seemed to require.[86] What was happening to the church was, of course, happening to the sacraments of the church:

> It is by no fortuitous coincidence then, that we find the spirit of sect since the Reformation, (as indeed before it also,) in close affinity with the spirit of theoretic rationalism, in its low estimate of the Christian sacraments.[87]

Again:

> The anti-sacramental tendency of the sect spirit is strikingly revealed under its true rationalistic nature, in the disposition so commonly shown by it to reject infant baptism. . . . If there be no objective reality in the life of the Church, as something more deep and comprehensive than the life of the individual believer separately taken, infant baptism becomes necessarily an unmeaning contradiction.[88]

Nevin's emphasis here colored his whole approach to Winebrenner. He attacked Winebrenner for his rationalistic approach to the sacraments and the nature of the church itself. It was Winebrenner's rationalistic approach that enabled Nevin to charge that Winebrenner gave the Church of God a fresh start "out of his own mind." [89]

Finally, in explaining the Winebrenner-Nevin materials (and, in fact, in explaining why Nevin wrote many of the things he did) the evidence points to the fact that Winebrenner had become for Nevin his final foil. He regarded Winebrenner as an apostate from the German Reformed Church in the 1842-1843 controversy. By 1849 Winebrenner was also an apostate from *The* Church. To be sure, there were other apostates and other heretical churches, but Winebrenner had compounded the crime by becoming a diabolical parodist of the true Church with his "Church of God." Winebrenner's system was "dangerous to souls" in the early

91

1840's. By the half century mark, "Winebrennerism" was no part of the "heavenly corporation." Again and again Nevin pointed to Winebrenner and "his church" as the ultimate result of contemporary tendencies in American Protestantism. "The most franctic [*sic*] disciple of Winebrenner" was the extreme extremist in the matter; the very opposite pole to Nevin's approach. Beyond Winebrenner, Nevin had no examples. Unrestrained revivalism, pernicious sectarianism, "unchurchly" rationalism, and Winebrennerism were one.

Such was John Winebrenner's contribution to John Williamson Nevin and the Mercersburg theology.

6

Antislavery

SILK WORM

As a reformer, Winebrenner faced no problem so continually vexing or personally agonizing as that of slavery. He never found the permanent answer; but he did spend a great deal of time looking for it.

Background

Winebrenner was not a stranger to slavery. His father, Philip, on April 30, 1828, "released from Slavery" a Negro servant, James Tooley, "for divers good causes and considerations . . . and . . . fifty cents current money, . . ." [1] How long Mr. Tooley had been a slave in the Winebrenner family is unknown. However, inasmuch as Philip Winebrenner's will made provision for the manumission of his "Negro man Daniel" after an additional five years of servitude to either his son Christian (John's younger brother), or son-in-law Ezra Cramer, it would seem that slavery was a continuing institution in the Philip Winebrenner household. [2] Inasmuch as both of these notices of slavery in the family deal with manumission, we would assume that Philip Winebrenner was one of the slave-holding "liberals" common to the border states. Very possibly the slaves on the Winebrenner farm were allowed to "work out" their freedom over a set number of years. It is implied in the case of Daniel, and reasonably may have been one of the "divers good causes and considerations" related to the liberation of James Tooley.

But even apart from his being born in a slave state and into a slave-holding family, Winebrenner lived close to slavery all his life. Although he attended Dickinson College in Carlisle, Pennsylvania; studied theology in Philadelphia; and after 1820 made his home in Harrisburg, Pennsylvania—in all of these locations he was never more than fifty miles from the Mason-Dixon Line. After removing to Pennsylvania permanently, he frequently returned to Maryland on family, church, or business matters. Living in Harrisburg, he and his south-eastern Pennsylvania contemporaries frequently were more apt to follow the Susquehanna River south to Baltimore and northern Maryland for the latest news of the world, country, and markets, than to look east to the more distant Philadelphia. The connections of southeastern Pennsylvania with northern Maryland were further reinforced by ethnic ties. Many of the Germans in northern and western Maryland, including the Winebrenner family, had entered the state from Pennsylvania and had relatives in the latter state.

Nor was slavery but a distant memory in Pennsylvania for most of Winebrenner's life in that state. Pennsylvania had passed a gradual emancipation act, largely due to Quaker pressure, in 1780. However there were still slaves listed in the 1840 census for Pennsylvania. Twenty-four of these were in Cumberland County, across the Susquehanna from Harrisburg. One of the last slave cases in the Pennsylvania courts was not settled until 1849, eleven years prior to Winebrenner's death.[3]

Yet if, by virtue of his residence in Maryland and southeastern Pennsylvania, Winebrenner was not a stranger to the existence of slavery, probably he also absorbed the prevalent optimism with regard to its ultimate extinction which was so much a part of his home territory. During his lifetime he witnessed slavery's disappearance (by 1860) in Pennsylvania, and its gradual decline in Maryland. In 1790, seven years prior to Winebrenner's birth, Maryland listed 103,036 slaves in the national census—a number exceeded only by Virginia's 292,037 and South Carolina's 107,094. This figure climbed to 111,502 slaves in the 1810 census, but declined after that. Maryland claimed 87,189 slaves in the 1860 census. This decline was due to a number of factors, not the least of which was the opening of cotton and cane fields in the lower south and southwest, which drained slaves from the depleted fields of Maryland and the eastern seaboard. But another important factor was Maryland's high rate of manumission. In 1860 there were more free Negroes in Maryland than in any other state in the Union. In fact, in Maryland in 1860 there were almost as many free Negroes as there were slaves.[4]

The strength of the antislavery impulse in Maryland (and other border states) partially can be gauged by the continuing concern expressed by states farther south. In 1849 the editor of the daily *Chronicle and Sentinel* in Augusta, Georgia, could write: "By degrees the spirit of emancipation has ever progressed and is now progressing south. Maryland, Kentucky, and Virginia are [now] discussing its practicability. . . ." [5] Ten years later *The New Orleans Daily Crescent* sadly commented on the passing of slavery in the border states, lamenting that Maryland was "well nigh abolitionized" and becoming Northern in outlook.[6] The terrors of isolation were beginning to be felt by the Black Belt. The fact that Maryland was a state with a well developed system of fugitive slave routes likewise was not calculated to improve her image with slave states farther south.[7]

It should be recalled that Winebrenner was born and raised in Frederick County, in northern Maryland. The small proportion of slaves to the free population in Maryland's northern tier of counties, which included Frederick, frequently led to their being termed the "free counties." Illustrating the trends in Frederick County was the fact that whereas the county had 3,641 slaves in the 1790 census, and 4,445 slaves in the 1840 census, by 1860 there were only 3,243 slaves listed in the census. Over the same period, the free Negroes in the county increased: from 213 in 1790; to 2,985 in 1840; to 4,957 in 1860.[8]

Roger Brooke Taney practiced law in Frederick County between 1801 and 1823. In 1819 Taney was called upon to defend one Jacob Gruber, a Methodist Presiding Elder, against the charge of instigating Negro slaves to "commit acts of mutiny and rebellion." The charge was the result of a sermon preached by Gruber at a Washington County, Maryland, camp meeting in August of 1818. During the course of the sermon, Gruber named slavery as a national sin (along with infidelity, intemperance, and profanity), quoted relevant passages of the Declaration of Independence, and compared slaveholding Maryland to Pennsylvania—for all practical purposes a free state. Slaveholders in the audience succeeded in getting Gruber arrested. Taney had the case moved to Frederick, and in the course of the defense argued that:

> A hard necessity, indeed, compels us to endure the evil of slavery for a time. . . . It cannot be easily, or suddenly removed . . . every real lover of freedom confidently hopes that it will effectually, though it must be gradually, wiped away. . . . And until it can be accomplished, until the time when we can point without a blush to . . . the Declaration of

Independence, every friend of humanity will seek to lighten the galling chain of slavery. . . .[9]

Here was a frank admission by the outstanding lawyer of Frederick, the second city (next to Baltimore) in the state, of slavery as an evil. Yet at the same time the lawyer appealed for endurance of the evil, hoping for its obliteration—gradually. Taney knew the feelings of his Frederick County citizens. Gruber was acquitted.

About this same time the future Supreme Court Chief Justice was involved in manumitting his own slaves and, in at least one instance, purchasing slaves in order to keep a husband and wife together—and then freeing both. Living close to Frederick City and studying there, Winebrenner must have known of Taney. He later followed his career rather closely in the columns of the *Church Advocate.*

Sources telling us about Winebrenner's relations with either the slave or freedman in Maryland and Pennsylvania are disappointingly scarce. The only reference to his connections with Negroes on the family farm in Maryland is provided by Winebrenner's daughter, Emma Winebrenner Christman. In 1897 she prepared a brief biography of Winebrenner to be read at the centennial celebration, at the Harrisburg First Church of God, of her father's birth. Concerning his interest in the salvation of all his "kindred and friend," she wrote that "on his visits to his Maryland home during the days of slavery he always requested that the colored people be allowed to be present during family prayers." [10] The implication is that Philip Winebrenner owned more than one slave. However, it is also possible that the "colored people" included freedmen hired annually. It is remarkable that aside from Mrs. Christman's somewhat ambiguous reference to the "colored people" on the Philip Winebrenner farm, there is no hint of the Winebrenner family's connection with slavery in Winebrenner's correspondence with his family or in later polemical material written by Winebrenner, or the attackers and defenders of his shifting positions on the slavery issue. Probably the existence of slavery in his father's household was regarded as an extremely delicate matter by all concerned, and out of deference to Winebrenner's feelings the matter was never broached.

In Harrisburg, Winebrenner was involved in the development of a Negro Sunday School.[11] Persons of color attended Winebrenner's revival meetings. Bishop Seybert approved of Winebrenner's preaching to "the wicked and the good, among the high and the low, the rich and the poor, Methodist, white or black." [12]

Negroes were converted in, and baptized by, the early Churches of God in Maryland and Pennsylvania. For example, at the 1845 East Pennsylvania Eldership, Elder J. Keller from the Uniontown, Maryland, Church, reported thirty-three baptized, "22 white— 11 persons of color." [13] In 1848, the East Pennsylvania Eldership licensed its first Negro minister. From his journal kept in the month of January, 1826, we read of Winebrenner marrying "R. Gilmore to M. Bartlet, colored people (Fee 50 [cents])," on January 12. (On January 5, he had married a white couple and received $3.00.) [14]

Winebrenner undoubtedly had slaveholding friends and fellowshipped with them in some of the early Maryland churches of God. On October 31, 1850, G. U. Harn, a Church of God pastor in eastern Pennsylvania—but originally from Maryland—wrote a letter to the Church Advocate, outlining the "history" of slavery in the Church of God. He emphasized that

> five or more persons holding slaves had been members of the Churches of God, or fellowshipped and baptized as Christians—that repeatedly Camp-meetings had been held on extensive slave-holder's lands, and they fellowshipped as Christians—that ministers holding slaves had occupied the stands with our preachers—that twelve or fifteen Churches in Maryland and in the edge of Pennsylvania had been in regular communion with those persons—that not until very recently had two persons, the only ones that I ever knew to apply and not succeed on those grounds, been denied the rite of baptism— that one of those members had attended two sessions of the Eldership in East Pennsylvania . . . that more than thirty of the oldest and ablest of the ministers in Pennsylvania and Maryland had communed at the Lord's table and washed feet with these slave-holding members, and knew them to be such.[15]

Inasmuch as churches of God were not established in Maryland until the early 1830's, Harn's "history" covers about a fifteen to twenty year period. Without question Winebrenner is included in the "more than thirty of the oldest and ablest of the ministers in Pennsylvania and Maryland." He was personally responsible for the establishment of several of the churches in Maryland in the early and middle 1830's.

All in all, our sources tell us very little about Winebrenner's relationship to the slavery problem prior to 1835. We can only surmise that while closely acquainted with slavery he looked forward, with many of his northern Maryland and Pennsylvania contemporaries, to its decline and demise. Beginning in 1835, the picture becomes clearer.

1835-1838: Winebrenner and Abolitionism

On June 5, 1835, the first number of the biweekly *Gospel Publisher and Journal of Useful Knowledge* appeared. It was edited and published in Harrisburg by John Winebrenner in the interests of the Church of God.

Throughout 1835 the paper expressed a general interest in the antislavery movement, but hardly more than any "Journal of Useful Knowledge" might. There was mention of the public burning of the abolition tracts sent from New York to Charleston, South Carolina; notice of a rumored slave insurrection in Mississippi and the operation of "Lynch law" following; and an article from the *Charleston Observer* stressing the importance of religious instruction for Negroes. Several articles on African colonization appeared, all of them favorable toward the project. All of the articles dealing with slavery were clipped from exchange papers and not much of Winebrenner comes through. What we do see of him indicates a general interest in colonization and a none too favorable attitude toward the American Anti-Slavery Society. To a sympathetic article dealing with the progress of colonization in Liberia, Winebrenner added, "We are glad to see this work advancing." [16] He further approved an article from the *Cincinnati Journal* advocating gradual abolition rather than giving in to, in Winebrenner's words, the "ultra doctrines" of the American Anti-Slavery Society. [17]

This image of a moderate antislavery colonizationist was broken with the issue of January 29, 1836. This issue of the *Publisher* proclaimed the establishment of the Harrisburg Anti-Slavery Society, an affiliate of the American Anti-Slavery Society. Winebrenner was listed as one of the three managers of the Harrisburg group. A year or so later, the Harrisburg Society claimed 109 members, eleventh in size of the 126 societies in the Keystone State. [18]

Winebrenner gave no hint of what led him into active affiliation with the abolitionist movement. However the irregular abolitionist publication (of the American Anti-Slavery Society), the *Emancipator*, told of the presence in Harrisburg in late December, 1835, or early January, 1836, of the revivalistic abolitionist, Samuel L. Gould. [19] Gould was one of Theodore Dwight Weld's earliest "agency men." [20] In the course of delivering a series of antislavery lectures in Harrisburg he so aroused the local citizenry that the Town Council was petitioned to request Gould to desist. They did; but Gould did not. He stayed in the area, whipping up support for the antislavery cause. While certainty is not possible, in all likelihood one result of Gould's appearance in Harrisburg was Winebrenner's decision to identify himself with the "ultra doctrines" he had noted disapprovingly but a few months before.

The Constitution and "Declaration" published by the Harrisburg Anti-Slavery Society were modelled after the Constitution and "Declaration of Sentiments" approved by the American Anti-Slavery Society at its inaugural meeting in Philadelphia in December of 1833. William Lloyd Garrison, John Greenleaf Whittier, and the Rev. Samuel May were the authors. The Preamble to the Constitution read in part:

> Whereas, the most High God "hath made of one blood all nations of men to dwell on all the face of the earth," and hath commanded them to love their neighbors as themselves; and whereas our national existence is based upon this principle, as recognized in the Declaration of Independence, "that all mankind are created equal . . ."; and whereas slavery is contrary to the principles of natural justice, of our republican form of government, and of the Christian Religion, . . . and whereas we believe it to be the duty and interest of the masters, immediately to emancipate the slave; and whereas we believe that it is practicable by appeals to the consciences, hearts and interest of the people, to awaken a public sentiment throughout the nation, that will be opposed to the continuance of slavery. . . . WE DO HEREBY agree, with a prayerful reliance on the Divine aid, to form ourselves into a society, . . .[21]

The "Declaration" in the Harrisburg Society implied, upon casual reading, an "extremist-abolitionist" position. The "Declaration" insisted:

> That the slaves ought instantly to be set free, and brought under the protection of law:
> . . . .
> That all those laws which are now in force, admitting the right of slavery, are therefore before God utterly null and void: and ought to be instantly abrogated.
> We maintain that no compensation should be given to the planters emancipating their slaves, . . .[22]

To emancipate the slaves immediately, to appeal to a higher law, and to deny compensation to slaveholders for freeing their slaves, was generally regarded as irresponsible Garrisonianism—the most extreme abolitionist option available.

Winebrenner signed his name to the Constitution and "Declaration." His slaveholding father and his friends in Maryland must have winced.

With the notice of the formation of the Harrisburg Anti-Slavery Society, Winebrenner began an attack on slavery through the pages of the *Publisher* throughout 1836, 1837, and well into 1838. Occasionally he penned a scathing condemnation dealing with slavery in the states. More often, however, he relied upon his exchange papers, primarily the *Emancipator*, to do the job for him. The progress of abolitionism was noted in nearly every issue of the paper. His readers were kept in touch with items relating to the petition fight in Congress, the murder of Elijah Lovejoy in Illinois, fugitive slave cases, the possible admission of Texas as a slave state, etc. The *Gospel Publisher* maintained a healthy interest in the Gospel. Antislavery articles did not crowd out the usual revival news. However, by 1838 the paper had earned the distinction of being classed as an abolitionist sheet, as the following item from the *Richmond Whig,* for October 26, 1838 illustrates:

> A barrel full of abolition papers and pamphlets were burned in the Main Street of our city Richmond, Va. on Saturday last, by the police of the city. They were handed over by the Postmaster. Among them were—New York Evangelist; Gospel Publisher, Harrisburg, Pa.; Friend of Man, Utica, N.Y. . . . Liberator, Boston; . . . Philanthropist, Cincinnati; . . . Zion's Watchman, New York. . . . It is a great display of folly for the abolitionists to send their incendiary matter South; with a view of having it distributed among the people. . . . The vigilance of our Postmasters . . . will commit it to its proper element.[23]

At this time the *Publisher* probably had fewer than 400 subscribers. To be listed with papers like the *New York Evangelist* and *Liberator* was to be moving in heady company, even in a burning cause.

During 1837 and 1838 Winebrenner's involvement in abolitionism deepened. He was selected a delegate from the Harrisburg Society to the State Anti-Slavery Convention held in Harrisburg early in February, 1837.[24] In May of that year Winebrenner, with the other managers of the Harrisburg Society, defended the cause of abolitionism in Pennsylvania against the charges levelled against the movement by an antiabolition convention—the "Convention of the Friends of the Integrity of the Union"—which met in Harrisburg in May.[25] (This was the meeting which Thaddeus Stevens, at that time a delegate from Adams County, broke up by amending all resolutions to the effect that they were valid only insofar as they did not conflict with either the Bill of Rights or Declaration of Independence.) [26] In January of 1838 Winebrenner was appointed delegate, from Harrisburg, to the first annual meeting of the Pennsylvania Anti-Slavery Society which met in Harrisburg on January 16, 1838.[27] On January 22, 1838, Winebrenner, now corresponding secretary of the Harrisburg Society, read the report of the managers for the past year.[28]

Meanwhile, Winebrenner kept in touch with the struggle on a national level by means of the work done in the Harrisburg area by representatives of the American Anti-Slavery Society. Lewis Tappan announced the curtailment of the tract campaign and adoption of the Agency System (Weld's "70") by the national office at the Anti-Slavery Convention in Harrisburg, attended by Winebrenner in February of 1837. At least three of Theodore Dwight Weld's "agency men" operated for a time in the Harrisburg area. By January, 1837, Jonathan Blanchard was active in Dauphin, Adams, and Lancaster Counties (apparently succeeding Samuel Gould) converting Pennsylvanians to the cause (including Thaddeus Stevens) [29] and getting local antislavery societies started.[30] The seeds sown by Blanchard were watered by antislavery agent William Burleigh in the first part of 1838.

References to both Blanchard and Burleigh appeared in the *Publisher*. Blanchard used its columns to promote his cause in the Harrisburg locality and among the churches of God. Prior to his departure from Harrisburg in October of 1837, he wrote Winebrenner a letter, evidently intending it for publication. Winebrenner obliged in the *Gospel Publisher* for December 2, 1837. Portions of it are valuable for the light they throw on the "nationalization" of the local movement and the way in which abolitionism was now being identified as an essential of the Christian faith.

> Dear Brother Winebrenner: —An Anti-Slavery Society was formed in Middletown, Dauphin County, the day before yesterday. . . . Its constitution declares slave-holding to be a "foul sin in the sight of God," and affirms that slave-holders aught [*sic*] to be considered unworthy of communion in any Church of Christ.
> . . . .
> Do not fail to obtain the Anti-Slavery almanac, and other anti-slavery reading for your families the coming winter.
>
> Use all diligence, to circulate petitions whenever there are any to be circulated.
>
> Do not fail faithfully and affectionately to rebuke those Methodist, Presbyterian, and Lutheran brethren who do not lift up their voice against the slave-holding ministers in their respective churches.
> . . . .
> Yours for the slaves, J. Blanchard

In the *Gospel Publisher* for April 19, 1838, under the caption "Spirit of Anti-Abolitionism" Winebrenner wrote his longest editorial (only half a column) dealing with the issue of abolitionism. It was in response to an article in the *Keystone,* a Harrisburg paper, which claimed that while there were "many pious persons" who supported abolitionism at the beginning of the antislavery controversy, its increasingly political nature warranted its being handled now by the politicians alone. Winebrenner denied that abolitionism was a political question and, in addition, had a few well chosen words relative to Negro colonization:

> It [abolitionism] is not now, and it never was a political question. Politicians or rather, colonizationists and anti-abolitionists have long tried to make it such . . . but hitherto, they have not succeeded, and we hope never will. African colonization has assumed much more of a political character, than abolitionism. . . . Abolitionism aims at the destruction of a corrupt tree; . . . whilst, colonization only contemplates the preventing of it.

Winebrenner had reversed his position on the principle of colonization. In 1835, he was pleased "to see the work advancing"—a stand he was once again to adopt in later years. In 1837, however, colonization was the politicians' "out." He would have nothing to do with it.

When Winebrenner rejected the colonization program, he reflected the position taken by a number of rigid abolitionists in the 1830's. For these "extremists," colonization was simply a way of diverting attention from the real moral problems involved in the slavery system.

Yet it is difficult to determine how much of an extreme abolitionist Winebrenner actually was during this period. He did not do a great deal of editorializing in the *Gospel Publisher,* and we can not say with certainty that he personally accepted everything included in the *Publisher* from exchange papers. To be sure, he signed the Constitution and "Declaration" of the Harrisburg Anti-Slavery Society, which documents were based upon the Constitution and "Declaration of Sentiments" of the American Anti-Slavery Society, and which were written in part by the prince of the "ultra abolitionists," William Lloyd Garrison. However close examination reveals that the Constitution and "Declaration" of the Harrisburg Anti-Slavery Society, as printed in the *Gospel Publisher,*[31] omitted several statements found in their prototypes. These included, for example:

That every American citizen who retains a human being in involuntary bondage as his property, is [according to Scripture] a MAN-STEALER.

. . . .

We further believe . . . that all persons of color who possess the qualifications which are demanded of others, ought to be admitted forthwith to the enjoyment of the same privileges . . . as others; and that the paths of preferment, of wealth, and of intelligence, should be opened as widely to them as to persons of a white complexion.

. . . .

We shall aim at a purification of the Churches from all participation in the guilt of slavery.[32]

These and many other omissions indicated a much more cautious acceptance of the American Anti-Slavery Society's platform than at first might have been supposed. Whatever personal feelings might have been in the matter on the part of the Harrisburg Anti-Slavery Society's membership, they undoubtedly were aware also of what their fellow non-abolitionist Pennsylvanians were thinking. The equality of Negro and white, especially in terms of education and job opportunities, was not at all popular in Pennsylvania in the 1830's. Reversing a previously liberal attitude, the state limited the voting franchise to white freemen in 1837. To what extent the above omissions represented Winebrenner's general attitude is unknown. At any rate, he signed both the Constitution and "Declaration" as amended by the Harrisburg Society.

In the matter of "immediate abolition," the Harrisburg Society did modify its stand. Whereas in 1836 the Society declared that "the slaves ought instantly to be set free," by 1837 the Society felt it necessary to redefine what was meant by "instantly." In explaining the term "immediate emancipation" to the "Friends of the Integrity of the Union Convention" meeting in Harrisburg in May of 1837, the managers of the Harrisburg Society (including Winebrenner) suggested that

by immediate emancipation . . . we mean that measures shall be immediately taken to deliver the slave from the arbitrary will of the master, and place him under the salutary restraints and protection of law. We see no absurdity in the use of immediate as applied to these measures, nor do we transcend the ordinary force of language when we call an important and complex public measure an immediate one, *if it be promptly commenced, with the honest determination or urging it on to its completion.*[33] [emphasis mine]

This explanation of "immediatism" was based upon a similar one offered by national antislavery headquarters in New York. It undoubtedly reflected the influence of Theodore Weld's "immediate emancipation, gradually accomplished" doctrine upon the abolition movement as a whole. In accepting it, Winebrenner and the Harrisburg Society rejected the "immediate emancipation, immediately accomplished" doctrine of the more extreme "Garrisonian" wing.

Winebrenner was an abolitionist by 1836. There can be no doubt about that. However, it would appear that perhaps due in part to state and local sentiments and perhaps in part to his own background, Winebrenner actually represented abolitionism of a somewhat more tempered variety—at least in contrast to the later doctrines of Garrison (which included, for example, denouncing the United States Constitution as a proslavery document).[34]

In the *Gospel Publisher* for August, 1838, Winebrenner once again attacked the principle of colonization, indicating that, among other things, the southern slaveholders had stolen the wages of men by enslaving them and then returning them to Africa. In the north, by contrast, workers were paid their due and allowed to go wherever they wanted.

After this issue, the *Publisher* fell silent on the issue of slavery. For over a year next to nothing appeared in the paper which even faintly had an abolitionist ring to it. When once again, late in 1839, matters pertaining to the slavery struggle were reintroduced to the *Publisher*, they tended to be highly routine and were without editorial comment.

What happened? Available sources point to a reaction against Winebrenner's policies on the part of his friends in the Church of God and subscribers to the *Publisher*. In January of 1838, James Mackey, a Church of God minister, wrote to Winebrenner, evidently a little worried that the editor of the *Publisher* was in danger of losing his Christian zeal in his excessive interest in abolitionism. Mackey had a high regard for Winebrenner and was antislavery himself. But he wrote:

> Dear Brother: —I am preaching up temperance, and abolitionism with all my might,—not however alone the temperance of whiskey drinkers, but "Let your moderation be known to all men," and, I generally add, in all things. . . . "The abolition of sin," is what I am at likewise. Of course when slavery comes in my way, I lift it out of the way, and if I can, I try to let it fall out of my hands hard enough to kill it. After all, you will think as to you appears best, and sure I have no objection, provided, these things get not the

ascendency in my dear brother's mind; so much as to crowd out the more important graces and abilities, with which the Lord has so bountifully, stored it; and which in years gone by, has made him such a successful, Herald of the cross . . .[35]

Mackey was gracious, but obviously concerned.

Then too, abolitionism was causing trouble for those churches of God which espoused the cause. The Union Bethel was stoned and several of its windows broken because Jonathan Blanchard was allowed to speak from the pulpit.[36] In the recollections of Jacob Flake, a Church of God minister, appearing in the *Church Advocate* for April 18, 1867, the following appeared:

> Human slavery was another question that as early as the years 1835 and '36 caused some considerable contention, especially at Harrisburg and Middletown; Our Bethels were opened for abolition lectures and anti-slavery meetings, when stones, rotten eggs and fire, slander and persecution were the only arguments of our opponents, and professed Christians and whole churches among them.

The fact of opposition to abolitionism in the churches at Harrisburg and Middletown is confirmed by letters to the editor appearing in the *Publisher* beginning in 1838.[37] While Winebrenner said nothing about it at the time, a reasonable surmise would be that increasing dissension in the Church of God, and a threatened if not actual loss of subscribers to the *Publisher* (which was in continual financial difficulty anyway), were influential in Winebrenner's decision to drop abolitionism from its columns.

There were other factors, without doubt. The Panic of 1837 and following depression had cost Arthur Tappan, prime mover of the American Anti-Slavery Society, his fortune. In addition, contributions to the national office from local antislavery societies dropped off sharply in the late thirties and especially after the Panic. Also, in the late 1830's the American Anti-Slavery Society was experiencing those personality and policy difficulties which led to its division in 1840, and the formation of two "shadow" national societies. The Pennsylvania Anti-Slavery Society disappeared as did many of the local societies. The meeting in 1838 is the last of the Harrisburg Anti-Slavery Society meetings noted in the *Publisher*. Across the country, the late 1830's saw a reaction against the "ultraism" of the mid-thirties, though abolitionism, especially as it moved into political realms, was far from dead.

Too, Winebrenner himself was getting interested in other things. A craze involving the growing of silk worms and mul-

MORUS ALBA MULTICAULIS

berry trees (especially the *morus multicaulis*) swept the eastern states in the late 1830's and early 1840's. Winebrenner became deeply involved with *morus multicaulis*, and eventually suffered financial reverses because of it. Winebrenner's involvement in the silk industry may be related to his interest in abolitionism in that, about this same time, some northern abolitionists were recommending the use of silk instead of slave grown cotton. Winebrenner was also showing an interest in the sugar beet, from which the abolitionists hoped sugar could be extracted more economically than from slave produced sugar cane.[38] Winebrenner's concern with silk culture and sugar beets was illustrated by the large number of articles in the *Publisher* in 1839 dealing with both—but especially with the *morus multicaulis*, which Winebrenner sold. These appeared not long after articles devoted to abolitionism disappeared.

As far as our records go, Winebrenner's abolitionist days ended abruptly in August of 1838. After that, he no longer attacked the colonization principle or advocated "immediate" emancipation, however interpreted. He remained opposed to slavery, of course, just as he remained opposed to all sin. But his problem now became one of satisfactorily relating—in his own mind and in the minds of others—the fact of the existence of slavery to the fact of the existence of the Christian Church, particularly the Church of God.

1839-1845: Winebrenner, Antislavery, and the Church of God

In the years immediately following his abolitionist period, Winebrenner and his friends attempted to persuade the Church of God to take a definite stand against slavery.

There was opposition. In the *Publisher* for January 31, 1840, Winebrenner inserted an article clipped from the *Oberlin Evan-*

106

gelist which gave resolutions on moral subjects passed by the "Congregational Association of Central Ohio." These included resolutions promoting antislavery, temperance, Sabbath-keeping, and moral reform (anti-sin) in general. Winebrenner added, with almost certain reference to his detractors in the Church of God,

> ... there are other churches [like the Congregational Association of Central Ohio] who deem it their bounden duty to express their mind fearlessly in favor of righteousness, and against all sin, the croaking of time-servers and the fearful-hearted notwithstanding.

Winebrenner's "fearful-hearted" were those in the church who, whatever their personal feelings in the matter might have been, were convinced that the slavery question was not an issue for the church to decide without imperiling its unity. Slavery was a secular matter and should be left to the politicians. The *Gospel Publisher*, moreover, as a religious periodical, should concern itself with "religious" rather than "secular" intelligence. Winebrenner did not agree. Slavery was no more a secular matter, beyond the reach of the church, than was any other form of sin— only "time-servers," those who obsequiously complied with the spirit of the times, would hold the contrary. But the existence of the *Gospel Publisher* was at stake, apparently. In the issue of January 3, 1840, he agreed to abridge the "secular department" of the paper because of "anti-secular brethren," although anti-slavery articles, primarily from exchange papers, continued to appear.

Yet, opposition or not, the early and mid-1840's saw a gradual acceptance by the Church of God, as a church, of antislavery principles.

Winebrenner edited the *Gospel Publisher* until April 1, 1840. At that time the editorship passed to John F. Weishampel, who held the position until the end of 1843. He was succeeded by George McCartney, who continued as the *Publisher's* editor throughout 1844 and 1845. In 1845 financial problems resulted in the non-appearance of the *Publisher* for several issues, and with the December 12 issue it suspended publication altogether. The paper then reappeared as the *Church Advocate*, edited by Winebrenner again, on May 1, 1846. He continued as editor until 1857. During the entire period, the paper was published in or near Harrisburg, generally weekly.

Weishampel and McCartney were, like Winebrenner, from northern Maryland. Also like Winebrenner, they were antislavery men, and continued the antislavery emphasis Winebrenner had established before he left the *Publisher* in 1840, and which he resumed when editing the *Advocate* from 1846 on.

Items of concern to the editors during the 1839-1845 period included the "Armistad affair," [39] which dragged on for several years in the columns of most northern church papers; President Tyler's slaves, again a cause of national scandal and prayer for antislavery papers; articles vindicating the Bible from the charge of sanctioning slavery; fugitive slave cases; and the division of the Methodist and Baptist Churches over the slavery issue. The impression received is not that the editors were actively agitating. The approach was much more sedate than in the mid-1830's. The Millerite and Temperance movements appeared to be of greater concern, especially to Weishampel. However, the *Publisher* did keep the slavery controversy simmering if not at full boil. The "Anti-secularists" still opposed an open discussion of either abolitionism or slavery in the paper, and probably were not too happy with antislavery exchange articles which did appear. But an editor's righteous indignation occasionally got the better of him. Commenting on the report of a South Carolina man who was condemned to death for helping a slave to escape, George McCartney was moved to express himself on such "legal murder":

> It is not our desire or intention to open our columns to discuss, advocate or condemn the measures of the abolitionists. We know that many of our readers are opposed to the discussion of the slavery question, and as our paper was not instituted for such purposes, we shall not offend them by taking part in such discussion. But . . . there is not a man in this community who will not join with us in the . . . condemnation of such an unchristian act as putting a man to death for advising a fellow creature to escape from the bonds of Slavery . . .[40]

In 1844 I. D. Rupp's *He Pasa Ekklesia* appeared. The article setting forth the Church of God was written by Winebrenner. In listing the twenty-seven points covering the "leading matters of faith, experience, and practice" of the church, Winebrenner included as the nineteenth point: "She believes the system or institution of involuntary slavery to be impolitic and unchristian. (Matt. vii 12, xix 19; Gal. iii 28)."

Winebrenner's judgment concerning the antislavery nature of the church was confirmed by the first General Eldership of the Church of God which met at Pittsburgh in 1845. At this meeting, the position of Winebrenner and the *Gospel Publisher* was reinforced by delegates from the "western elderships" (West Pennsylvania and Ohio) who tended to represent a more clearly defined antislavery attitude than the churches in the East Pennsylvania

Eldership (which included the Maryland churches of God). The result was the passage by the General Eldership of the following "Resolutions on Slavery," drawn up and offered by Winebrenner himself:

Whereas, it is the duty of the ministers of God to testify against sin in every form and place, Therefore,

1. Resolved, That it is the unequivocal and decided opinion of this General Eldership of the Church of God, that the system of involuntary slavery, as it exists in the United States of North America, is a flagrant violation of the natural, unalienable and most precious rights of man, and utterly inconsistent with the spirit, laws and profession of the Christian religion.

2. Resolved, That we feel ourselves authorized by the highest authority, and called upon by the strongest ties and obligations, to caution our brethren in the Church of God, against supporting and countenancing, either directly or indirectly, the said iniquitous institution of involuntary slavery; and should any of our ministers or members ever become guilty of this great and crying sin, we do most earnestly and religiously recommend and advise, that all such be excommunicated, or cast out of the church, and denied the right of Christian fellowship among us.[41]

By 1845 the Church of God was officially an antislavery church. The "anti-secularists," "fearful-hearted," and "time-servers" had been defeated.

1846-1852: Church Membership for Slaveholders?

The years following the passage of the General Eldership Resolutions on Slavery saw a general extension of antislavery feeling in the Church of God. The Indiana Eldership, organized in 1846, resolved that the Bible taught slavery to be an evil and that the eldership would have nothing to do with slaveholders.[42] In 1849, the Journal of the first Michigan Eldership resolved "that we the brethren of the Church of God, prohibit anyone from uniting with us who holds slaves or belongs to secret societies." [43] The Illinois and Iowa Elderships, organized prior to the Civil War, took similar actions.

Letters from individuals concerning slavery began to appear in the *Church Advocate* following its establishment by Winebrenner in 1846. In the *Advocate* for December 15, 1846, John Hickernell, one of the outstanding western missionaries in the pre-Civil War period, wrote from Marshall County, Virginia (later West Virginia):

It is here that men will plead the propriety of buying and selling the temples of the Holy Ghost, and separate man and wife, and even snatching the child from the mother's breast: yet, withal, taking the Bible for their counsellor. . . . Among these tyrants, in human form . . . you will find the professors of Christianity. . . .

I have been frequently asked whether I would take slave-holding men into the church. I answered, No! I think all whom God sets at liberty, ought to let the oppressed go free.[44]

Another indication of the accelerating interest in slavery and antislavery in the Church of God during this period was the increase in the number of major news items dealing with both in the *Church Advocate*. Whereas in 1844, the last full year of the *Gospel Publisher*, articles on slavery appeared irregularly, by 1848 the *Advocate* was carrying items on slavery averaging more than one a month. By 1850, the year of the Compromise,[45] articles related to slavery and antislavery appeared every bit as frequently as in the *Gospel Publisher* in Winebrenner's abolitionist days. The editor's concern for the feelings of the "anti-secularists" seems to have disappeared. Numerous articles indicated that Winebrenner was confident of general church support for his antislavery policies.

One might suppose that by 1848 Winebrenner would have been satisfied with the attitude of the Church of God toward slavery. The church had taken an antislavery position. Winebrenner was free to express himself in the *Advocate* with regard to slavery and to present antislavery articles and letters. His abolitionism of the 1830's had been at least partially justified by the passage of time. He was no longer regarded an extremist in antislavery matters.

Here was, in fact, a problem. Winebrenner was not only no longer an "extremist," he was beginning to find himself a "conservative." The church was willing to go further down the antislavery road than he.

In the July 1, 1848 *Church Advocate* Winebrenner for the first time editorialized on the question of church membership for slaveholders, in the context of a general discussion on war and slavery. He wrote:

We are opposed to War and Slavery. Yet we believe there are Christian soldiers and Christian slave holders. Though, therefore, we go with all our might for the abolition of War and Slavery, yet we cannot feel free to unchristianize and condemn everybody who is a warrior or a slave holder.

No one picked up the statement and compared it to the 1845 "Resolutions on Slavery" which advised excommunication of, and denial of fellowship to, slaveholders. But it did become increasingly clear that the church lacked a consensus on the subject and that John Winebrenner himself was now trying to moderate what he considered an extremist antislavery position.

Winebrenner's attitude on church membership for slaveholders remained unchallenged until 1850, when the problem surfaced during the East Pennsylvania Eldership late in mid-October of that year. Elder G. U. Harn, an East Pennsylvania pastor, visited the General Conference of the Free Will Baptist Church (which met at the beginning of October, 1850, in Providence, Rhode Island) as a fraternal delegate. In his report to the *Church Advocate* of his visit, he mentioned presenting the 1845 General Eldership "Resolutions on Slavery" to the Baptists, which resolutions were "greeted with much enthusiasm" by the General Conference. But then he added a qualification:

> . . . You will, however, permit me to remark, that, although I endorse the sentiments contained in these resolutions, yet I never understood them to advise the Churches of God to withhold the hand of fellowship from or disconnect themselves with a brother, merely on the ground that he sustains the relation of master to a slave.[46]

Harn's understanding was not the understanding of the majority of the East Pennsylvania Eldership. When he gave a similar report to that group, the result of his qualification was the disapproval of his whole report. The vote rejecting the report was close, nineteen to seventeen, Winebrenner and, generally, the older members of the Eldership (including most, but not all, of those with Maryland connections) voted with the minority for accepting the report. Harn, whose antislavery views branded him as an abolitionist and "amalgamationist" in his home state of Maryland, where he had involved himself in antislavery debates, was amazed by the vote. He shortly thereafter wrote a long letter to the *Advocate* [47] defending his position and mentioning that in the past slaveholders had had fellowship with members of the Church of God.[48]

A month later, the Rev. A. D. Williams, representing the Free Will Baptists, wrote Winebrenner, asking him what his and the East Pennsylvania Eldership's position on slavery actually was.[49] (Williams had frequently visited among the local churches of God and knew Winebrenner personally.) Harn had reported to the General Conference of the Free Will Baptists that the 1845

Resolutions "presented the sentiment of the ministers and churches generally." Yet, Harn's report had been rejected by his own eldership.

Williams' letter to Winebrenner and Winebrenner's reply appeared in the *Church Advocate* of December 2, 1850. We quote portions of Winebrenner's reply, entitled "Position of the Eldership on . . . Slavery." It is true, Winebrenner told Williams, that the East Pennsylvania Eldership does have a position on slavery.

In respect to the Institution of American Slavery, the East Pennsylvania Eldership of the Church of God entertain but one opinion, and that opinion is fairly and fully expressed in the resolutions passed by the General Eldership, held in Pittsburg, Pa., in the year 1845.

However,

. . . on the question, "Is the relation of master to slave a bar to Christian fellowship?" the body is divided—some taking the affirmative, others the negative.

Those who take the negative side of this question, [including Winebrenner] think that the decision of it ought always to be made to turn on the circumstance of the case— that there are *mitigating circumstances* [emphasis mine] connected with many cases, which require the exercise of Christian toleration and forbearance, and hence the bare relation of master to slave does not, always under all circumstances, furnish a sufficient bar to Christian fellowship.

Winebrenner was pleased to say, however, that

. . . this difference of opinion has not led to strifes and divisions among ourselves, as unfortunately it has done in other bodies.

"Those who err," he continued, "ought to be instructed, reproved, and warned according to . . . the Bible"; but,

. . . there is no warrant to expel them from the church, or declare them unworthy of Christian fellowship, so long as they, in the judgment of Charity, may be deemed in favor with God.

Slavery, as far as Winebrenner was concerned, is sinful, but tolerable:

Faults and errors are not all alike sinful and injurious. Some . . . strike . . . at the very foundations of religion; and these, when embraced, will soon work out the destruction of Christian character. Others are less injurious, and must be tolerated, or the principle of Christian forbearance must be abandoned.

After noting that the vote in the East Pennsylvania Eldership "shows nothing but disrespect to Brother Harn," Winebrenner concluded with a plea for the golden mean:

> Howbeit, on the aforesaid question there is an honest contrariety of opinion among the brethren of the Eldership; yet through grace, they have charity to bear with one another, and are neither intolerant nor latitudinarian in faith or practice. "Mittel mass die beste Strass." [Roughly, "Moderate measures are best."]

Unfortunately, in this open letter to Williams, Winebrenner did not provide his readers with the "mitigating circumstances" which might allow a slaveholder Christian fellowship, a positive estimation of his "favor with God," and require of nonslaveholders an "exercise of Christian toleration." However, G. U. Harn, writing on "Politics, Religion and Slavery" in the *Church Advocate* for December 8, 1859, gave several instances "relied on by Mr. Winebrenner" as extenuating circumstances in privately interpreting Winebrenner's *Letter on Slavery* written in 1858.[50] Probably they were what Winebrenner had in mind in his letter to Williams. They included:

> . . . where the State law inhibits manumission without first giving . . . security . . . for the maintainance of the slave through life . . as the master is unable to afford it; when the State forbids manumission, unless the slaves be removed from its bounds, and this the master may be incapable of doing . . . ; or their release might be under such circumstances as would render their return to relentless bondage almost certain and inevitable. Or, again, all a man's estate may be invested in slaves—to manumit them would be to reduce himself and family to poverty. Again, some slaves may be so young and others old, that they are not capable of doing for themselves.

Williams replied to Winebrenner's answer to his question in the *Morning Star,* a Free Will Baptist publication.[51] In the reply he said that, among other things, he could not reconcile the General Eldership Resolutions, "according to their obvious meaning," to the "mitigating circumstances" which would allow a slaveholder to be received into the church.

Winebrenner answered Williams in an editorial headed "Our Position on Slavery Re-Defined," in the *Church Advocate* for January 1, 1851. He challenged Williams concerning the "obvious meaning" of the 1845 Resolutions, stating that only an "ultra" would say they were irreconcilable with the possibility of slaveholding membership in the church. He told Williams that there were other "great evils in the world besides slavery," and proceeded to name them; intemperance, covetousness, sectarianism, and war. "Each of these master evils," Winebrenner held

> . . . to be "utterly inconsistent with the spirit, laws, and profession of the Christian religion." Peradventure the Free-Will Baptists do likewise. If so, will brother Williams and his brethren apply the lash of discipline with as much severity upon these sinners in Zion as upon the slave-holding sinner?

He then offered an interesting hierarchy of sin, in which slavery came off reasonably well. "Is it true," he asked,

> . . . that slave-holders, under all circumstances, are sinners above all men? We say nay—sectarianism, war, etc., are greater evils than slavery. These facts are almost self-evident.

Without giving substance to his "etc." or illustrating how "these facts are self-evident," Winebrenner proceeded to argue his position by showing Williams the absurdity of his:

> I ask, then, does brother Williams hold and teach that there are no mitigating circumstances that will entitle the RUM-SELLER, the COVETOUS MAN, the SECTARIAN, and the WARRIOR, to exercise of Christian toleration and forbearance? . . . If these evils are utterly inconsistent with the spirit, laws, and profession of the Christian religion, (and who will dare to deny it?) then, according to brother W[illiams]'s reasoning, strange indeed, that they should not "always, and under all circumstances, furnish a sufficient and an unmistakable bar to Christian fellowship!"

In conclusion, Winebrenner denied that "one leading minister" (Winebrenner) used "all his influence to secure votes for the adoption of brother Harn's report on the ground of courtesy" and that Brother Harn's church had "changed its position without acknowledging it" on the slavery question. This remained Winebrenner's position on church membership for slaveholders until 1860, the year of his death.

Why did Winebrenner take this position on church membership for slaveholders?

To begin with, I feel we must be careful not to assume that because he was at one time an abolitionist, at least in the conventional sense of the term, he therefore necessarily was opposed to slaveholders in the church on principle. It was indicated earlier that, as a member of the Harrisburg Anti-Slavery Society, he represented a considerably more cautious abolitionism than that advocated by Garrison and other northerners. That item relating to the "purification of the Churches from all participation in the guilt of slavery" in the "Declaration of Sentiments" of the American Anti-Slavery Society was omitted from the similar "Declaration" of the Harrisburg Society as printed in the *Gospel Publisher*. During the mid-1830's, Winebrenner did print at least one letter in the *Publisher* which urged that there should be no slaveholders in the church.[52] Similarly, when the issue was raised by churches of God ministers and laymen beginning in 1846, Winebrenner printed the letters in the *Advocate*. However, Winebrenner did not comment positively on letters of this type before 1848. Further, as editor of both the *Publisher* and *Advocate* he published letters and articles with which he disagreed (as long as they were legibly written and in good taste).

Winebrenner's first statement on the subject was the short editorial in the July 1, 1848 *Church Advocate*.[53] This editorial could very well reflect feelings that he long had maintained privately, even during his abolitionist days. At least, there is no evidence to the contrary in his letters or the files of the *Gospel Publisher* and *Church Advocate* from 1835 to 1848. If we assume this to have been his position consistently, then we must also assume that even when drawing up the 1845 "Resolutions on Slavery," he meant them as a general expression of the Church of God rather than as a categorical denial of church membership to slaveholders at all times and at all places. The fact that the Resolutions only "religiously commend and advise" that slaveholders be excommunicated would allow for individual interpretation and evaluation on the part of the local elderships.

But at best, given our sources, we can only conjecture about how Winebrenner related his position on church membership for slaveholders expressed in the last dozen years of his life to his earlier abolitionism. We are still faced with the fact that an abolitionist in the mid-thirties, and antislavery advocate thereafter, argued "mitigating circumstances" for slaveholders from 1848 on; and that he argued against excommunicating slaveholders at a time when in the north it was increasingly popular to deny categorically the possibility that any slaveholder could be a Christian, let alone a member of a Christian church! Why?

In his open correspondence with Williams in the pages of the *Advocate*, Winebrenner made it clear that though he was opposed to slavery as a sin, he was not an ultra-perfectionist in the matter. The church was a body of converted Christians, not sinless ones. With this understanding of the church and the Christian life, he found no more justification for a complete expulsion of slaveholders from the church than for expelling without exception a person who went to war or one who was involved in the liquor traffic. Circumstances governing each case were important. General Christian character had to be taken into consideration. Further, Christian charity should be exercised in determining a person's character (even though he be a slaveholder). The assumption was, of course, that some slaveholders in certain circumstances were "in favor with God."

On a less theological and more practical level, Winebrenner was aware of the disastrous schisms which had occurred in the American church over the slavery issue. The *Church Advocates* bore constant reference to them. The matter of church membership for slaveowners—ministers or laymen—was a frequently discussed issue in these divisions.[54] In the face of what had happened to the Methodists, Baptists, Presbyterians, and Lutherans, Winebrenner, by 1848, undoubtedly felt he had a responsibility to keep together a church for whose origin he was in a large measure responsible. This was especially true in view of the fact that the Church of God by 1848 listed churches in Maryland and Virginia, and that slaveholders were (or at least had been until very recently) in fellowship with some of these churches. In his correspondence with Williams, Winebrenner emphasized that though there "is an honest contrariety of opinion," the brethren "have charity to bear with one another." By 1850, he probably felt it was as important to make the point with the membership of the Church of God as with A. D. Williams.

That a potential division in the church was a motivating factor with Winebrenner during this period was made clear in 1852 in correspondence from William Loveland. Loveland, from Charridon, Ohio, wrote in the *Advocate* for June 19, 1852, that he wanted Winebrenner's opinion on a matter which was causing local excitement, i.e., fellowship with churches which had any connections with slavery. He mentioned that he knew of some in the Church of God who would like "close Communion" and to have nothing to do with Methodists, Baptists, and Presbyterians. Winebrenner replied that such "close communion brethren" are "sincere but erring," and proceeded to relate the matter to division in the church in general. "I would say," wrote Winebrenner in the same number of the *Advocate,*

> ... that we have undoubted right to "withdraw ourselves from every brother that walketh disorderly," but we have no right to withdraw from the Church of God. The Church is the body of Christ, and to withdraw from the body is to withdraw

from the Head, and such a withdrawal must be fatal to every Christian.

This issue of "come-outism" was an increasing source of agitation from the 1840's on.[55] Abolitionists were divided on it. For Winebrenner, the issue was clear. To withdraw the hand of fellowship from an erring brother was one thing; to withdraw from the Church of God—which was to be identified here with the "true" church—was quite another.

Finally, there was the matter of Winebrenner's lifelong ties with slavery among his family and friends in his home state of Maryland. The churches of God in Maryland had had at least a tangential relationship with slaveowners up to 1850. These churches, a part of the East Pennsylvania Eldership, had fellowshipped with men holding slaves and had held camp-meetings on their lands. Elder G. U. Harn had reported that upwards of thirty of the "oldest and ablest" East Pennsylvania ministers had fellowshipped at the Lord's Table and washed the feet of slaveholders at ordinance meetings. Without question, Winebrenner would have been included in the thirty. His ties with several of the Maryland churches were extremely close. Similarly, he maintained a close connection with his slaveholding family in Maryland, especially his father. He visited the homestead often and wrote solicitous letters to his father in the latter's declining years.[56]

Winebrenner knew that not all slaveholders, including those in his Maryland family, were the ogres many northern churchmen made them out to be. He for one, opposed to slavery as he was, was not about to tar all slaveowners with the same hard-bristled abolitionist brush. Moreover, it was demonstrably true that slavery was on the decline in Maryland, and especially in the northern counties where the Church of God was located. What would be the sense in pushing a categorical excommunication of slaveholders—largely an abstract issue in the remaining non-slavery portions of the Church of God anyway—when slavery was disappearing from those sections of Maryland where the Church of God and slavery co-existed? By not getting excited, by following a moderate course, the situation probably would take care of itself. I do not believe that we assume too much in suspecting that Winebrenner's background, by itself, could have provided for his "mitigating circumstances" argument.

1853-1857: Dissension

The years 1853-1857 saw an intensification of concern in the churches of God over the slavery problem. Reflecting a national apprehension scarcely diluted by the Compromise of 1850, almost every issue of the *Advocate* had something to say about slavery both in the church and out.

Winebrenner, who remained editor of the *Advocate* until the end of April, 1857, used the paper to continue to promote what he, at least, felt was a determined antislavery position. Fugitive slave cases received extensive coverage as did the various antislavery and slavery-oriented activities going on in Congress. A number of kidnappings of free colored men received scathing denunciation. *Uncle Tom's Cabin* and *Uncle Tom's Key* were the subject of short approving editorials as was Frederick Douglass' *My Bondage and My Freedom.* Winebrenner commented on the *Key,* that it presented "a sight that will make your heart ache and your blood boil with indignation." [57] When antislavery speakers like Elihu Burrit and Henry Ward Beecher appeared in Harrisburg, Winebrenner gave them favorable coverage in the *Advocate.* [58] When asked by a reader what the differences between the Church of God and Missionary Baptists were, Winebrenner gave as one of the differences, "the Baptists are pro-slavery in some places, whereas the Church of God is anti-slavery, everywhere." [59] An exchange paper which Winebrenner used in the *Advocate* and advised his friends to receive was Dr. Gamaliel Bailey's firmly antislavery *National Era,* printed in Washington.

Yet tones of moderation were apparent. From 1849 on, Winebrenner was inserting articles or writing short editorials favorable to the principle of colonization. [60] This was in contrast to his anti-colonization sentiments expressed in the *Publisher* in the mid-1830's and in spite of the fact that the good abolitionist in the 1850's was no more in favor of African settlement than he was some twenty years earlier. The February 14, 1856 *Advocate* carried without comment a favorable article on the general improvement of slaves in Virginia. Illustrative of his deliberate attempt at a moderate course was an extract from the report of the Committee on Slavery of the General Conference of the Methodist Episcopal Church, which in the June 5, 1856 issue of the *Advocate* Winebrenner laid before his readers

> . . . as a reasonable and readable document—a document that breathes a Christian and conservative spirit, and contains, we think, the middle, Scriptural and feasible ground of this much debated and debateable question.

Once again, Winebrenner found strength in a middle ground, especially now that he found the middle ground Scriptural as well as expedient.

But while Winebrenner emphasized moderation in his antislavery approach, at the same time he also witnessed the development of slavery-related problems in the Church of God which were to threaten seriously its unity.

One of the problems was politics. For years Winebrenner had kept both *Publisher* and *Advocate* readers aware of political action related to slavery. In earlier years the *Publisher* carried numerous items covering such matters as the presentation of antislavery memorials to Congress and John Quincy Adams' victorious struggle against the "gag rule." After the Compromise of 1850, Winebrenner was given to frequent editorializing on affairs of state. While counselling observance, he nevertheless let his feelings be known on what he considered was one unjust, "pro-slavery" law after another coming from Washington.

His reaction to the Fugitive Slave Law, one of the Compromise provisions, was fairly mild. In his open letter to A. D. Williams in the *Advocate* for December 2, 1850, he wrote:

> Ministers are always best engaged when they give themselves to prayer and the ministry of the word. Nevertheless, they enjoy equal rights with all other citizens, under the Constitution and laws of this land. . . . But, nearly all the ecclesiastical bodies in the country, who have ventured to say anything on the subject of this law, have said it with too much feeling and fire. Christians are bound to "let their moderation be known," and to "do nothing rashly." Wrong legislation should never be set aside by resistance. Redress lies in the right of repeal. . . . Resistance and evasion of law is criminal, and we have no right to do a criminal act that good may come.

Winebrenner was not to be counted among the growing number of those who were once again appealing to a "higher law" in order to justify nonobservance of Congress' "unjust" laws. "Moderation" was the key.

However, even the moderates were pressed when the 1854 Kansas-Nebraska bill came before Congress. The most appalling feature of the Compromise of 1850 had been the Fugitive Slave Law. Utah and New Mexico were organized as territories without reference to slavery; but even southerners granted there was little possibility of an economically profitable slave system being successfully established in these areas. The moderate and conservative north generally felt it could live with the Compromise as a relatively permanent settlement. With the Kansas-Nebraska Act it was another matter. An amendment to the Act repealed the Missouri Compromise and opened Kansas and Nebraska to slavery on the basis of "squatter" or popular sovereignty. While the bill was in Congress early in 1854, a number of New York clergymen signed a petition protesting it. Winebrenner, who was opposed to the extension of slavery regardless, ran the petition in the *Advocate* for March 18, 1854. Appended to it was the following preface:

> The Clergy of New York and its vicinity have at last spoken out against the Nebraska iniquity. A petition . . . circulated during a few days has been signed by 151 names of the various denominations . . . embracing the most conservative and moderate of the clergy, and uniting with common consent against the half-finished crime at Washington. These signatures represent many thousands of men and women, likewise the most conservative and moderate classes of our community: . . . Read and ponder it well, traitors of the Capitol: . . . Read it and ponder well before you consummate the crime of tyrants drunk with success and defying justice and truth: . . .

These were rather strong words on a touchy subject for the *Advocate*. However, Winebrenner was doubtlessly reinforced in his printing of the petition by the fact that it was endorsed by a considerable number of "conservative and moderate" clergymen and citizens.

Winebrenner's interest in political affairs increasingly was shared by the membership of the Church of God from the late 1840's on. By the mid-1850's it was not unusual for a local eldership at its annual meeting to recommend repeal of the Fugitive Slave Law and the Nebraska Act or a return to the Missouri Compromise.[61] Yet, there was not unanimity about the church's role on the political antislavery scene. One of the Church of God missionaries sent out to Texas in 1856 found himself having to convince the surrounding slaveowners that he was not an abolitionist in disguise after several copies of the *Church Advocate* with its antislavery articles were distributed in the neighborhood. Accordingly he wrote the editor of the *Advocate* that his "honest impression" was

> that politics should never be brought into our ecclesiastical matters. . . . I think the minister of the Gospel who converts his pulpit to a political rostrum, is hard up for matter, or has forgotten his commission.[62]

Similar sentiments, at one time frequently expressed during Winebrenner's early *Publisher* days, were still present to a degree in the northern elderships of the Church of God. Generally speaking, however, these northern elderships eschewed political neutrality.[63]

120

The acceptance of political antislavery activity by the churches brought with it problems not unique to the Church of God. The February 22, 1855 *Advocate* carried an impassioned letter from "Republican" excoriating the Know-Nothing Party for its temporizing on slavery and taking issue with some of the brethren in the church who supported the Know-Nothing ticket. A further burden of the letter was to advertise the Know-Something Party, an antislavery group which developed in Ohio in the late 1850's.

As early as 1849 Winebrenner himself had to deal with the Church of God in Greene County, in the southwest corner of Pennsylvania, which reportedly had excluded members who voted for "pro-slavery" candidates in the recent national election. This was later denied by a member of the congregation, but the divisive nature of antislavery politics in a local church situation was described in his letter to Winebrenner. He wrote, for example, that

> During last winter religion was almost forgotten by some; politics was all the go. Cass and Taylor pro-slavery, Van Buren and anti-slavery, were the bones of contention. . . . . But there was no final decision until in June, when Elder J. Hickernell came out and brought the church right up, where, in my opinion . . . she ought to have been long before. . . . Since then she is quit, [quiet?] and is considered a cooperative branch of the Church of God. The consequence of which was the loss of a few brethren, by withdrawing from the church.[64]

Winebrenner could only advise, "He that loves his brother as Christ has loved us, will never have a hand in casting him out of the church for opinion's sake." [65]

A far more critical problem developing during this period was that caused by the dissidence on the part of some from the heretofore generally accepted antislavery ("moderate" or otherwise) position of the church. This dissent, which made use of proslavery arguments, and an accompanying extreme antislavery reaction, seriously threatened Winebrenner's program of "moderate antislavery" and his position of leadership in the church.

In September of 1853, Winebrenner attended the "World's" Temperance Convention in New York City's Metropolitan Hall. He was accompanied by a former editor of the *Publisher*, J. F. Weishampel, Sr. Also attending the meeting were the Rev. Antoinette Brown, women's rights enthusiast, and Wendell Phillips of temperance and also abolitionist and disunion fame. The Convention was noteworthy for its discord. Dr. J. McCune Smith was barred because he was a mulatto; Miss Brown, because she was a woman; and Wendell Phillips, apparently because he was Wendell

Phillips. (The grounds given were because "the temperance society he represented had been too recently organized."[!])[66] Winebrenner, in a letter to his wife, did not hint that there was trouble. [67] However, in a resume of events which he or Weishampel sent to J. F. Weishampel, Jr., who was editing the *Advocate* in Winebrenner's absence, the editor *pro tem* received the details. Weishampel, Jr.'s account in the *Advocate* noted that the Convention was broken up by "Wendell Phillips, the noted abolition and Disunion agitator and Rev. Antoinette L. Brown, a female speaker, with others of the fanatic species so common in the north . . ." [68] J. F. Weishampel, Jr., was from Baltimore, Maryland.

Weishampel was answered by Samuel Fasig from Ashland, Ohio in the October 15, 1853 *Advocate*. Fasig was a devout abolitionist. "Now dear brother," he wrote,

> I would like to know of you, what ground you base upon to insinuate that there is more fanaticism in the North than in the South, among the ungodly, heaven daring, God provoking, hypocritical slaveholders; . . .

Weishampel replied in the October 22, 1853 *Advocate*. In the course of his defense he presented several arguments used by the southerner in defense of his "system." It is the sort of thing the *Advocate* readers had not seen before. We quote extensively (with original spellings) :

> That there is more fanaticism of every shape in the North than the South, is undeniable. . . . The circle of agitators there has brought out Abolitionism from its original favorable phase, into a question of politics, and by improper discussion rendered it so dangerous that the separation of our Union was for a time probable. Wendel Phillips, . . . Wm. Loyd Garrison . . . and several other prominent anti-slavery speakers, openly denounced our sacred federal compact, preferring . . . to plunge the country in civil war, rather than await the peaceable adjudication of a matter which God and time alone can settle.
> . . . .
>
> From the same hot-bed, we receive daily accounts of the progress of Womens' Rights—based on ultra democracy, Socialism, and a Liberalism truly French. The advocates of Abolitionism in the North, are the advocates of Fourierism, Bloomerism, Womens' Rights and a disbelief in Christianity. . . .
>
> Can any reader produce such a list of isms originating in the South as dangerous to society as these? It is because anti-slavery has such upholders that I reprobate all present agitation on the subject. What humane slave-holder will yield his property when black-guarded by such a party of visionar-

ies, reprobates and their deluded associates? . . . It is only through COLONIZATION that this evil will eventually be abated.

. . . .

Having seen the condition of our slaves, I can truly say that the free blacks in Baltimore, as well as those in the Free States that I have notices [*sic*], are in a worse condition in regard to morals and social happiness than the slave. . . . The chivalrous sons of the South are not more heartless than the task-masters of the Northern factories.—Nay! I will weigh the plantation against the factory, and in the balance God will see, if many will not, the woe of the white slave!

Fasig answered in the *Advocate* for November 24, 1853, giving conventional northern responses to conventional southern assertions. He found Weishampel's article,

. . . the most extravagant assertions and misrepresentations I have witnessed for a long time. The course of this apologist for one of the most damning and hell-born institutions that has ever been hatched out by arch-Lucifer . . . must be exceedingly disgusting to every lover of God and humanity; . . .

After listing Winebrenner with Washington, Jefferson, John Adams, Finney, and Beecher as "good and patriotic lovers of God and humanity" he continued:

He says the slave is better off than the free black man in the North. Well if this be true, why is it that those free men do not go South and become slaves, seeing that happiness is the great aim of man? And why do so many almost daily run away from their humane masters, . . .

Weishampel's answer to Fasig was extremely mild and defensive (possibly Winebrenner or Weishampel, Sr. had interceded), but at this point John W. Kerr from Hancock County, Virginia (later West Virginia, in the West Pennsylvania Eldership), took over for Weishampel and completed the southern argument. In his letter printed in the *Advocate* on February 4, 1854, he defended slavery as an Old and New Testament institution. He continued this theme in a letter printed on April 8, 1854, in which slavery, or the basic inferiority of the Negro, became the wise purpose "of Almighty God concerning the human race, as presented to us by his servant Noah . . ." The "distinction of races" was God's law.

Surprised at finding proslavery sentiments in their midst, the West Pennsylvania Eldership's standing committee met to admonish Kerr, finding him "blame-worthy," and hoping that "he will in the future desist in giving publicity to similar articles." [69] Meanwhile, the Fourth General Eldership gathered at Wooster, Ohio, beginning May 29, 1854. It met three days after the passage of the Kansas-Nebraska Act, and with the recent proslavery articles in the *Advocate* by Weishampel, Jr. and Kerr doubtlessly in mind. Totally convinced that the "slave power in this country seeks to occupy Territory pledged to Freedom," the Eldership reaffirmed its 1845 "Resolutions on Slavery" and added in explication:

> That we understand them [the 1845 Resolutions] to teach in their practical operation, that any person sustaining the relation of master to slave is disqualified for membership in the Church of God.[70]

James Colder, who had joined his father-in-law, John Winebrenner, as assistant editor of the *Advocate* for about a year beginning in May, 1854, used the pronouncements of the 1854 Eldership to close the columns of the *Advocate* to further debate on slavery. (Colder—sometimes "Calder"—had married Winebrenner's daughter Ellen. A Methodist missionary in China, 1850-1853, Colder joined the Church of God when he returned to the United States. After the death of Ellen and a prolonged quarrel with Winebrenner, Colder joined the Free Will Baptists. He was well educated. After several years in a Baptist pastorate in Harrisburg, he became president first of Hillsdale [Michigan] College, and then of Pennsylvania State College.) He wrote in the issue of June 15, 1854:

> If anyone is still in doubts as to her [the Church of God's] position, we invite his attention to the minutes of the last General Eldership. . . . In view of this plain and oft-repeated declaration of the Church, the question can no longer be considered an open one; and therefore we see no necessity for its further discussion in the *Advocate*.

But it was not to be that easy. By 1857 the *Advocate* was once again dealing with dissent from the Church of God's antislavery position, only this time on the part of a whole eldership.

Up to this point, Winebrenner had not been directly involved or identified with those who reacted against the antislavery views of the church, "moderate" or "extreme." While his plea for "mitigating circumstances" was followed by only a minority in the Church of God, up to 1857 his position of leadership in the church was not seriously questioned. His role in the establishment of the Church of God, his abilities as a preacher and theologian, his education, and his apparently determined (if only moderate) antislavery stand made him the subject of deference on the part of the church as a whole. "Mitigating circumstances" could be allowed as a personal weakness in one otherwise so strong (especially if it were known that his father owned slaves). Events surrounding the "Texas Mission" program were to jeopardize seriously both Winebrenner's "mitigating circumstances" and his leadership in the church.

In 1855, the East Pennsylvania Eldership authorized sending missionaries into Texas. Winebrenner, who was in large part responsible for originating the idea, enthusiastically endorsed the program. Why Texas—apart from the fact that a few Church of God families had settled there—is unknown. While there was some opposition, the plan generally was conceived to be feasible. These missionaries, Benjamin Ober and Enoch Marple—both ordained by the West Pennsylvania Eldership—soon discovered they were surrounded by slaveholders who regarded them as representatives of a northern abolitionist church. The *Church Advocate*, with its antislavery articles and the proceedings of its antislavery elderships was all the proof the southerners needed. Fearing for the complete failure of their mission work, and at times for their personal safety,[71] Ober and Marple wrote the *Advocate* on April 1, 1857, requesting that nothing more appear in the *Advocate* "which our enemies can take advantage of." [72]

Had Winebrenner still been editor, perhaps he might have been able to do something. However, in April of 1857, he had sold his interest in the paper to James Colder. The reasons are obscure. Very possibly, Winebrenner needed the money. (Colder was from a well-to-do Harrisburg family.) At any rate, as editor of the *Advocate* Colder followed an extreme abolitionist line. He would have nothing to do with his father-in-law's "mitigating circumstances" which might allow certain slaveholders to become members of the Church of God. Colder's reply to the missionaries was in the "I will add to your yoke" tradition; in the *Advocate* for June 11, 1857, he reviewed with favorable comments the actions on slavery of the General Elderships from 1845 to 1857, none of which could be calculated to help the cause in Texas. In the article he further equated the slavery situation in Texas with that in northern Maryland and western Virginia when he wrote of Church of God ministers:

Their well-known views on the Slavery question have not hindered their success in slave states, nor will they, we think, wherever they are frankly avowed and conscientiously maintained.

Colder was a northerner and it showed. He certainly had little appreciation of the vast differences between the attitude toward slavery in Texas and the northern parts of border states. There followed a considerable correspondence between Ober and Colder, primarily related to the binding force (on individual elderships or churches) of any General Eldership resolution on slavery.[73]

In the meantime, Winebrenner had come to the defense of the Texas mission. Without question he looked upon the project as uniquely his. He had helped to finance Ober's and Marple's trip to Texas out of his own pocket.[74] At the 1857 General Eldership which met at Harrisburg, beginning June 1, Winebrenner offered the following resolution:

> *Whereas,* the form of church government as taught in the Scriptures is a free, independent family, or congregational form, which admits of no extrinsic legislation. . . . And whereas, Our brethren in the South, and especially in the State of Texas, are likely to be brought into serious difficulties, in consequence of the passage of ultra resolutions, by Northern Elderships on the subject of slavery . . .

> *Resolved,* That whilst we hold it to be our right and duty to express our sentiments freely and fully on any and every subject of civil or ecclesiastical policy, nevertheless, we adjudge it inexpedient and unnecessary to do anything more at present than to reaffirm our sentiments, as set forth in the resolutions on slavery, passed by the first General Eldership . . . and that, apart from those resolutions, we go for the doctrine of non-intervention, and therefore are satisfied to let our brethren at the South and everywhere else, enjoy their natural and indefeasible right and liberty; . . .[75]

By stressing congregational polity, Winebrenner was emphasizing the advisory nature of General Eldership resolutions—an emphasis which Ober proceeded to use against Colder. (It was also an emphasis which Winebrenner had not used in almost thirty years. The elderships, in practice at least, did exercise some authority over local churches.) Allowing the southern brethren their own "natural and indefeasible right" was an argument Winebrenner was to expand shortly.

Winebrenner's resolution was in response to communications from the Texas missionaries to the General Eldership which apparently informed the delegates that progress of the Church of God in Texas was dependent upon the admission of slaveholders into membership.[76] The resolution, which Winebrenner later claimed had the support of the "conservative brethren" was not acceptable.[77] Nor, apparently, was one which condemned the missionaries.[78] The resolution finally adopted asserted that inasmuch as previous General Elderships had "covered the ground" on slavery, further action was unnecessary.[79] It was obviously a compromise.

On June 16, 1857, Winebrenner wrote the editor of the *Advocate* a letter, taking exception to Colder's attack on the Texas missionaries in his editorial, "The General Eldership on Slavery," in the issue for June 11.[80] Colder had, according to his father-in-law, "injudiciously spread before the public the very things which our friends in Texas deprecated." [81] Winebrenner emphasized that he was "no apologist for the system of slavery" but, at the same time, confessed that he was no "ultraist." Rather, he was opposed to "extreme measures." Explaining in more detail his view of a southern churchman's "natural and indefeasible right," mentioned in his resolution before the General Eldership earlier in the month, he insisted that

> I accord the right of *opinion* to our brethren in the Southern States and everywhere else. They have an unquestionable right to think and judge for themselves. . . . If the slaves have a natural right to their freedom, the masters have an equal right to form their opinions. . . . Whilst, therefore, I contend for the rights of the slave, I would respect, also, the opinions of the master.

"Church officers in the South," he continued,

> are clothed with the same power and authority that they are here in the North. Where, therefore, a slaveholder applies to them for church membership, it is their prerogative to say whether there are any mitigating circumstances that will justify them in receiving him into church fellowship.

Calling his views "liberal conservative" he concluded on an expansive note in the final paragraph of the letter:

> . . . I have charity enough to believe that there are many Christian slaveholders, as well as Christian soldiers, Christian Masons, Christian Odd Fellows, Christian Pedo-Baptists, and Christian Catholics.

Winebrenner's concept of "mitigating circumstances" in the past had carried with it the understanding that northern churchmen would do the interpreting of the circumstances. To allow the same option to the southern church doubtlessly would help the Texas missionaries, but the reaction by the northern membership of the church understandably would be cool. The only reason that Winebrenner did not experience difficulty from his northern brethren is that Colder refused to print the letter, together with several others on the same subject, in order to avoid (among other things) disrupting the "peace of the Church."[82]

Winebrenner continued to assist Ober as best he could. They were in direct communication at least by the summer of 1857, and probably before. In a letter dated August 23, 1857, Winebrenner told Ober that he sympathized with him in the position in which he had been placed by the "unprudent and hasty course of the editor of the *Advocate*." [83] Privately he wrote to Ober what he had heretofore published openly, that he was opposed to slavery, that he held it to be antiscriptural and unchristian, but that he would not "unchristianize anyone for the simple reason of being a sectarian, warrior or slaveholder." The relationship between the two was close enough that by the latter half of 1857 Winebrenner was rewriting, presumably for better effect, some of Ober's correspondence against Colder for the *Advocate*.[84]

Yet whatever Winebrenner could do—and he was the only conspicuous defender of the Texas missionaries in 1857—it was not enough. At the East Pennsylvania Eldership which met at Middletown, Pennsylvania, beginning November 4, 1857, a resolution was offered which would have cut off the East Pennsylvania Eldership's financial support to the Texas missionaries. (This was actually a formalization of what had already taken place.) Winebrenner offered a counter-resolution granting the missionaries their money ($200.) and further resolving that "we highly disapprove of the editor's [of the *Church Advocate*] course, in reference to our missionaries in Texas, and advise him to be more careful and prudent in future." Winebrenner's resolution lost by a fifteen to ten vote, with an unusually large number of abstentions. The older ministers and those with Maryland connections tended to support Winebrenner.[85] The West Pennsylvania Eldership, from which Ober and Marple had received their ordination papers, had met a few weeks earlier and disfellowshipped the missionaries.[86] Probably expecting the above actions, the Texas brethren had formed an eldership in Texas in July of 1857. The Texas Eldership refused to take action on slavery because of its "political" nature. Further, the eldership protested the General Eldership "resolutions on slavery," advising "our brethren in general to have nothing to do with them, and [to] secede from everything that presents itself among us (in the form of human legislation) as a test of church-fellowship . . ." [87] (The Texas Eldership was not received into the General Eldership until 1875.)

Clearly, by the end of 1857, Winebrenner was in trouble. The editor of the *Advocate,* son-in-law or not, had turned the paper against Winebrenner, his "mitigating circumstances," and "moderate antislavery" position. Colder was, in fact, becoming the leader of a fairly well-defined opposition to Winebrenner. Both the General Eldership and East Pennsylvania Eldership had refused to accept Winebrenner's resolutions dealing with slavery and the Texas mission. The East Pennsylvania Eldership further had cut off its financial support for the Texas missionaries—missionaries Winebrenner had been instrumental in sending to Texas a few years earlier. Worse and better was to follow.

1858-1860: Winebrenner's "Letter on Slavery"

In the *Church Advocate* for December 17, 1857, James Colder carried the following item from the *Religious Telescope* of the United Brethren in Christ:

> It seems from some letters that have lately appeared in the *Church Advocate*, that Rev. .... is in favor of opening the door of the church with which he stands connected, to men who own their fellow men. The present editor of the *Advocate*, Br. Colder, we are happy to see, is not disposed to join hands with oppressors. We hope that Mr. .... will not be able to drive him from his position.

Colder used blanks in place of Winebrenner's name, but for anyone who had been following the Texas controversy in the *Advocate*, it was obvious to whom the *Telescope* was referring.

The above item provided Colder with an opportunity for an attack upon Winebrenner and his supporters. He wrote in the same issue:

> We assure the Editor of the *Telescope* that there is no danger that the brother referred to, and the few who hold his peculiar sentiments, will "be able to drive" us "from our position" of hostility to the admission of slaveholders into the Church. . . .

> The position of the Church on the subject of Slavery as it exists in our Southern States is so plain, and can so easily be understood, that it is a marvel how any one laying claims to a sound mind, and professing a desire to promote the peace and harmony of the whole body, can pursue the course which a few ministers have taken. While prating about law and order, . . . they shut their eyes to the actions of both Annual and General Elderships; and mounting the hobby of Lawlessness, which they call Gospel Liberty, cry out, Open the doors to every one who professes to be a Christian, though he be a Slaveholder, a Drunkard-maker or a Mormon! The goodness

of their motives may be great, but is imperceptible; . . . They have always been in the minority, and whilst the Lord delights in the Church He will keep them there. . . .

As might be expected, Winebrenner was stung by his son-in-law's criticism and immediately began to prepare a lengthy reply. Colder, however, apparently indicated that he would not print his father-in-law's reply (he previously had refused to print several of Winebrenner's articles) and so the former editor of the *Advocate* found himself forced to petition the General Eldership Board of Publication for the right to answer in the present editor's columns.[88] The Board granted Winebrenner the opportunity and Colder reluctantly began to carry Winebrenner's answering letter in the *Advocates* for May 27 and June 10, 1858. But then Colder refused to print any more of what he considered a proslavery article in his abolitionist-oriented paper. The Board of Publication, for some reason, would not compel Colder to finish printing Winebrenner's letter. Therefore, Winebrenner was instrumental in a call for an extra session of the East Pennsylvania Eldership to consider this and several other matters relating to Colder. The special session, reluctantly attended by most, referred the matter of Winebrenner's rejected letter and other articles to the Board of Publication which printed them (or allowed Winebrenner to have them printed) as Winebrenner's *Letter on Slavery, with an Appendix Containing Various Rejected Articles Addressed to Elder James Colder, Editor of the Church Advocate.* The pamphlet, totalling twenty-eight pages (nineteen of which were the *Letter*), appeared sometime before the end of August, 1858.

In his *Letter* Winebrenner stated the issue at hand as being

. . . whether slavery is necessarily, and under all conceivable circumstances, a sin; and whether, therefore, slaveholders, in all places and under all circumstances, are unworthy of church fellowship; and whether, moreover, ministers baptizing and receiving such into membership, ought themselves to be disciplined, and cut off from support and Christian fellowship? . . . You [Colder] affirm and I deny. . . . The debatable question is not the moral character of slavery and its *abuses.* On this point we agree. But the real question is ultra and fanatical views on the subject, as I conceive them to be.[89]

Winebrenner suggested that neither Colder nor "anybody else in the whole ultra abolition fraternity" could make good their position on the above issues inasmuch as "they are not the doctrine of the Church of God, on this subject." After once again emphasizing the *advisory* nature of General Eldership resolutions dealing with slavery, he insisted:

But the Church of God, unlike the sects, denies the right of human legislation in matters of faith and practice. Christ, her founder, is her only law giver. . . . All her true and free-born sons hold this doctrine, notwithstanding the insidious attempts of some to sectarianize her.[90]

To insist that slaveholding was a sin and heinous crime *per se* was to reduce the whole matter to the point of absurdity, said Winebrenner. If the "Church North" used this argument to "justly claim the right to discipline and expel her slaveholding brethren in the South"; then,

> . . . it may also be alleged that War, Monarchy, Free Masonry, Sectarianism, etc., are all *mala per se* . . .; and therefore she [the South] . . . can claim the right to discipline and expel her erring brethren in the North. A good rule, all admit, must work both ways. But who does not see the disastrous results of such a rule? Naught but interminable broils, schism and desolation would flow from such a system.[91]

In Colder's reply to the *Telescope* he had written: "They [Winebrenner and his friends] have always been in the minority, and whilst the Lord delights in the Church he will keep them there." This became the occasion for Winebrenner to give several pages of proof-texting from various authors and groups who supported Winebrenner's "minority" opinions in the Church of God. This parade of witnesses in Winebrenner's behalf was the primary thrust of the letter. It was also the primary cause of scandal following its publication. Winebrenner used Dr. Francis Wayland, Dr. Richard Fuller, Dr. William Paley, William Ellery Channing, Alexander Campbell, George Whitefield, the Old School Presbyterian Synod of Ohio, and the General Conference of the Methodist Episcopal Church, North (Colder had been a Methodist) to support positions that: (1) Slavery was sanctioned in the Old and New Testaments; (2) Slavery was not a sin or immoral by simple virtue of its existence; (3) There were such things as mitigating circumstances which might allow slaveholders to be Christians; and (4) The Northern abolitionists were fanatics who had enthusiastically done wrong. Winebrenner was careful to point out that he did not endorse all the sentiments of several of the men mentioned; but sandwiched between quotations from Fuller (a Baptist lawyer-clergyman with a distinguished record at the Seventh Baptist Church in Baltimore, Maryland), Winebrenner penned some lines which must have seemed remarkable to those few who remembered his abolitionist days over twenty years earlier:

Now what is the sum and true meaning of these texts? I return, for answer, the following syllogistic exegesis:

1st. Whatever relation the New Testament does not forbid, but recognize and regulate, cannot be in itself sinful.

2d. The New Testament does not expressly prohibit, but recognize and regulate the relation of master and slave.

3d. Therefore, the relation of master and slave cannot be in itself sinful.

Here is good logic, if not also good theology. Here is something more than ranting, and high wrought pictures of the wrongs and cruelties inflicted by despotic and tyrannical masters. Here are sound arguments by men of sound minds, free from bias, bigotry and prejudice.

From the foregoing quotations it is evident, and the whole Bible does most explicitly, both by precept and example, bear me out in the assertion, that slavery is not necessarily always, and amid all circumstances, a sin. Hence, the simple holding [of] men in bondage ought not to be a ground of ecclesiastical excommunication.[92]

While not proslavery by any means, Winebrenner had reached the point where he could accept the southern arguments for the permissibility of slavery. It certainly represented a new stage in the evolution of his thought on the question. His old argument allowed slaveholders in the church, sinners though they were, on the basis of his belief that the church was made up of converted rather than sinless Christians. Hence, warriors, rum-sellers, and sectarians might, with slaveholders, be a part of God's church. Now, however, there was some question as to whether slavery was always, *per se*, a sin according to the Bible. "Abolition is no Bible test of church membership," he told Colder. "Hence, where there is no law, there is no transgression; and when there is no transgression, there is no sin." [93] The question for Winebrenner no longer was: Which "mitigating circumstances" would allow a slaveholder to be a member of a Christian church? Now the question had become: Under what circumstances is slavery—approved by the Bible as it is—a sin?

In his closing paragraphs, Winebrenner once again returned to the *reductio ad absurdum* theme:

The "infernal and unchristian fruits" you speak of are the abuses of slavery, not slavery itself. Marriage is an institution of God, and yet how often is it abused? Government is an ordinance of God, yet how often does it yield "infernal and unchristian fruit"?

But who would justify and eulogize us for repudiating marriage and civil government, because there are great evils and abuses often found attending these divine institutions? The abuses of a thing is no argument against the thing itself. If it were, we would have to repudiate everything for every good thing has been more or less abused.[94]

Did Winebrenner actually mean what seems to be implied, that slavery was to be included under "every good thing"? In the context of the *Letter*, the statement is at best equivocal. At worst, it is a repudiation of all he had stood for since his abolitionist days. As he said no more about it we can only speculate. However, the explanation probably is related to his recently developed reliance upon the Scriptures in dealing with the slavery issue. This reliance was presented forcefully in the *Letter's* conclusion. The Gospel

> . . . may be a little too slow in its operations for abolitionists; yet after all, the Gospel is the only effectual panacea for the sins and wrongs of humanity . . . your [Colder's] arguments will not bear to be weighed in the balance of logic and gospel truth. They are all unsound and unscriptural.[95]

In fact, suggested Winebrenner, Colder's position was more than "unscriptural." It was even "anti-scriptural," as he proceeded to point out:

> And as for your position, from which you say you cannot be driven, this is, in my judgment, unreasonable, fanatical and anti-scriptural, and therefore wholly indefensible.[96]

Yet, in spite of Colder's "anti-scriptural" position, Winebrenner graciously would not give his son-in-law up

> for lost to all improvement. You are yet a young man, capable of amendment, and you can and may learn, if you will to understand the way of the Lord more perfectly.
>
> Yours, paternally, John Winebrenner [97]

The reception accorded the *Letter* in the church was less than enthusiastic. In response to its earlier portions which had appeared in the *Advocate* (May 27 and June 10, 1858) Colder himself replied in the *Advocate* for May 27, 1858:

> It is painful to see a brother who ought to be an example to the flock, and whose harsh and bitter speeches indulge, in nearly every paragraph of a long article, in very objectionable language.

This was to be expected. Winebrenner's daughter and Colder's wife, Ellen, had died on March 24, 1858. Ellen had been the last wholesome link between the two men. Whatever the relationship was before, it certainly was no better after her death.

In the *Advocate* for September 16, 1858, Pastor A. B. Slyter of the West Ohio Eldership attacked Winebrenner because of the *Letter* and suggested punitive measures. Winebrenner's pamphlet, according to Slyter, was "calculated to do more injury to the advancement of the church . . . than all the infidels . . . in this western world." He continued:

> I think the East Pennsylvania Eldership would do him due justice if they would disfellowship him, or at least give him a severe reprimand, for such an unreasonable course.

The East Ohio Eldership, an extremely antislavery group led by abolitionist G. U. Harn, discussed the *Letter* at length. The impression received is that the eldership could not bring itself to associate Winebrenner with a scriptural defense of slavery, even though they felt the evidence pointed to it. Rather, they kindly suggested that the *Letter* was "a feeble effort to sustain and bolster up a weak and confused theory," referring no doubt to Winebrenner's "mitigating circumstances." [98]

The strongly antislavery Illinois Eldership, meeting near Freeport a month or so after the Lincoln-Douglas debate at that place, was inclined to be much less generous. A special committee appointed to review the pamphlet found that it inculcated "principles repugnant to the doctrine of the Church of God . . ."; was "at variance with the Bible"; and was "calculated to sow the seeds of discord among us." The committee finally was of the opinion that the Illinois Eldership should "discountenance . . . the circulation of said monster." Also, the eldership applauded Colder's "noble stand." [99]

Such open opposition in the Church of God was a new experience for Winebrenner. But though severely handled by some, and his image tarnished in high abolitionist places, all was not lost for either Winebrenner or his *Letter*.

In Texas, Ober later wrote in his recollections for the *Church Advocate*, the pamphlets which Winebrenner sent to him "no doubt saved my life, and our lives in the future." [100] According to the Texas missionary, he had been told in a certain Texas town to "leave in ten minutes or be hanged"; upon which he produced Winebrenner's *Letter on Slavery* and was allowed to remain. (Colder could have made a great deal of that.) While perhaps not the primary reason for the *Letter*, Winebrenner may well have felt the eyes of Texas upon him while he wrote it. He wanted to save the mission field in a growing southwest.

Several elderships meeting in 1858, unlike East Ohio and Illinois, made no mention of the *Letter* though doubtlessly familiar with it. The East Pennsylvania Eldership, meeting on November 3, 1858, not only did not mention the *Letter*, but instructed its Board of Missions (which included Colder) to "settle with the Missionaries in Texas according to contract," [101] thus reversing eldership action of a year earlier. In the East Ohio Eldership, which had taken action against the *Letter*, the delegates took exception to Elder A. B. Slyter's attack on Winebrenner [102] and invited Winebrenner to move to the west and "spend the balance of his life . . . and labors among us." [103] The West Ohio Eldership highly disapproved of the editor of the *Advocate's* derogatory remarks about "some of our ministerial brethren." It also felt that Elder Slyter's letter was "entirely unjustifiable." [104] Elder Slyter himself apologized in the *Advocate* for November 18, 1858. When Elder G. U. Harn took exception to Winebrenner's position on slavery in his "Politics, Religion and Slavery" in the December 30, 1858 *Advocate*, immediately Elders Shoemaker and Price from East Pennsylvania rose to defend Winebrenner. In the *Advocate* for April 7, 1859, Elder Rockafellow from Carroll County, Maryland, pleaded "mitigating circumstances."

Winebrenner's support was at least partially due to the simple fact that there were those in the Church of God, particularly in Pennsylvania, Maryland, and portions of the "west," who basically agreed with Winebrenner's views on slavery. Another reason was to be found in the trip west Winebrenner made about the same time, or shortly after, his *Letter* was published in its pamphlet form. On the trip Winebrenner spent considerable time preaching, visiting elderships, selling the harrow and clod cutter he had invented, and giving his version of the quarrel with Colder.[105] Unquestionably, however, Winebrenner's greatest strength was Colder's increasingly hostile behavior. His attacks on Winebrenner and others in the *Advocate* on slavery and other issues, regardless of possible justification, did not sit well with a people which had come to identify Winebrenner as the "grand old man" of their church. Winebrenner's age and increasing infirmities helped his image at this point. More important yet was a schismatic tendency associated with Colder throughout the second half of 1858 and into 1859. Charges relating to Colder's mishandling of *Advocate* and church matters led to his censure by the 1858 East Pennsylvania Eldership which met in November of that year.[106] In February of 1859, he precipitously abandoned his editorship of the *Advocate*. Elder E. H. Thomas, a long-time friend of Winebrenner's, was appointed in his place. By April 1, 1859, the

Harrisburg First Church, which Winebrenner had established about 1825, declared itself independent of the Church of God. Its pastor was James Colder. The East Pennsylvania Eldership thereupon removed Colder and appointed Winebrenner pastor. Colder refused to leave and there followed a long litigation eventually settled in favor of the eldership. Meanwhile, Colder was disfellowshipped from the Church of God with a warning to all pastors to have no further dealings with him. The opposition to Winebrenner's position on slavery which had gathered about Colder had been fragmented.

Outside of eastern Pennsylvania, the most able and consistent critic of Winebrenner's position on slavery in the latter half of the 1850's was Elder G. U. Harn. A member of the East Pennsylvania Eldership but pastor at Wooster, Ohio, Harn was an avowed abolitionist who later died in battle during the Civil War. However, he remained on genuinely good terms with Winebrenner, even though taking strong exception to his *Letter on Slavery.*

All in all, Winebrenner had stood the challenge to himself and his *Letter* fairly well.

Winebrenner had little further to say on the subject of slavery prior to his death on September 12, 1860.

In a letter to the editor in the *Advocate* for March 8, 1860, Winebrenner supported Simon Cameron for President of the United States. Cameron was a long-time resident of Harrisburg. His land had been used for camp meetings by the Church of God. However, Winebrenner based his support of Cameron upon his position on slavery. "General Cameron stands," Winebrenner wrote,

where every wise and good man ought to stand; on the platform of non-interference with it where it now exists, and the non-extension of it where it does not exist.

This was Winebrenner's solution in 1860 to the political problems associated with the slavery controversy. (At the Chicago Republican Convention later in the year, Cameron exchanged his "Peoples' Party" votes for a spot in Lincoln's cabinet.)

At the end of May, in 1860, Winebrenner attended the sixth General Eldership meeting at Upper Sandusky, Ohio. As reported in the *Church Advocate* for June 21, 1860, the Eldership's Committee on Slavery reported an extremely severe (from Winebrenner's point of view) series of resolutions which disallowed "mitigating circumstances"; any Biblical sanction, toleration, regulation, or permission of slaveholding; and "the course of the Texas Missionaries." Elder E. H. Thomas offered a substitute series of resolutions which reaffirmed the actions of the General Eldership at Pittsburgh in 1845 and at Wooster in 1854. The Eldership adopted Thomas' substitution by a twenty-one to fourteen vote, Winebrenner voting with Thomas. The substitute resolutions incorporated that action on slaveholding ("that any person sustaining the relation of master to slave, is disqualified for membership in the Church of God") which Winebrenner had refused to vote for in 1854. Whether Winebrenner voted for it now out of conviction or in an attempt primarily to defeat the original resolution is conjectural. Regardless of the rationale, the resolutions voted for by Winebrenner cannot be reconciled with the positions set forth in his *Letter on Slavery.* But then, the year was 1860. Across the country former positions on slavery were being abandoned by many as the nation polarized into more rigid stands prior to the Civil War.

What then can we conclude about Winebrenner's relationship to the antislavery movement?

All of our sources indicate that Winebrenner was opposed to slavery. It is true that his *Letter on Slavery* introduced a rationale for the existence of slavery based upon Scriptural authority and that in it he wrote disconcertingly about the sinfulness of the *abuses* of slavery rather than of the sin of slavery itself. However, it is also true that the *Letter* was hardly a paean raised in behalf of the poor, misunderstood slaveholder. Winebrenner would not debate with Colder about "the moral character of slavery and its abuses. "On this point," wrote Winebrenner, "we agree." A negative evaluation was implied. So also, while allowing that the Scriptures gave permission for the existence of slavery, and therefore the system could not be *per se* sinful, the conclusion of the *Letter* indicated a general feeling that the Gospel ultimately was antislavery in emphasis. Winebrenner wrote:

> . . . I fully agree with the sentiments expressed by Dr. Wayland, when he says: "If the principles of the Gospel are faithfully inculcated and applied, they will work out the extinction of slavery." It may be a little too slow in its operations for abolitionists; yet after all, the Gospel is the only effectual panacea for the sins and wrongs of humanity.[107]

The best approach to the *Letter on Slavery* probably is to regard it as a desperate attempt in the face of mounting pressures in both church and state to preserve a moderate, "mitigating circumstances" position. At all odds, it is futile to attempt to reconcile one portion of the *Letter* with another, let alone reconcile it with Winebrenner's position on slavery before and after. In my judgment at least, the *Letter* is internally self-contradictory.

Some clarification of Winebrenner's position on slavery during the period of his *Letter on Slavery* is received from those contextual writings available. In his private letter to Benjamin Ober in Texas (written no more than five months before the *Letter*) Winebrenner, while allowing southerners their "birth right opinions," nevertheless held slavery to be "anti-scriptural and unchristian." [108] On his trip west following the publication of the *Letter*, Winebrenner stopped off at Decatur, Illinois, where he heard Stephen Douglas speak at a rally. Winebrenner observed:

> Judge Doughlas [*sic*] addressed a political meeting here yesterday. There was a great rally of the Anti-Lacomsston [*sic*] Democracy. The Judge spoke about an hour and a half, and was greatly applauded. His speach [*sic*] was a hard bore on the administration and the Black-Republicans. The little giant is a good democrat, but a bad christian.[109]

Winebrenner was no northern "dough face." Douglas was regarded generally as the chief perpetrator of the infamous Kansas-Nebraska Act by antislavery forces in the north. Winebrenner's opinion of Douglas fits in nicely with his later support of Cameron and, I would imagine, Lincoln, had Winebrenner lived.

But having said this much, it is also true that when we deal with Winebrenner we are dealing with a man who did considerably alter his approach to the slavery problem in the twenty-five years prior to the Civil War. In his abolitionist days, Winebrenner was concerned about the sin of slavery; by the time of his *Letter on Slavery*, in 1858, the sinfulness was in its *abuse*. The procolonizationist of 1835 and the 1850's bore little resemblance to the staunch anticolonizer of the later thirties. Most obvious to one who follows his statements on slavery between 1836 and 1858, is the gradual diminution of antislavery zeal. This was especially true after 1848 when Winebrenner was forced to the defensive in behalf of his "mitigating circumstances." By 1858 he gave every indication of a man who had repented numberless times of ever having, in his earlier years, opened an antislavery Pandora's Box in the church. Then there is the further problem of relating the 1860 General Eldership, where Winebrenner voted for a non-"mitigating circumstances" resolution, to his statements on church membership for slaveholders from 1848 to 1858.

There are many factors to take into consideration when explaining Winebrenner's shifting antislavery attitudes. Some of these have been mentioned previously. Winebrenner's close acquaintance with slaves and slaveholders, especially in his own family, in Maryland; his apparent admiration for "moderates" like Judge Taney, Richard Fuller, and Francis Wayland; his desire to save the Texas Mission (which he probably did); his increasingly Bibliocentric approach to solving the slavery problem, which approach was usually a real southern point-maker—all of these enter into the picture.

We should also consider Winebrenner's concern for the Union and fear of a civil war. It was mentioned earlier that in his article on the Church of God in Rupp's *He Pasa Ekklesia*, point nineteen under the church's leading matters of faith was a declaration that the system of involuntary slavery was "impolitic and unchristian." [110] The twentieth point was: "She [the Church of God] believes that all civil wars are unholy and sinful, and in which the saints of the Most High ought never to participate." There followed a long list of supporting Scripture verses; a longer list than the one following the antislavery point. Winebrenner's unionism reflected the feelings of a great many in Maryland (and other border states) who equated a civil war with armies marching back and forth across their towns and fields.[111] History has supported their premonitions.

Winebrenner's changing attitudes toward slavery were, of course, not unique. As previously noted, the abolitionist movement was fragmenting by the late 1830's. By 1840, the national office of the American Anti-Slavery Society had been reduced to two shadow organizations. The antislavery thrust increasingly carried with it political overtones, although there was the appropriate amount of moral indignation present both in and out of the halls of Congress. The "curse of slavery" soon attached itself to all sorts of national issues including the annexation of Texas, the Mexican War, establishment of territories, and admission of states. Slavery petitions disturbed the Congress. The Wilmot Proviso angered the President. The Compromise of 1850 did not solve anything for long, while the Kansas-Nebraska Act succeeded only in promoting a growing northern sentiment that an insidious "slavepower" would not be satisfied with anything less than the extension of slavery into the free states. The Dred Scott decision confirmed this feeling. The Whigs disappeared as a national party, the Republicans arose, and the Democrats divided—largely because of the slavery issue. In addition to all of this, sectionalizing of the churches over the slavery issue began in the 1840's.

With happenings such as these, it comes as no surprise that the antislavery movement itself should manifest some subtle and some not-so-subtle shifts. The abolitionists of the thirties made their peace with changing conditions in a number of ways. Some simply dropped out of sight or lost their first love in the course of deep involvement in other reform movements, especially temperance. William Lloyd Garrison cursed the Constitution as a proslavery document and advocated disunion. Nathan Lord, an officer of the American Anti-Slavery Society organized in 1833, and later president of Dartmouth College, moved in an entirely different direction. By 1854 he had retreated far enough from 1833 that he could write a book defending slavery on the basis of its being a divine institution; hence, antislavery advocates were interfering with the will and purpose of the Creator. Other former abolitionists like Winebrenner aligned themselves somewhere on the spectrum between Garrison and Lord. They maintained their interest in antislavery until the Civil War; each one relating in his own way—and not always consistently—national, sectional, and local pressures to his essential antislavery convictions.

7

Peace

Pacifism has deep roots in America. The ravages and threats of war in the Old World have been responsible for the settlement of large numbers of Europe's dispossessed in the New. America, and especially Pennsylvania, was regarded as a haven for those with pacifistic sentiments. European "peace churches" like the Mennonites and Quakers flourished in the freedom of conscience offered by William Penn and the freedom from rapacious European armies offered by the Atlantic Ocean.

The virtues of peace were extolled in the eighteenth century by a number of well known Americans. Anthony Benezet and John Woolman, although perhaps better known for antislavery sentiments, also attacked the evils of war and military conscription in good Quaker fashion. Benjamin Rush, the Pennsylvania reformer of just about everything, suggested a "Peace Office" to balance the new American republic's "War Office." The ubiquitous Dr. Benjamin Franklin undoubtedly represented the feelings of a good number in the nation he had helped to bring to birth when he suggested in 1783 that "there never was a good war or a bad peace." [1]

As with the antislavery and temperance crusades, the peace movement in America began to organize in the early part of the nineteenth century; its early leaders were generally ministers or devoted Christian laymen; and it was fractured in the mid-1830's by an "ultraist" faction (which advocated complete nonresistance in opposition to those who allowed for the possibility of a defensive war). Early leaders in the peace movement included David Low Dodge, a Presbyterian businessman; Noah Worcester, a Congregational clergyman; William Ellery Channing, the leading Unitarian minister in America; and the prime mover of the American Peace Society, William Ladd, a devout and devoted retired merchant.

The Peace Society was organized in 1828 at the Dodge home in New York City. Open to all who pursued peace in principle, it advocated international arbitration to settle disputes and particularly denounced offensive wars. Such an emphasis might allow for the growth of the Society among those who were not of a purely pacifistic persuasion, but it was also a source of irritation to those who felt that the only road to peace was through total nonresistance. Where was the line, they asked, between "offensive" and "defensive" wars? Was there ever a nation which admitted engaging in an "offensive" war? The "nonresistants" in the society, including William Lloyd Garrison and Bronson Alcott, urged the condemnation of all wars. In 1838, the split in the peace movement was formalized by the organization of the New England Non-Resistance Society.[2]

Winebrenner and the Peace Movement

The first intimation that Winebrenner was adding the peace movement to his list of reforms came in the *Gospel Publisher* for March 11 and 18, 1836—about ten months after the first issue of the paper. On March 11, an article entitled "War, Unlawful," probably clipped from an exchange paper, is given first page prominence. Its message was to prove that "the apostles and primitive Christians understood their religion to interdict all physical war" and that "physical wars of all kinds—offensive and defensive—convertible terms among belligerents, are unnecessary." The March 18 article was a continuation, entitled "Consequences of War."

Why at this point did Winebrenner become interested in the peace crusade? There is nothing in his earlier writings to indicate a concern and he offers no explanation in the *Publisher*. Probably, his antiwar efforts were generated by his general reformist tendencies. Many evangelical clergymen in the North saw the fight to free the slaves, abolish rum (and sometimes tobacco), and end war as a package deal. Looking closely at the time sequence involved suggests that possibly Winebrenner's recent acceptance of the abolitionist platform may have been the immediate cause for his assumption of the pacifistic mantle. Many, if not most, of the strongly antislavery leaders in the 1830's were also strongly antiwar. (It took the Civil War, a generation later, to point out the luxury of such a position.) Garrison, Lewis Tappan, and John Greenleaf Whittier are but a few of the more important examples. Just a month before, in the *Publisher* of January 29, 1836, Winebrenner had revealed his abolitionist stance. He no longer could be counted upon as a colonizationist—a moderate—where slavery was concerned. It does not seem unreasonable to suggest, therefore, that the same reform forces which prompted him to espouse abolitionism also prevailed upon him to support the peace movement and probably in its more extreme form. (The articles on March 11 and 18, 1836, essentially promoted a nonresistance position.) At any rate, pacifism would not be a strange custom to Winebrenner. Both Mennonite and Quaker peace testimony were near at hand to anyone living in eastern Pennsylvania.

Most abolitionists, if they were indeed pacifists as well, tended to subordinate their pacifism to their concern to free the slave. In the 1830's, after all, war was not a paramount concern for most Americans while slavery was on the road to becoming just that. Winebrenner apparently shared these feelings. Consequently, throughout his editorship of both the *Publisher* and the *Advocate* articles extolling the virtues of peace and the evils of the war system appear, but only at irregular intervals. The exception to this was during the war with Mexico, about which we shall have more to say shortly.

In both the *Publisher* and *Advocate* war was assumed to be unreasonable, tragic, wasteful, immoral and anti-Christian. Peace was, of course, the opposite. Positions in support of both non-resistance and defensive wars were presented, largely through clips from exchange papers. One of the most extensive articles in behalf of the cause appeared in the *Gospel Publisher* for December 30, 1836. Entitled "Peace Societies—What They Have Done and What They Could Do," it summed up the role of the peace groups and their relation to Christianity. The object of the peace societies was nothing more than "to render peace co-extensive with Christianity." Therefore, "Christian Churches of every name, should consider themselves as societies divinely appointed for the universal spread of peace and good will." The article was a reprint from the *Philadelphia Observer,* but Winebrenner's later writings indicate that he shared its sentiments.

In the late 1840's and early 1850's Winebrenner kept his readers informed of the international peace congresses being held in Europe, in which the American peacemaker, Elihu Burritt ("the learned blacksmith") took so notable a part. As he urged a political decision with regard to temperance, he also strongly supported attempts to legislate in favor of peace through the arbitration process in the United States Congress. Illustrative is his editorial on "Peace Petitions" in the January 1, 1853, *Advocate*:

> The American Peace Society is issuing memorials for signatures addressed to the two houses of Congress, praying

for the adoption of a substitute for war by incorporating a clause in all treaties with foreign powers, providing for the reference of all disputes to umpires . . . A petition is addressed to each House, and the two should be therefore signed by those who would promote this safe and desirable reform.

Winebrenner regarded the Church of God as a peace church, an evaluation which was not challenged by the membership. In his article on the Church of God in *History of all The Religious Denominations in The United States,* he presented the Church as believing that "all civil wars are unholy and sinful, and in which the saints of the Most High ought never to participate." [3] This pacifistic stance was reinforced by Winebrenner's occasional descriptions of the Church of God's beliefs in response to letters of inquiry printed in the *Advocate.* For example, when asked by a correspondent in Victoria, Texas, to distinguish between the Church of God and the Missionary Baptist Church, one of the differences noted by Winebrenner in the *Advocate* for December 1, 1855, was:

The Baptists are a military or war people, whereas the Church of God are an anti-war people. If my kingdom, said Christ, were of this world, then would my disciples fight, but because it is a spiritual kingdom and not of this world, therefore they will not fight, except in a spiritual warfare.

It was a point Winebrenner felt worth making. After all, there were hot heads around who were predicting that only a war between the South and the North would finally solve the slavery problem.

The agonies experienced by Winebrenner—an antislavery pacifist—as the nation reluctantly pressed toward the Civil War were detailed in Chapter Six. What was a man to do if he were opposed to both the slave and war systems, but was being forced to choose between the two? Winebrenner chose slavery. Thus, in the *Advocate* for January 1, 1851, he could announce that "sectarianism, war, etc., are greater evils than slavery." Winebrenner disliked the slave system. He opposed the Fugitive Slave Law. The Kansas-Nebraska Act was an abomination. His support of Simon Cameron for President in March of 1860 was in part predicated on the Cameron platform which would restrict slavery. But, he would not support war—a greater evil—in order to eradicate slavery—a lesser one. Let "nonresistance" Garrison approve the violence of John Brown. Let Theodore Parker discard his antiwar stance and approve the Civil War as a necessity. Winebrenner for his part would remain a consistent pacifist.

The Mexican War

It was the War with Mexico, 1846-1848, which provided Winebrenner with the best opportunity to elaborate upon his pacifistic principles.

The Mexican War was not one of the United States' most popular military ventures. Northern abolitionists regarded it, with some justification, as an attempt by the South to extend slavery—and they reacted accordingly. Those who were opposed to both slavery and war, as Winebrenner was, found the sin compounded. There was simply no justification for military action against a smaller and weaker southern neighbor.

Regular readers of the *Advocate* had absolutely no trouble following the progress of the conflict. In almost every issue of the then biweekly paper, Winebrenner carried the latest from the Mexican front, frequently with a rather hostile observation appended. From the beginning of hostilities it was as though Winebrenner regarded the war as the final case study in human depravity. In the May 16, 1846, issue he announced the war:

> Hostilities have commenced between the United States and the Republic of Mexico . . . Thus, then, the calamities and horrors of war, the greatest and worst of scourges, have broken in upon us. As a nation, we are guilty, and have long since deserved to to be punished for our great and crying sins. May the Lord give us repentance and save us from the horrors and desolations of war.

The four horsemen of the Apocalypse had been let loose! Moreover, there was no doubt where the fault lay. The United States was guilty of perpetrating the worst of all possible "scourges."

A month later, in the June 15 issue, editor Winebrenner dwelt on the cost of the war and the necessary army in "News from Mexico":

> What an oppressive burden will the supplies for such an army impose upon the country, not to say anything of the loss of time, the stagnation of business, the shedding of blood, the destruction of life, and the ruin of souls. May kind Heaven save us from the awful calamities of war!

The whole thing was as unreasonable as it was immoral.

Winebrenner was not alone in his condemnation. Grumbles were heard throughout the General Eldership of the Church. Jacob Flake, a minister of the Church and an old friend of Winebrenner's, frequently handled editorial duties while Winebrenner was away. In the *Advocate* for December 15, 1846, under "The World in 1846—War," Flake put the war in a theological context:

> War may and perhaps will continue among the nations of the earth until Christ the Lord returns again to claim the kingdom and dominion for himself. But let the children of this world fight if they wish to have it so.—The disciples of Christ, the children of the kingdom have a higher and holier calling: they are the sons of peace.

Another Church of God minister, member of the Pennsylvania legislature, and long time friend of Winebrenner's, was James Mackey. In the *Advocate* for February 15, 1847, Winebrenner gave prominent attention to a "Sermon on Patriotism" preached by Mackey at the Shippensburg Church. Mackey wrote:

> This brings us to say some few things on the subject of WAR. Our idea of war is, that it is always unlawful, except in cases of necessary self-defense.

> Whenever, therefore, war is got up for, and its object is merely for political purposes, for wealth, glory, or the extension of territory, it is the most horrid of all crimes; for every crime almost is involved in it, and every calamity produced by it.

Mackey was no nonresister. He allowed for defensive wars. But the Mexican adventure clearly was not that. It was the United States which was guilty of "the most horrid of all crimes." As the prophet Nathan rebuked David, so Mackey pointed his finger at his own country:

> If a nation, already possessed of sufficient territory, should wantonly attempt to dispossess other nations by spreading among them promiscuous distruction [sic] or oppression, whatever pretentions [sic] they may make of love to their own country, they are but plunderers of the rights of their fellow-creatures, and real humanity will weep at their success. Such was the boasted patriotism of the ancient Romans.

His audience knew what nation he was speaking about.

> California had fallen to the Americans. Colonel Kearny had proclaimed the annexation of New Mexico to the United States. But still the war dragged on. When General Zachary Taylor defeated General Santa Anna, president of Mexico, at Buena Vista in February of 1847, Winebrenner acidly noted:

> Another memorable and sanguinary battle has been fought between the American and Mexican armies . . . This is inglory enough for two Christian nations. We hope there

146

will now be a speedy cessation of hostilities and an honorable peace.[4]

Neither cessation of hostilities or an honorable peace was near at hand, however. The American government had decided to send an expeditionary force to capture Mexico City, and hopefully thus to end resistance by opening a second front. The 13,000 troops under the command of Winfield Scott landed on Mexico's east coast, captured Vera Cruz, and pushed inland toward the capital. Mexican and American casualties, costs of the struggle, and opposition to it continued to increase. Theodore Parker in Boston called the war a sin; Henry Thoreau in Concord refused to pay his taxes; and John Winebrenner in Harrisburg boiled over in an editorial in the July 15, 1847, *Advocate*. The editorial was titled, "Fourth of July."

> This day happening to fall on the Sabbath this year, seemed to set aside the usual celebration in this place . . .
>
> That which seemed to attract the most attention was a military parade of the Harrisburg Cadets, under Capt. Partridge.
>
> These youthful soldiers were out with a six pounder, firing federal and honorary salutes, at stated hours, from morning till evening.
>
> This may do well enough for the people of this world, but we are surprised at some of the good people of Harrisburg, who profess to be Christians, to send their sons to military schools, and have them trained for carnage and bloodshed. Between the spirit of war and the spirit of Christianity there is an utter incompatibility. That system of government, which, for the same deed, will punish the *citizen* and reward the *soldier*, is not congenial with the righteous government of the Prince of Peace.

Rarely, if ever, had Winebrenner found the American government so culpable.

In his excoriation of the American position in the war, Winebrenner did not at the same time absolve Mexico completely. "The fact is," he wrote in the December 15, 1847, *Advocate*, "the fault lies on both sides. Both nations are guilty before God. . ." What he did object to was the government's attempt to place the blame for the war on Mexico. President Polk was doing just that and, in addition, linking peace to the American annexation of Mexican territory. Winebrenner tried to reason with the government:

> Now, if we must have the province of New Mexico and the two Californias added to the United States as an indemnifica-

F. Brenneman's Dyspeptic Medicine.

BROTHER FREDERICK BRENNEMAN, near Maytown, requested us to give notice, for the benefit of suffering humanity, that he prepares a most excellent medicine, for the cure of dyspepsia, or indigestion, which he will be happy to furnish, wholesale or retail, to all person who may see proper to give him a call or send their orders. The Medicine is for sale also at this office. Advertisement and certificates of cure in our next.

President's Message.

THE last annual Message of President Polk, is a long and elaborate document.

After recounting the distinguished mercies of a gracious Providence, our unequalled domestic happiness and prosperity, and our venerated and Pacific relations abroad, the President congratulates the nation, on the immense additions to our territorial possessions, in our late treaty of peace with Mexico. By the acquisition of Texas, California and

Church Advocate, December 15, 1848

148

tion for the expenses of this cruel and aggressive war, then what will poor distracted Mexico have to repair her loss? Strong and rich nations have no more right to wrong and oppress poor and feeble nations, than rich men have thus to treat the poor. The doctrine of the Bible is, to do justly and love mercy. We had better contend for religious toleration than for territory. If we must have territory, let us buy it. And at the same time, let us 'buy the truth and sell it not.'

If Winebrenner thought in terms of the "manifest destiny" of the United States, he saw it in a spiritual context rather than in a territorial one.

On September 19, 1847, Mexico City fell. Santa Anna abdicated the presidency and the war was effectively at an end. By the Treaty of Guadalupe Hidalgo the United States agreed to pay Mexico 15 million dollars and assume the $3,250,000 American claims against Mexico. In return, Mexico ceded Upper California and New Mexico, and confirmed Texan claims to land north of the Rio Grande. Winebrenner reported on "Peace with Mexico" in the June 15, 1848, *Advocate,* adding "This was the best news we have recorded for some time." The *Advocate* for August 1 announced the return of the American volunteers from Mexico (without comment) and carried an article discussing the wastefulness of the recent conflict. Plainly, Winebrenner the pacifist saw little glory or honor in the whole affair. But Winebrenner the farmer was on hand to note a beneficial thing or two arising from the experience of the Americans in Mexico. In the August 1 *Advocate* was the following short item:

A MEXICAN SQUASH, produced from seed brought from Vera Cruz, is growing in Mobile, one of the fruit measured in circumference two feet five inches by two feet two and a half. The fruit is . . . in flavour, far superior to the best American squashes.

Even war clouds might have a silver lining.

8

Temperance

Throughout the colonial period and into the early years of the American republic, the generous consumption of alcoholic beverages was more or less taken for granted by the American people. Fermented drinks were routinely used at the family table. Ale and beer might be passed around to young and old alike in a communal mug.

There were many factors contributing to this situation. Frequently water was regarded as unhealthy (as at times it undoubtedly was, given the primitive sanitation standards). Tea, coffee, and chocolate—water substitutes—were not widely available until well into the eighteenth century. Surplus fruits and grains easily could be turned into money making crops by their conversion into ciders, wines, beers, or ales. Moreover, the concept of the beneficial nature or medicinal value of alcoholic beverages remained generally unchallenged throughout America's early years.

As early at 1619, in the southern colonies, Frenchmen were imported to establish a colonial wine industry. Farther north, from the 1640's on, Puritan shipowners brought wines from Spain and the Madeiras home to Boston and Newport for the well- and better-to-do Puritan families. By the end of the seventeenth century, New England was distilling large quantities of rum from West Indian molasses. The rum was used both for home consumption, and, far more infamously, for bartering for slaves on the west coast of Africa. In other colonies, and especially on the American frontier, whiskey was distilled from various grains and competed with rum for "hard liquor" popularity.

From contemporary accounts it would seem that second only to the church, the tavern or public house was the most important gathering place to the colonial American. Taverns generally served as a sort of community club house where civic groups, city councils, and the local militia, as well as the local citizenry, might regularly meet over something alcoholic. By the late 1620's in New Amsterdam, the Dutch Colony on Manhattan Island, one out of four houses served grog (liquor generally diluted with water) or sold tobacco and beer. In Philadelphia, in 1752, there were 120 licensed taverns, the number continuing to increase until the Revolutionary War.

The pervasiveness of alcoholic addiction as the United States moved into the nineteenth century was the source of some despair to the Methodist circuit rider, Peter Cartwright (1785-1872). Cartwright, an older contemporary of John Winebrenner's, recounted in his *Autobiography*:

> From my earliest recollection drinking drams, in family and social circles was considered harmless and allowable socialities. It was almost universally the custom for preachers, in common with all others, to take drams; and if a man would not have it in his family, his harvest, his house-raisings, logrollings, weddings, and so on, he was considered parsimonious and unsociable; and many, even professors of Christianity, would not help a man if he did not have spirits and treat the company.[1]

Other writers from the same period support Cartwright's recollection. Methodist revivalist James Finley (1781-1856), riding circuit in Ohio, found spirits considered a necessity. Horace Greeley (1811-1872), of editorial and political fame, in recounting his boyhood days in Vermont indicated that there was hardly a casual gathering of two or three neighbors without alcoholic beverages being passed around. Election days, funerals, weddings, house and barn raisings—all were "drinking days." Anything to save the water!

Nor were the children exempt. "Cobb's Juvenile Reader Number Three," printed in Utica, New York, in 1838, counted among its "interesting, moral and instructive reading lessons" for youngsters an informative description of the composition of the various alcoholic beverages, from beer to whiskey, then available.

A glance at American clergy and churches during the eighteenth and early nineteenth century does not change the story much. Liquors frequently were served at the ordination and installation of pastors and at other churchly functions, including baptizings, weddings, and funerals. On occasion, a minister might even receive a portion of his salary in the form of ardent spirits. One of the recurring themes in Peter Cartwright's *Autobiography* was his difficulty with drunken frontier preachers and churchmen of varying denominational persuasions. Cartwright usually emerged victorious in his bouts with demon rum in the church although it did not necessarily assure his popularity with well lubricated ministers or parishioners. Indeed, he might even lose a family to the church because of his refusal to take a "cherry bounce" with the man of the family.[2]

The Temperance Movement

But addiction to things alcoholic did not go unchallenged, especially where excessive drinking was involved. The doughty Puritan theologian, Cotton Mather, by the 1690's expressed the fear that heavy drinking might in time inundate Christianity. In 1735 the London trustees of the newly developing Georgia Colony ruled that spiritous liquors could not be brought into the colony and that existing stores of the same should be destroyed. By such legislation it was hoped to protect both the morals and, to the extent it kept the soldier-farmers sober, the frontiers of the colony. Seven years later, in 1742, the trustees reversed themselves and repealed the prohibitionary statute. One of the reasons given for the reversal by the trustees was that it appeared to be the experience of colonial Americans that water in the colonies was better when "qualified" with spirits of some sort. And, as the trustees suggested, it was certain that no water needed "qualification" more than the water in Carolina and Georgia. More to the point was the potentially profitable trade with the West Indies— Georgia's lumber for West Indian rum.[3]

Probably the best known advocate of temperance in eighteenth century America, and in some ways father of the American temperance movement, was Dr. Benjamin Rush (1746-1813) of Philadelphia. His "Enquiry Into the Effects of Spiritous Liquors on the Human Body and Mind" in 1784 took issue with the widely held notion that alcohol was an American necessity. Highly influential as a resource book for later generations, the "Enquiry" went through eight editions between 1784 and 1815. The American Tract Society alone was responsible for reprinting 172,000 copies. Rush also used his influence to promote temperance principles before the Pennsylvania Legislature, the United States Congress, and the Presbyterian Church.

The first American temperance society was formed in 1808 in Moreau, in upstate New York, by a small group of townsmen. Known as the Moreau Society, its associates agreed to abstain from alcoholic beverages—except at public dinners where toasts were liable to be drunk. The Society's work was not crowned with tremendous success, but by the early 1800's other more promising currents were moving in the country. The American churches were beginning to bestir themselves in the interests of temperance.

As early as the 1740's, the Quaker saint, John Woolman (1720-1772), protested strongly against the "use of more strong liquor than pure wisdom allows." Quakers generally adopted Woolman's concern and by the last quarter of the eighteenth century were laboring for a reformation in the use of spiritous liquors. The Methodists also went on record in the eighteenth century in opposition to ardent spirits. Their 1780 General Conference opposed both the making and consumption of distilled liquors. Yet it was not until the early nineteenth century that concern over temperance began to assume crusade-like proportions. The prestigious New England preacher, Lyman Beecher (1775-1863), was deeply influenced by Benjamin Rush's "Enquiry". After witnessing with some distaste the abundant supply of liquors available at a Plymouth, Connecticut, ordination service, Beecher became actively involved in the fight against intemperance on the part of both ministers and laymen. The Massachusetts Society for the Suppression of Intemperance was founded in 1813 by Presbyterian and Congregational Churches. The fact that Boston itself could support a licensed grogshop for every 21 males who were 16 and older probably provided incentive enough.

The growing concern of the churches and increasingly intense activities on the part of a large number of highly influential ministers and academicians led to the founding, in 1826, of the American Society for the Promotion of Temperance. By 1834 the Society reported approximately a million members in 5,000 local societies. While the movement was nationwide, it was especially strong in New England, New York, and John Winebrenner's Pennsylvania.[4]

The temperance movement in Pennsylvania historically had its rootage among the Quakers in the eastern part of the state. Quaker preachers and writers like Thomas Chalkey, John Woolman, and Anthony Benezet emphasized the dangers of alcohol in the early and mid-1700's. In all probability, Dr. Rush's "Enquiry Into the Effects of Spiritous Liquors . . ." was influenced by his Quaker contemporaries, if not his own Quaker background. Although Quaker influence had waned considerably by the nineteenth century, the temperance movement had not. In 1827, the Pennsylvania Society for Discouraging the Use of Ardent Spirits was founded. Of far more significance was the founding, in Philadelphia in 1833, of The United States Temperance Union. The Union was a rather loose federation of the officers of the American Temperance Society and representatives from state societies and local organizations. At the first national convention of the society in 1836, its name was changed to The American Temperance Union. It had many Pennsylvania affiliates and was reported on regularly by Winebrenner (together with the meetings of the American Temperance Society) in the pages of the *Gospel Publisher*.

Winebrenner and Temperance: The Beginnings

Winebrenner's writings prior to 1835 do not indicate an extensive concern with temperance. In the few sermons we have which date from his German Reformed connection (1817-1825), there is no mention of the "sin of drunkenness" or the need for temperance. In his *The Truth Made Known,* published in 1824, he made passing mention of the "children of the world" who "very often drink, swear, frolic, dance, and gamble all night." [5] But this was standard fare for the time. Winebrenner's *Brief View of the ... Church of God* was printed in 1829.[6] In it Winebrenner gave as one of the qualifications of Church Elders that they be "not given to wine." This was explained to mean that the elder "must not drink to excess, nor unnecessarily." [7] Deacons similarly should be "not given to much wine." [8] Such statements indicate a general concern; hardly a passionate interest.

It is with the first issue of the *Gospel Publisher* on June 5, 1835, that Winebrenner is revealed to us as a temperance crusader. As laid out by Winebrenner, the *Publisher* had a weekly Temperance column in which was recorded the activities of the temperate around the world, but especially in the United States. Thus, the first issue of the *Publisher* told of the projected *Temperance Recorder* to be published by the Pennsylvania Temperance Society in Philadelphia; the "progress of the temperance cause among our German population" in Pennsylvania; John Wesley's "testimony against the distillation and sale of ... 'liquid fire' "; and, the "Combustion of a Drunkard." This last item, a reprint from the Kingston, Canada *Gazette,* was representative of a great number of supposedly true accounts floating around in temperance circles at that time of the "spontaneous ignition" of flagrant alcoholics. The article reported the doleful testimony of a Dr. Peter Schofield. According to Dr. Schofield:

> It was the case of a young man about 25 years old. He had been a habitual drinker for many years. I saw him about

nine o'clock in the evening on which it happened. He was then, as usual, not drunk, but full of liquor. About eleven on the same evening I was called to see him. I found him literally roasted from the crown of his head to the soul (sic) of his feet. He was found in the blacksmith's shop just across the way where he had been. The owner all of a sudden discovered an extensive light in the shop, as though the whole building was in one general flame. He ran with the greatest precipitancy, and on flinging open the door, discovered a man standing erect in the midst of a widely extended silver coloured blaze, bearing, as he described it, exactly the appearance of the wick of a burning candle in the midst of its own flame. . . . There was no fire in the shop, neither was there any possibility of fire having been communicated to him from any external source. It was purely a case of spontaneous ignition.

For all his exuberance for any cause, Winebrenner could be skeptical when the occasion demanded. In the *Publisher* for December 2, 1836, he noted "another instance of supposed spontaneous burning of the human body" in a French paper, and then commented:

It is remarkable that in all these instances, the commencement of the combustion, as we recollect, has always taken place when the individual was alone. No case is on record in which the human body was seen to take fire spontaneously. This leads to the presumption that in the cases of supposed spontaneous combustion, fire has been accidentally communicated to the clothing.

A reformer's life could be trying at times.

In later years, Winebrenner dated his attachment to the temperance cause around 1830. In an October, 1853 address, prepared for the voters of Harrisburg and Dauphin County, in support of a proposed Prohibitory Liquor Law (Maine Law) for Pennsylvania, Winebrenner began by first establishing his credentials as a reformer:

Men and Brethren: You that know me, need not be told that I have occupied the position for many years, in this community, of a *Reformer* [emphasis Winebrenner's] of the errors and wrongs of society. This position I hope to occupy as long as I live.[9]

He certainly would be known to his listeners as a church leader—a schismatic or reformer, depending upon the point of view. Building on this image, he continued:

I claim to be not only an ecclesiastical reformer, but also a Temperance reformer: and one of the oldest if not altogether *the* oldest Temperance reformer in Dauphin county. Thirty-three years ago, when I commenced my reformatory movements, in Harrisburg and the surrounding country, the Temperance Reformation had no organized form in this country, but irreligion and intemperance abounded to a fearful degree. . . . Single handed and alone, I raised my voice against the errors and sins of the people, and especially against this giant sin of intemperance.

Thus, according to Winebrenner, it was 33 years earlier (1830) that he embarked upon reforms of both church (probably the establishment of the General Eldership of the Church of God in October, 1830) and an alcohol oriented society.

What moved Winebrenner in the direction of the Temperance movement? Probably it was the natural outgrowth of his general reformist policies. It was the nature of the American "evangelical" clergyman to be involved in social reform and "good causes" generally. Anti-slavery, anti-alcohol, anti-war, anti-tobacco—all of these movements, especially in the North, were regarded as important reforming adjuncts to the Gospel message which offered rebirth of the soul through Christ. Consequently, Winebrenner used the *Gospel Publisher* to publish not only the Gospel but also to record the activities of the Young Men's Temperance Society of Harrisburg, organized in 1833, as well as the activities of the Harrisburg Anti-Slavery Society, organized a few years later. The two movements were so closely interwoven in Winebrenner's mind that on occasion he ran anti-slavery news in his Temperance column.

But there were also personal dimensions to Winebrenner's concern over alcoholism. His first wife, Charlotte, spent many of her early years in a home upset by hard liquor. Charlotte's apothecary father, Michael Reutter, died in 1805 in Harrisburg when Charlotte was but three years old. In 1811, her mother, Mary, married George K. Nutz. Mr. Nutz, it turned out, was given to heavy drinking bouts which afflicted the whole family, but especially Charlotte. Years later, while Winebrenner was involved in litigation related to Charlotte's estate, a number of friends and neighbors were called upon to testify concerning Charlotte's treatment by her stepfather. According to one Esther Hoover, for example:

Sometime when her stepfather was in liquor, Charlotte had to wash up after him and when he was sick she attended him . . . when he puked she had to carry the pots up and down [and] to bring him liquor and water and whatever he called for . . . he always called Charlotte, never Eliza [Charlotte's older sister] or his wife . . . When he was sober he was good to Charlotte, but when in liquor he would swear and scold and holler at her.[10]

Other witnesses corroborated Esther Hoover's testimony. Her stepfather was a drunkard. Her mother was sick most of the time—in her final illness—and apparently unable to assist her daughter. Her older sister left home (March 14, 1821) and shortly thereafter got married. Her older brother, Daniel, apparently was on good terms with Mr. Nutz and seemingly not too sympathetic to his sister. Charlotte could take only so much. On June 26, 1822, she left home. After "working in" with friends for several months, she cast her lot in marriage, on October 8, 1822, with the young, earnest, and undoubtedly temperate pastor of the Reformed Church, John Winebrenner. One suspects that Winebrenner's later concern over alcoholism in the *Publisher* might well have been fashioned in some measure by his wife's experiences.

Temperance in the Publisher and Advocate: 1835-1857

While editor of the *Gospel Publisher* (June 5, 1835-April 1, 1840) and the *Church Advocate* (May 1, 1846-April 23, 1857), Winebrenner kept his readers abreast of the latest temperance news in almost every issue. The *Publisher's* temperance column was dropped in the *Advocate* (as were other specialty columns), but temperance concern was not. As noted earlier, Winebrenner regularly carried reports of the national temperance groups. Also, reports of state and local temperance meetings were carried, usually through the courtesy of exchange temperance newspapers. From these same exchanges, on occasion the reader was treated to the rout of demon rum all over the world, from France to the South Sea Islands. Winebrenner, of course, paid particular attention to the progress of temperance in Pennsylvania. It was quite a chore and often disheartening. Unlike a number of neighboring states, Pennsylvania never adopted a prohibitionary liquor law in Winebrenner's lifetime.

Both the *Publisher* and *Advocate* contained the usual genre stories about the degradation of body and soul attributable to alcoholism. The following article headings are illustrative: "Intemperance, Gambling, Fire and Death;"[11] "Temperance vs. Cholera;"[12] "Alcohol Curses Generations to Come;"[13] "The Home of a Drunkard;"[14] "The Drunkard's Son;"[15] and, "The Drunkard's Wife."[16] Some of the articles are macabre; some are merely garish; some are genuinely touching. Still, over-all, there is an optimistic flair to much of what Winebrenner included in the church paper about the anti-alcohol struggle. The temperance cause was seen as one which combined in itself the forces of reason, religion, and men of good faith everywhere. While there might be (and were) reverses, victory was inevitable.

In the 1830's, Winebrenner's temperance articles, whether original or from exchanges, gave evidence both of the rapid, enthusiastic development of the temperance movement *and* of the serious dissension which split the camp toward the end of the decade.

Early advocates of temperance took the word quite literally. They were for a "temperate" or "moderate" approach to the alcohol problem. Like their British counterparts, late eighteenth and early nineteenth century American temperance reformers wanted to do something about a situation which allowed tavern signs to offer prospective patrons the opportunity to become "drunk" for a penny and "dead drunk" for two cents. Many of this type of temperance reformer in fact *urged* the use of wine and other fermented drinks in place of the much more potent distilled beverages. By the late 1820's and early 1830's this view was being challenged, especially on the national level, by those like Lyman Beecher, Justin Edwards, and western temperance leaders, who equated temperance with abstinence. When the first national convention of the American Temperance Union met in Saratoga, New York, in 1836, it was dominated by the abstinence party (the "ultras"). It passed resolutions which effectively defined temperance as abstinence, and obligated those temperance societies in connection with the American Temperance Union to condemn the drinking of all fermented drinks—wine, beer, cider— as well as "ardent spirits." However, when the "new pledge" condemning all intoxicating beverages was taken back by delegates from the national convention to state and local societies, chaos resulted. Many of the grass roots societies were oriented toward thinking of temperance as moderation and refused to accept the leadership of the national Temperance Union. Consequently, the temperance movement suffered a severe jolt as the "old pledge" ("O. P.") temperance people—those who believed in moderation— did battle with their "teetotal" ("T" for "total") cousins—those who believed in *total* abstinence from all intoxicants.

Reflections of the changing temperance climate are found in early *Gospel Publishers*. In several articles in the 1835 *Publisher*, temperance is identified with abstinence from ardent spirits— fermented drinks seemingly excluded.[17] However, in the *Gospel*

Publisher for March 4, 1836, Winebrenner reported favorably on the New York State Temperance Society which had met recently at Albany and which had adopted "the pledge of abstinence from all fermented liquors, wine, beers, cider etc. as well as from all ardent spirits." Winebrenner hoped that New York's example would be followed "throughout the land," and

> . . . that the intemperance which has found a countenance and refuge from those who sanction the use of fermented liquors though they do discard ardent spirits, will no longer slay its thousands, and tens of thousands.

Temperance in the *Publisher* was henceforth to be defined as abstinence. Winebrenner was following the lead of the national temperance leadership.

Harrisburg temperance circles did not greet the move from moderation to teetotalism with enthusiasm. On April 12, 1836, the Young Men's Temperance Society of Harrisburg met to consider, among other things, the following preamble and resolution:

> Whereas the pledge of this Society prohibits the use of Ardent Spirits only, and it has been clearly proven that many of our brethren have fallen into temptation by the use of vinous and fermented liquors . . .

> Resolved, That the following be the form of a Pledge to be hereafter used by this Society: "Whereas it has become necessary, in furthering the cause of Temperance, to adopt, as a fundamental principle, that great law of Christian love 'not to drink wine or any thing whereby thy brother stumbleth or is made weak, or is offended,' therefore the undersigned agree and solemnly pledge ourselves to abstain from the use of all intoxicating liquor as a beverage."

After "some debate," further consideration was postponed.[18]

The dissension within was not the only problem. In the late 1830's the temperance crusade was beginning to lose support generally, for a number of reasons. The open advocacy by some temperance societies of prohibitory laws to support if not replace moral suasion led to the disaffection of many who felt such an approach a threat to their personal freedom. The fact that many northern temperance leaders were also vocal abolitionists did nothing whatsoever for the cause in the South. Just as anti-slavery in the 1830's moved from a congenial colonization policy to rigid abolitionism, so also temperance moved from a genteel moderation to teetotal abstinence. As both reformatory movements became increasingly dominated by "extreme elements," increasingly also they alienated increasing numbers of the American people. The logic of the teetotaler that wine and whiskey were equally harmful and damning did not penetrate the masses. This was especially true in Pennsylvania where beer and wine drinking immigrants from northern and central Europe could scarcely fathom why the beer and wine they had always drunk without obvious ill effect should suddenly be regarded by the fiat of a few as a frightful sin, if not a heinous crime. Added to these factors was the Panic of 1837 and the ensuing depression which dampened the exuberance of Americans generally, and diminished funds in temperance society coffers.

Articles in the *Publisher* indicate that the malaise had begun to spread in the Harrisburg area as early as 1836. At the previously mentioned meeting of the Young Men's Temperance Society of Harrisburg in April of that year, the managers of the Society rapped the collective knuckles of the Society in their annual report:

> Your managers have been deeply grieved, that they cannot congratulate you upon the extensive spread of your principles, nor the adoption of your pledge, within the bounds of your Society, during the year that is past: That during said period they cannot present you the name of a single new member— that they cannot produce one . . . instance of a wretched inebriate reformed through your influence and example,— not point you to a deserted dram-shop . . .—nor a dilapidated distillery . . .[19]

But better days were ahead.

While it is true that the temperance movement faced a series of exacerbating frustrations in the late 1830's, the total effect was not one of debilitating despair. There was, for example, no overall fall off of significant temperance articles in the *Publisher* after 1836. Rather, it was a period of retrenchment perhaps, as temperance forces assimilated the actions and reactions of the earlier part of the decade.

Moreover, even though the "extremist" ideology of the temperance groups might have been initially rejected by a majority of the citizenry, temperance propaganda gradually was being assimilated into the American conscience. The research of temperance forces showing the damaging effect of alcohol to local, state, and national economies could not be ignored completely. Overindulgence in alcohol indeed had been a problem. It continued to be. Something was going to have to be done; and it was. The frustration of the late '30's was followed by an unparalleled expansion of the temperance movement in the 1840's and '50's.

In the years after 1840, the emphasis on moral suasion continued. It was promoted as at least one approach to the problem of drunkenness by many temperance societies on both local and national levels. Particularly effective were the Washingtonians, a non-religiously oriented society of ex-inebriates founded in 1840, and the semi-secret Order of the Sons of Temperance founded in 1842 as an abstinent fraternal order. But while moral suasion continued as a technique, its limitations were obvious. Some, both "traffickers" in and users of demon rum, could not be morally persuaded. What to do? Pass a law! Increasingly, from the late 1830's up to the Civil War, considerable effort was expended on securing statewide prohibition laws. Of these laws, by far and away the most popular was the Maine Law. Passed in 1846 by the Maine Legislature, the Maine Law became the prototype of similar prohibitory statutes enacted in most of the northern states—Pennsylvania being one of the few exceptions.

The *Church Advocate* between May, 1846 and April, 1857 (while Winebrenner was editor) kept its readers informed of expanding efforts in the direction of both moral suasion and prohibitionary law.

The Order of the Sons of Temperance was followed more or less closely. This was in part because the Order was a secret society of sorts and the Church of God was opposed to secret societies. The moral dilemma was obvious. Could an abstinent member of the Church of God (and by the middle of the nineteenth century it was hoped there were no other kinds of members) be a member of an abstinent but nonetheless secret society? In a letter to Brother Winebrenner in the *Church Advocate* for March 15, 1848, a correspondent from Elizabethtown, Pennsylvania, allowed that Church of God members indeed must be wary of secret societies. Certainly, the perfidy of the "wily Jesuits," who met in "secret cliques," was as well known a fact as any in church history. However, it was the correspondent's opinion that the Sons of Temperance were not a secret society, at least any more than the church itself was. They were open in their purpose. Therefore, a member of the Church of God could join the Sons of Temperance in good conscience. The correspondent signed his name "Adelphus"—thus keeping his identity a secret.

On the other hand, there were those in the church who could not agree with "Adelphus." About the same time his letter was appearing in the *Advocate*, the Mechanicsburg Church of God in the East Pennsylvania Eldership was experiencing schism over the issue. Apparently the church generally agreed that it was possible to be both a Son of Temperance and a member of the Church of God. But there were those, including Jacob Coover—one of the 1828 organizers and original elders of the Mechanicsburg congregation—who were "not satisfied with W. Hinney and others for so much conforming with world and neglecting the rule wich [sic] we have taken for our faith and practice, wich [sic] is Old and New Testament." Coover and his friends were charged with being "blameworthy for not submitting to the will of the church." In spite of the efforts of a goodly number to effect a reconciliation, the issue was solved only when Jacob Coover, J. Singeisen, J. Leininger, and H. Leas were expelled "For Aposing [sic] the Order of the Sunes [sic] of Temperance in their marches and regaily [regale, regalia?] for Christians." [20]

Winebrenner had introduced the concept of using laws to discourage the liquor traffic as early as May 16, 1839, when the *Gospel Publisher* carried an American Temperance Union article entitled, "Temperance Cause—Legislation Needed to Protect the People." But it was not until his editorship of the *Advocate* that concern over prohibitionary laws became a constant theme in the Church of God paper. While Winebrenner still carried numerous articles supporting friendly persuasion of the liquor interests, it is evident from other articles that this approach was undergoing sustained criticism from a growing number in the temperance movement. When, for example, in 1850, a temperance convention at Lisburn, Pennsylvania (near Harrisburg), suggested that ". . . if Temperance men were more vigilant, they could accomplish more by moral suasion than coercion," [21] this conclusion was attacked by "A. D. W." in an article entitled "Moral and Legal Suasion" in the *Church Advocate* for June 15, 1850. "A. D. W." was the Rev. A. D. Williams of the Free Will Baptist Church, a frequent contributor to the *Advocate,* especially on matters pertaining to slavery and temperance. As far as Williams was concerned, if there are laws prohibiting thievery and murder, there also ought to be laws prohibiting the rum-seller—whose product led to early graves, pauperism, and social misery generally—from plying his trade.

In the Spring of 1852, a restrictive liquor bill failed of passage in the Pennsylvania House by four votes. Winebrenner was rather pleased. The bill would have given Pennsylvania the "31 Gallon Law" of Massachusetts, by which traffic in liquor was restricted to amounts in excess of 31 gallons. As Winebrenner noted, such a bill "closed the grog only on those who are too poor to buy a barrel of 'the crittur' at once." Hence, in the interest of fairness, he was happy to see it defeated. Temperance people should not lose heart, at any rate. Even in defeat Winebrenner could see the Resurrection Day ahead in all its glory.

> The crisis has come. King Alcohol's reign is over. His days are numbered. And soon the Temperance jubilee will come.

Before that day, however, there would have to be an Armageddon.

> The great Temperance battle will be fought next fall,—Victory will crown the Temperance army;—and next winter a Temperance Legislature will give us the prohibitory Liquor Law, not in a crude, jumbled and rickety form, but in all its *Maine* symmetry, beauty and glory.[22]

It was an apocalyptic vision of the finest sort.

Winebrenner's hopes were not realized that next fall, although the Maine Law Party men made a respectable showing. In October of 1853, Winebrenner and the *Advocate* supported the Maine Law candidates of Dauphin County—William Bishop and Joseph Ross—for the Pennsylvania Assembly. Campaigning under the banner "Lead us not into Temptation," Bishop and Ross lost, but not by much. They carried Harrisburg itself, but could not offset large Whig and Democratic totals in the county. The *Advocate's* "Temperance Platform," run in the October 8, 1853 issue, three days before the election, is probably a fair representation of the feelings of the Church of God on the issue:

> The enforcement of existing laws against the sale of liquors on the Sabbath-day.
>
> The removal of the polls and political meetings from all places where liquor is sold.
>
> The enactment and due execution of just and sufficient laws for the *Total Prohibition* of the sale of intoxicating liquors as a beverage.
>
> The elevation to office of just, able and worthy men, who will aid in securing these results.

As noted earlier, "total prohibition" for Pennsylvania did not occur in Winebrenner's lifetime. Pennsylvania voters turned down the Maine Law for their state by a bare majority (approximately 3,000 out of 300,000 votes cast) in October of 1854. (In fact, the Keystone State did not adopt statutory prohibition until the federal government forced it to do so in the twentieth century.) However, the political efforts of the churches did bear fruit, and by the mid-1850's the *Advocate* was appreciatively recording the adoption by Pennsylvania of "half way" or restrictive temperance legislation. For example, in the *Advocate* for September 28, 1854,

Winebrenner reported that a recently enacted law prohibiting the sale of liquor on the Sabbath, and to the intemperate and minors, helped to explain "the remarkable good behavior of the people at our camp-meetings this season"—which should add a new dimension to our concept of a nineteenth century Winebrennerian camp meeting.

It was with a spirit of philosophical acquiescence that in the *Advocate* for April 19, 1855, Winebrenner applauded a recently passed anti-saloon bill, prohibiting less than a quart sales of liquor:

> This law is a great victory, all things considered, for Pennsylvania. Although not a prohibitory liquor law, it comes as near to it, perhaps, as public sentiment would sanction. It will completely break up the worst features of the liquor traffic, and will prove a powerful entering wedge for final and entire prohibition.

He did not applaud the repeal of the bill a year later. By the late 1850's "powerful entering wedge" temperance legislation was being blunted not only in Pennsylvania, but across the entire nation.

As the country marched toward the Civil War, the involvement over slavery considerably diminished support for the temperance crusade. Moreover, the states which had passed prohibitive and restrictive legislation often found it difficult to enforce. Much temperance legislation was amended or repealed on constitutional grounds. By Winebrenner's death in 1860, the pre-Civil War temperance ship had foundered. While some temperance legislation remained on the books in Pennsylvania, and Winebrenner legitimately could ascribe its being there to the efforts of men like himself, still one suspects that the general declension of the movement must have been a disappointment to him. Perhaps, at least, we can be thankful that he did not live long enough to witness the demise, in 1865, of his close organizational friend, the American Temperance Union.

Winebrenner and Temperance: An Evaluation

On the basis of *Gospel Publisher* and *Church Advocate* articles and his own miscellaneous writings, John Winebrenner's relationship to temperance reform seems somewhat less complex, on balance, than his relationship to the antislavery and peace movements.

In his attempts at the reformation of the slavery system, Winebrenner moved from the position of a moderate antislavery colonizationist to that of an abolitionist in late 1835 or early 1836. By whatever criteria are applied, it was a radical step. It was also a directional change when, in the late 1850's, he moved to a stance whereby he could rather unenthusiastically permit slavery on biblical grounds. As bad as slavery was, Winebrenner considered a civil war even worse. If it came to a choice between the two, Winebrenner would have to go with allowing slavery—a reasonable enough approach, I suppose, especially if one was not a slave.

From what sources are available to us, it would appear that Winebrenner was concerned over intemperance in more or less conventional ways as early as the 1820's. By his own reckoning he came to regard himself as a temperance reformer about 1830. In all probability his early interpretation was "moderation." This was in keeping with prevailing patterns in the temperance movement at that time, and involved opposition to ardent spirits (as a beverage) while allowing a moderate use of fermented drinks like wine, beer, or cider. In general, the concern was the avoidance of drunkenness and not alcohol. In 1836, about the same time as he adopted the "ultra" or abolitionist position on slavery, he also adopted the "ultra" or total abstinence position where intoxicating beverages were concerned. This was the growing edge of the temperance movement, and although it meant dissension in the temperance ranks, by the 1850's it was the dominant approach. In all probability Winebrenner maintained his teetotal thrust throughout the rest of his life, although we have very little information to go on after he gave up the editorship of the *Advocate* in April of 1857.

The best overall clarification of his later personal position with regard to temperance was given during the course of his campaign for the election of the Dauphin County Maine Law candidates in October of 1853. In the same speech in which he claimed to be one of the oldest, if not *the* oldest temperance reformer in Dauphin County, he also carefully defined his understanding of the issues at hand. "By the *Maine Law*," he meant

> . . . nothing more or less than a law to prohibit the sale of intoxicating liquors, as a beverage. This is all we want. Give us a prohibitory statute . . . and we are content.

Winebrenner had no desire to argue against any possibly beneficial use of alcohol by society. That was not his intent in supporting the Maine Law.

With the manufacture and sale of liquors for medicinal, mechanical, and sacramental purposes, we wish not to interfere. We have no controversy with any man or party, on the subject.

"But," he continued,

... against the abominable liquor traffic for drinking purposes, and the odious license law, legalizing the traffic, we must, and do declare, an uncompromising warfare; ... And for it we know no remedy, but moral suasion and prohibition.[23]

It is of at least passing interest that, at a prohibition rally, Winebrenner would emphasize "moral suasion" as well as "prohibition" as the means for bringing in true temperance reform. Probably it indicated an attempt at securing the broadest possible base for electing Maine Law candidates. Probably also, it indicated Winebrenner's own conviction in the matter. As pastor, camp meeting preacher, or as editor, Winebrenner's job was to *persuade* his listeners and readers of the rightness or wrongness of a religious or social position. He recognized that unless there was personal commitment to abstinence, laws could not be expected to solve the problem.

Winebrenner's warfare against "the odious license law," which in effect legalized the liquor traffic, was a part of his teetotal approach to the liquor question. Prior to his adoption of the total abstinence standard, the matter of license laws was a source of concern to Winebrenner, but apparently, on balance, he felt them to be proper. Thus, musing over the 1835 recommendation of the American Temperance Society that license laws governing the traffic in ardent spirits be repealed, in the December 11, 1835 *Gospel Publisher*, Winebrenner allowed that while he had thought about the matter "for several years," he was "not ready to give a positive opinion." Indeed, he suggested, "the man who is ready, we suspect, must be one who has studied the subject very much, or very little."

In assessing Winebrenner's personal temperance position, it is of particular importance to recognize that this opposition to intoxicating liquids was far from absolute. He believed in abstinence, to be sure, but only abstinence from intoxicants used "as a beverage," or common drink. He assumed, and nowhere questioned, the "manufacture and sale of liquors for medicinal, mechanical, and sacramental purposes."

Winebrenner and his contemporaries, in and out of the temperance movement, generally expressed a firm belief in the medicinal value of intoxicating spirits. Between April 1, 1833, and

PROSPECTUS

OF A

New and Highly Interesting Work.

THE Standing Committee, or Board of Publication of the General Eldership of the Church of God, propose publishing by subscription, a work entitled,

Biographical Sketches

OF THE

First One Hundred Ministers

OF THE

Church of God in North America.

These sketches will comprise a brief account of each minister's birth and education, his conversion and call to the ministry, and his travels, experience, scenes, labors and success therein, from its commencement down to the present time.

Such a work, it is believed, will be highly interesting and useful, both to parents and children—professors and non-professors of religion.

The work will contain some 5 or 600 pages, in *deo descimo* form, neatly printed and bound, and delivered to subscribers at $1 per copy, payable on the delivery of the book.

Dow's Family Medicine.

AS sundry persons, here and there, are beginning to complain of Bilious Fevers, Dysentery, Flower & Ague, &c., we would advise them to call and get Dow's Medicine, which is a most excellent remedy for these and other complaints.

For sale at the office of the *Church Advocate.* Price 50 cents per bottle. Aug. 1.

History of the Church of God.

THE history of the Church of God in the United States, as contained in the History of Denominations, is now published in pamphlet form, for distribution in cities and new places, where the principles of the Church are unknown. Price, 25 cents per dozen, and $1 50 per hundred.

From the October 16, 1848 *Church Advocate*

168

April 1, 1836, Winebrenner was operator and one-quarter owner of a "Drug and Book Store" on Market Square in Harrisburg— the result of a settlement of his first wife's guardian's estate. As such, he dispensed not only Bibles, Baxter on "Conversion," and Fuller on "Backsliding," but also patent and often potent cures like Lorenzo Dow's Family Medicine, John Oak's Hysterical Medicine, and Swaim's Panacea. Many, if not most, of the patent medicines at this time included alcohol as a "solvent" and/or "preservative," a fact with which druggist Winebrenner undoubtedly was familiar. Indeed, some nineteenth century patent medicines contained up to 40% alcohol and were sold in saloons by the drink! [24]

For those acquainted with Winebrenner's activities on behalf of temperance, but unacquainted with nineteenth century medicine, his occasional inclusion of recipes for making wine from small fruits (generally currant, strawberry, and blackberry) in the pages of the *Church Advocate* is likely to come as something of a shock.[25] (The potential shock value is considerably higher when such recipes are found in issues of the *Advocate* which also lavish praise on the Sons of Temperance or blister those who defend the use of intoxicating beverages in any form.) But here again, Winebrenner was expressing his faith in the health-producing powers inherent in the judicious use of a little alcohol. For example, an editorial in the June 18, 1853 *Advocate* advised:

> As currants, in many places, will soon be ripe, we give the following receipts for making wines from them, believing that in cases of sickness they are very excellent.

Directions for manufacture included the addition of a quart of French brandy "to every fifteen gallons of the [currant] liquor"— suggesting frequent usage over the year ahead. "Black currant wine," Winebrenner offered in the same article, "is also excellent in cases of sickness, such as for disease of the bowels." He apparently favored elderberries, as well. In an 1858 letter to his wife, he instructs her to "get the boys to gather a good many elderburries [sic] and make a good supply of syrp [sic], and wine." [26]

His *Advocate* readers did not object to Winebrenner's wine recipes as far as we know, apparently recognizing his intent. However, his sometime Associate Editor, J. F. Weishampel, did feel that Winebrenner had gone a bit too far when a recipe for potato jelly in the May 15, 1853 *Advocate* (probably clipped from an exchange paper), suggested the use of sugar, nutmeg, and wine for flavoring. Weishampel objected in the *Advocate* for May 22:

I was considerably mortified upon reading in the last number of the Church Advocate, a recipe for making potato jelly in which wine is recommended to be used, to flavor it; and I was as much astonished that our staunch tee-total editor should have so far forgotten himself as to have it in the paper. Intoxicating liquors of all kinds should be totally proscribed in eating as well as drinking, except for medicine; and then they should be prescribed and used with utmost prudence. . . . All temperance women should refrain from using it and all other intoxicating liquors in cooking. Be total abstinents, ladies.

Winebrenner did not respond. Weishampel had served as Editor of the *Gospel Publisher* between April 1, 1840 and December 26, 1843, succeeding Winebrenner at the post. As Associate Editor of the *Advocate* (a job he irregularly held) he apparently was given freedom to express himself on anything and he usually did. Much more inclined toward controversy than Winebrenner, he was also more inclined toward extreme positions than was the Editor of the *Advocate*. Winebrenner and Weishampel frequently disagreed on issues, sometime in the same issue of the paper.[27] On the basis of their *Advocate* contributions, it appears that Weishampel may have considered Winebrenner a bit "soft" on certain temperance issues. Winebrenner probably considered Weishampel's objection to the use of wine as flavoring as another example of his Associate Editor's tendency to run to extremes. Certainly Winebrenner—who ran wine recipes in the *Advocate* and had his family making elderberry wine at home—would have some reservations about Weishampel's insistence that "intoxicating liquors of all kinds" used as medicine be "prescribed." But, for all that, there was mutual respect if not admiration between the two men.

In his speech of October, 1853, Winebrenner also indicated that he had "no controversy with any man or party" regarding the "manufacture and sale of liquor for . . . sacramental purposes" —which translates into the fact that Winebrenner did not want to make an issue out of the propriety of serving wine at Communion. The early nineteenth century temperance movement, with a few exceptions, agreed that sacramental wine was an issue for the churches to decide.[28] By the 1850's however, temperance forces generally were pursuing the line that the "fruit of the vine" served at the Last Supper was unfermented "pure wine," *i.e.*, grape juice. Therefore, to serve fermented and potentially intoxicating wine at a Communion Service was a "perversion" of the Lord's ordinance.[29] Nowhere that we know of does Winebrenner analyze the biblical exegesis involved. The fact that he was a minister, and almost certainly in his early years had served sacramental wine in his churches, may have influenced his position. Possibly, in the 1850's Winebrenner's "sacramental exception" was not overly popular in the Church of God itself. Weishampel, for example, allowed the medicinal use of intoxicating liquors as the only mitigation.

Winebrenner's credentials as a temperance reformer are clear enough. He struggled against "the crittur" from the early 1830's on. Both the *Gospel Publisher* and *Church Advocate* were temperance papers. In Dauphin County he entered the political arena for temperance candidates. As one of the "veteran laborers in the great and noble cause of Temperance," he attended the World's Temperance Convention in New York City in September of 1853. At its conclusion he visited the World's Fair at the famous Crystal Palace between 40th and 42nd Streets and 5th and 6th Avenues. Impressed by the Palace (". . . well worth a jaunt or voyage to New York to see.") and the technological displays (". . . a wonderful display of the wisdom, ingenuity and skill of man . . ."), Winebrenner was depressed by the gaudy side-shows which operated "in open day in sight of the police." Particularly obnoxious was "a notable, or notorious rum saloon "fitted up with every possible enticement to decoy the idle and the vicious." Among the enticements was "a very strong cheese" furnished gratis "to provoke the thirst of the loungers." [30]

But, in understanding Winebrenner as a temperance reformer, it should also be remembered that he was given to somewhat more moderate views than many of his contemporaries, especially in later years. He maintained his opinion on the importance of moral suasion even in the midst of the prohibitory law drive in the 1850's. He would not contest the use of wine at Communion when it was becoming popular to do so. His estimation of the value of alcohol for medicinal purposes was probably higher than many of his contemporaries, like J. F. Weishampel. A firm believer in abstinence as an ideal, Winebrenner was nonetheless willing to compromise if he felt the compromise were in the direction of progress. Thus, while Pennsylvania's anti-saloon bill of 1855 was not a prohibitory liquor law, it was for Winebrenner, "all things considered" a "great victory," and the closest thing to prohibition as "public sentiment would sanction." [31] Maybe next year, after a little more persuasion, public sentiment would sanction something more. Until then—one step at a time. Within the Church of God itself he exercised caution in promoting his teetotal position. In his "History of the Church of God" in *He Pasa Ekklesia. An Original History of the Religious Denominations . . . in the*

United States, first printed in 1844, he presented the Church of God's temperance position as follows:

> She [the Church of God] believes that the manufacture, traffic and use of ardent spirits as a beverage or common drink, is injurious and immoral, and ought to be abandoned.[32]

This was written years after Winebrenner had adopted a total abstinence platform. Yet, almost certainly reflecting the fact that he recognized that his position was not necessarily that of the entire church, he mentioned only "ardent spirits" (rather than "all intoxicating beverages," which would include wine, beer, and cider) as "injurious and immoral." In fact, the Church of God was moving rapidly toward the teetotal position advocated by Winebrenner. At the 1845 General Eldership, it was resolved, "That we consider the traffic in intoxicating liquors as a drink, always sinful and demoralizing . . ."

Conjecture there must always be. However the evidence seems to suggest that for all of his enthusiastic support of the temperance crusade, Winebrenner's concept of "practical" reform, his native intelligence, and his pastoral interests combined to keep him from absolutizing his temperance (or ecclesiastical, or antislavery, or pacifistic) position. So, in his "Our Position on Slavery Re-Defined" in the *Church Advocate* for January 1, 1851, Winebrenner included intemperance as one of the "great evils" along with slavery. Yet, in the same article he could argue also that there might be "mitigating circumstances" which would allow the rum-seller, along with the sectarian and warrior, "to exercise of Christian toleration and forbearance."

Tobacco

Finally, a discussion of Winebrenner's relationship to temperance reform is not complete without at least a passing mention of nineteenth century attempts to reform America's use of the "noxious weed"—tobacco.

Tobacco culture was particularly important in the development of the border states, especially Virginia ("a colony founded on smoke") and John Winebrenner's own Maryland. In the days of the South's pre-cotton economy, the spread of tobacco determined the extent of agricultural growth patterns and slavery. Its usage by Americans was taken for granted from the colonial period on. Clergymen in Virginia often received their wages in tobacco. One of the New World's gifts to the Old, as early as the sixteenth century tobacco was regarded as a certain cure for every ailment man was heir to, including worms and toothaches. William Byrd II, planter, entrepreneur, and diary writer extraordinary, early in the eighteenth century suggested tobacco to counteract the plague.[33] By Winebrenner's time its medicinal value was not touted, but snuffs, chews, cigars and pipes abounded. Its use was a national pastime. Dolley Madison took snuff. Mrs. Andrew Jackson smoked a corncob pipe. Tobacco juice was spit everywhere—on streets and sidewalks by policemen on their beat, on the rugs of luxury hotels by wealthy guests, on the floors of Congress by congressmen who frequently missed their spittoon, and in churches by clergymen.

Frequently, although not inevitably, nineteenth century temperance reformers were also anti-tobacco. Even though he was born and raised in a tobacco state and lived the rest of his life near tobacco producing areas of Pennsylvania, Winebrenner was an anti-tobacco man. In the first issue of the *Gospel Publisher*, June 5, 1835, he included a bold-face memo on "Smoking":

That tobacco may kill insects on shrubs, and that one stench may overpower another is possible enough; but that thousands and tens of thousands die of diseases of the lungs and generally brought on by tobacco smoking, is a fact as well known as any in the whole history of disease.

Moreover, not only was it responsible for physical deterioration, but in the June 12, 1835 *Publisher*, under the heading "Insanity Caused by Tobacco" Winebrenner reported the following testimony of a physician who linked the "weed" to mental illness:

F. W. G. was put under my care in a state of insanity, caused entirely by the free use of tobacco. He was deprived of this stimulous and gradually regained his health; but some time after he incautiously returned to the use of tobacco again, and again became my patient. —From the polished gentleman of refined manners, and the utmost propriety of conduct, he had become profane, obscene, furious, and transformed into a savage, armed with a deadly weapon. Again he was interdicted the use of tobacco; and his reason was restored, he was again a perfect gentleman, and has continued so for many years.

If the danger to physical or mental health was not sufficient to make the user reform his ways, Winebrenner included articles intended to provoke disgust with the habit. Consider the following item from the *Publisher* of August 26, 1836, which also subtly suggested that the tobacco quid might have the effect of diminishing the love light in a fair young damsel's eyes:

Allow that a young man, who is a confirmed tobacco chewer, may live 25 years. In each day there will issue from his mouth half a pint of fluid too nauseously disgusting to describe. In 25 years this will amount to 550 gallons, or more than four hogsheads of this detested mass. In the same time, allowing him only two ounces a day, he will roll as a sweet morsal under his tongue half a ton of this hateful weed, which will sicken a dog or kill a horse; forming a heap of the size of a hay stack. . . . Now if such a young man could see 10 half hogsheads full of an abominable filth . . . a wagon load of tobacco and ten wheelbarrows heaped up with quids destined for an equally ultimate association with his lips, how would the prospect affect him? And if the delicate young lady, who is to be the partner of his life, could see the same, how enviable would be her emotion?

And if our hypothetical young man lived 50 years . . .

Then there was the economic argument. In May of 1855, Winebrenner visited the Newbury and Goldsborough Churches in York County, Pennsylvania, in order to assist with a protracted meeting. Noting that both churches, located in a tobacco area, needed to be enlarged, he suggested a way.

The annual expenditures for that useless and nauseous weed, tobacco, would more than accomplish the object in each place. This startling fact we gathered from the statements of several brethren in said places, who are well booked up in the tobacco trade. A good deal over $2000 worth of tobacco is consumed by the people of these villages and the surrounding neighborhood annually. Strange to say, it is used by almost every body; men, women and children.

Now if they would all quit the use of tobacco for one year, they would save enough to build two spacious and handsome Bethels—one in each place—and have enough left to pay the preacher's salary.[34]

We have no record of how Winebrenner's suggestion was received. We suspect, however, that giving up tobacco for any purpose whatsoever would have been considered a Draconian measure by a majority of Church of God males in the pre-Civil War period.

The fact of the matter was that, unlike the prevailing attitude toward alcohol, the use of tobacco was widespread in the Church of God on the part of ministers and laymen. In an article entitled, "Ministerial Tobacco-Users" in the *Church Advocate* for March 15, 1855, Winebrenner's son-in-law, James Colder, lamented:

The habit [tobacco] here condemned is fearfully prevalent among the ministers connected with the Church of God. Many carry their abomination with them around the circuits and use it in their stations—it accompanies them in their pastoral visits—goes with them to camp-meetings—is a sweet morsel during revivals, and seems indispensable to "liberty" in the pulpit.

Colder was frequently given to hyperbole, but there is reason enough to suspect that the use of tobacco was general among Church of God ministers in Winebrenner's lifetime. In the 1840's the Mt. Joy Church in Pennsylvania had a card on the back of its pulpit informing those preaching from that spot: "No spitting of tobacco juice from this pulpit." Nor were the laymen far behind the ministers. On the front page of the December 20, 1855, *Advocate* Winebrenner included a "Tobacco Memorial" which the ladies of the Wooster Church in Ohio had presented for approval to the Ohio Eldership that year:

> We . . . humbly petition your honorable body to take an action relative to the using of tobacco; the use of which creates so much filth in our Bethels and around our fire-sides, and consequently imposes on us so much unnecessary labor and cleaning after the same. Besides which, we believe it to be a nuisance and an idol that can be dispensed with without any real harm to those who use it, but rather to their health and benefit, and would certainly add greatly to their cleanliness.

Winebrenner was happy to say that the "memorial" was "favorably entertained and approbated" by the Ohio Eldership, an indication perhaps that changes were in the wind.

Changing America's tobacco habits was not Winebrenner's chief reforming concern. He tended to regard it as a form of intemperance, and used many of the same arguments against it that he used against alcohol. Still, he seemed to grant that whatever the arguments against its use, tobacco was not as dangerous as alcohol. The Church of God as a whole respected Winebrenner's beliefs in the matter, but with few exceptions apparently were not inclined to change their tobacco habits on account of their Harrisburg reformer. Still, on occasion, Winebrenner noted a glimmer of hope. On the front page of the June 7, 1855 *Advocate*, he included a note from brother R. T. McDowell of Shelbyville, Illinois:

> I save from my tobacco money more than enough to pay for all my periodicals. . . . Once I loved the "weed," dearly: it was my idol.—I rolled it, as a sweet morsel under my tongue. Now I am entirely saved from the love of it. Your paper has been a great service to me and my family. Your brother, R. T. McDowell.

A letter like that, even if infrequent, probably made it all worthwhile!

9. Everything of a business nature must be written separate and apart from other matters.

EDITORIAL DEPARTMENT.

NATIONAL FAIR.—A meeting has been called in Washington, to make arrangements to hold a National Fair.

THE CHOLERA.—Our Western papers bring us accounts of the spread of the Cholera in that portion of the country. At the quarantine at St. Louis, the disease had assumed a more malignant type than has ever before come under the observation of the medical faculty of that place.

Changes in Camp-meetings.

THE Camp-meeting at Eberly's, near Kritzer's, in Cumberland county, is recalled, on account of insufficient encouragement. Shame! on old mother Cumberland!

The Lancaster County Camp, for various good reasons, is removed to Mount Joy. See notices.

Cure for Scarlet Fever.

WE published in the Advocate, some time ago, a statement that the rubbing of all parts of the body, three times a day, with fat bacon, as soon as the scarlet fever disclosed itself, was a sure remedy for that disease. It has been tried in numerous instances with uniform success. The remedy is simple, and can do no harm; we therefore recommend its trial.

Church Advocate, August 1, 1851

9

Later Years

From the organization of the first eldership in 1830 to his death in 1860, Winebrenner generally was regarded as the Church of God's most knowledgeable and influential leader. However, in the glimpses we get of him after 1830, he in no way fits the traditional image of the ecclesiastical autocrat. The impression received from the files of the *Gospel Publisher* and *Church Advocate* is that while in matters theological he usually carried the church along with him, his more activistic, reform-oriented approach to "secular" matters like slavery was not always shared by a majority of the church. However, as noted in Chapter 6, the only time his leadership role in the church was seriously questioned was during the last few years of his life in the course of his dispute with James Colder over the slavery issue. Even here he emerged from the dispute with the respect, if not the full approval, of the Church of God.

It is difficult to generalize here, but in his later years especially, Winebrenner appears to have adopted and promoted a "moderate" approach to reform. He remained opposed to sectarianism, slavery, war, and rum; but, in opposition to a growing number in the Church of God, he would not categorically claim that an upholder of any of these four evils was not a converted Christian. The roots of his moderation undoubtedly extended into the past (especially would this be true of the slavery issue), but also it became increasingly obvious toward the end of his life that he was deeply concerned about holding together the first and greatest of his reforming interests, the Church of God. A polarity was developing in the Church of God over the slavery issue. Division was possible. The best approach, he felt, was one of caution and moderation. So his message became "Mittel mass die beste Strass." [1]

Winebrenner's reforming zeal was not restricted to the struggle against sectarianism, slavery, war, and rum. Other causes received his attention, although not on as intense a level. In the late 1830's, Winebrenner was for a while interested in homoeopathy and Thomsonianism as reforms of the then prevailing system of medicine.[2] More extensive was his interest in educational reform. He supported the *American Lyceum,* a movement built around educational self-improvement, in the *Gospel Publisher.* Both the *Publisher* and *Advocate* promoted the cause of public education, particularly in Pennsylvania. In 1849 Winebrenner regarded Massachusetts, with its "popular" education, reform schools, institution for "idiots," and state system for the education of the deaf, dumb, and blind, as a "pattern state," concluding that "she is from thirty to fifty years ahead of the age. Following her example, let us all endeavor to progress."[3]

Winebrenner was a staunch advocate of biblical revisions. He spoke and wrote in both English and German, used Greek and Latin on occasion, and probably was acquainted with Hebrew. Capable thus of comparing the English text to other translations as well as to the biblical languages (at least Greek), Winebrenner found the English Bible itself in need of reform. In the *Advocate* for July 5, 1855, under "Progress of Revision," he suggested that "friends of pure versions" would be "gratified to learn that the Bible Union is making rapid progress in the great work of revising the English Scriptures. . . ."

In the early *Gospel Publishers* especially, Winebrenner frequently strikes a reforming "Christian Union" chord. Thus, in the *Publisher* for October 14, 1836, he explained that:

> The disunion of the Christian Church is not to be perpetual. We are certain, that a period is hastening on when its divisions shall be healed, when its boundaries shall be enlarged, and when 'the name of Jehovah shall be one throughout all the earth.'

Editor Winebrenner, of course, saw the Church of God as the primary reform agency for effecting such a union. It was in the Church of God after all, that

> . . . the long lost Apostolic platform was revived and reasserted. Here the primitive character and polity, and the whole faith and practice of the Church of God, as set forth in the Scriptures, were avowed and vindicated.[4]

It is difficult to overemphasize Winebrenner's devotion to democracy and freedom of speech. They were hallmarks of a reformed, enlightened society, and essential to the work of a reformer. In his *A Brief View of the Formation, Government, and Discipline of the Church of God,* he asserted that "to a republican as well as to a Christian the rights of conscience and the liberty of speech and of the press, are precious and unalienable privileges." [5] Winebrenner could see some dangers, of course. "These privileges, however, ought not to be perverted from their proper uses, and made the occasions of strife, controversy and war." Winebrenner added that he was opposed to controversies, ". . . because there is generally more loss than gain by it—and because there is often more religion in not contending, than there is in that about which men contend." Perhaps this was a lesson learned in the course of his controversy with the German Reformed Church.

Submission to the government—to the will of the people—was integral to Winebrenner's reforming beliefs. Where the people took positions disliked by Winebrenner, he looked to elections, education, time, and Providence to bring them around to Winebrenner's stance. However, he did allow for civil disobedience in situations where the government was following a "manifestly unscriptural" course. In the fourth chapter of his *A Brief View . . . of the Church of God,* he wrote:

> The duty of subjection to them that are without, when clothed with magisterial authority, can, however, only remain a duty so long as they rule in the fear of God, or according to his laws. For whenever they abuse their power, by commanding things contrary to God's law, disobedience rather than obedience, becomes a duty.

That the matter was not wholly academic, is illustrated by the favorable attitude exhibited in the *Church Advocate* with regard to the "underground railroad" and various attempts in the 1850's to disobey the Fugitive Slave Law in the North.

After 1830, Winebrenner was most often a "preacher-at-large" or "general missionary" for the Church of God. He was stationed at the Harrisburg and Middletown churches in 1832, and again in 1840. In 1841 he was at Lancaster, and in 1846 at Lisburn in Cumberland County. Apparently he preferred not to serve a regular charge. This left him free to engage in general church work, frequently, but not always, related to the development of the Church of God. He was active, especially in his earlier years after the separation from the Reformed Church, in organizing, promoting, and preaching at protracted and camp meetings in Church of God areas in Maryland and eastern Pennsylvania. However his effectiveness, particularly while preaching

Gen. Joseph Markle was appointed messenger to carry the returns to Washington.

Notice to Debtors.

Those brethren and agents who know themselves to be indebted to us, for subscriptions for the Advocate, or on account of books, will oblige us much, by making remittances immediately. We stand in need of funds, and hope our debtors will relieve us.

The Cholera.

A ship from Havre arrived in New York last week, with this disease on board. Several cases have since occurred at the quarantine hospital on Staten Island, a majority of which terminated fatally. One case is reported in the city. A vessel from Bremen, has also introduced it into New Orleans.

New Subscribers.

Will not our friends make a little effort in behalf of the Church Advocate just now?— We should like to add a few hundred new subscribers to our list, to commence with the New Year.

Congress.

On monday, the 4th instant, Congress met

Church Advocate, December 15, 1848

180

in German, was such that his services were sought after as far away as Iowa. He was instrumental in the formation of the Ohio Eldership in 1836, and the General Eldership (comprising the East Pennsylvania [originally the General Eldership], West Pennsylvania, and Ohio Elderships) in 1845, being elected Speaker of both assemblies.

Without a settled charge for most of his life after 1830, and with a family to support, finances were a source of constant concern. Thrown on his own resources, Winebrenner became a writer and publisher. He is perhaps best known for his contributions to, and his extensive revisions and publishing of I. D. Rupp's *He Pasa Ekklesia. An Original History of the Religious Denominations at Present Existing in the United States.*[6] Winebrenner's revised editions of this work enjoyed a brisk sale and appeared from the late 1840's into the 1850's. His *A Brief View of the Formation, Government and Discipline of the Church of God* in 1829 became more or less the theological rationale for the existence of the Church of God. It was printed in German as well as in English. However, inasmuch as just a year after its first printing in English Winebrenner moved from a strictly congregational to a presbyterial polity, the book could not be considered wholly authoritative. It was widely read and appreciated by the membership of the Church of God, but with due reservation. Winebrenner reprinted it in 1847.

In 1831 he published in German a pocket New Testament.[7] By the time of his death his *Reference and pronouncing Testament . . . with a Short Dictionary and Gazetteer* was in its seventh stereotype edition.[8] Winebrenner's later approach to baptism, the Lord's Supper, feet-washing, regeneration, Christian union, and a number of other topics were contained in his *Doctrinal and Practical Sermons,* published in 1860 shortly before his death. The book was actually a compilation of sermons delivered over the years. Most, if not all, were contained in a magazine, *The Monthly Preacher,* which he issued for several months in 1859.[9] Among the other books and pamphlets which he wrote or published,[10] we would judge that his *A Prayer Meeting and Revival Hymn Book* first printed in 1825 was by far the most popular.[11] It had gone through some twenty editions in one form or another by 1860.

Another writing and publishing venture was the *Gospel Publisher.* Intended to be the periodical of and for the Church of God, the four page paper was nonetheless almost entirely in Winebrenner's hands. As he made clear to his readers, Winebrenner did not care particularly for editorial duties and was pleased to dis-

u Burritt's | spirit of that man appears before the mansions
ost any of | of the blest, the guardian angel will reject it,
is Scenery | saying—" go away, go away ! what business
te volume | have you here.—*Phil. Nat. Gaz.*

ournal.

es!

s a prac-
have been
seems to
ministers
ough the
ecially of
. We as
l alive to
general.
time and
cupied in
d printed
what has
ended to,
oid long
, as they
success

—an un-
nd pray-
ess to be
e other.
hat such
ber and
uch are
preach-
site, and
r the at-

Advertizements in Winebrenner's *Gospel Publisher and Journal of Useful
Knowledge.* Thursday, September 5, 1839.

pose of the *Publisher* to John F. Weishampel in 1840.[12] With scarcely more than 500 paid-up subscribers, the paper never was a financial success. It tottered on the edge of extinction for a number of years before finally succumbing in 1845. The *Church Advocate*, which replaced the *Publisher* in 1846, was largely the creation of Winebrenner who was convinced of the necessity of a church paper. Once again he became a reluctant editor. Although the *Advocate* formally was published by the "Publishing Committee" of the East Pennsylvania Eldership, for all practical purposes Winebrenner owned the paper. He was expected to finance the *Advocate* and make up any losses which might occur while the paper was under his editorship. Losses there were, especially in the earlier years of the periodical. We are left with the impression that, all in all, the *Church Advocate* was one of Winebrenner's unintentionally charitable enterprises. Although a growing list of subscribers brought with it black ink instead of red, in 1857, "weary of the toils and perplexities of editorial life," Winebrenner sold the paper and its good will to his son-in-law, James Colder.[13]

Winebrenner had other business enterprises to occupy his time. Between 1833 and 1836, he was one-quarter owner and operator of an apothecary and book store in Harrisburg. This came about as the result of an informal settlement of his wife's former guardian's estate. The store also served as the editorial office of the *Publisher*. Winebrenner never revealed how he actually felt about dispensing the "Mineral Horse Powder," "J. Weller's Vegetable Rheumatic Compound and Indian Panacea," or "John Oak's Hysterical Medicine" which he advertised in the early issues of the *Publisher*. But, for the remainder of his life, he maintained an interest in drugs and medicine. For years afterward he was an agent for Lorenzo ("Crazy") Dow's medicinal syrup, advertising its virtues in both the *Publisher* and the *Advocate*. On his travels he not only sold the Dow formula, but also gave smallpox vaccinations to his friends.[14]

Winebrenner seems to have done reasonably well in the drug business. This was not true of his experiments in silk culture. In the late 1830's and early 1840's, Winebrenner and the whole eastern United States, as we have seen,[15] became convinced that fortunes were to be made in sericulture through the cultivation of the fast growing *morus multicaulis*. Fortunes were made, but only by those who got in and out of the attendant speculation early. Winebrenner, chosen the recording secretary of the Pennsylvania Silk Society at its inaugural meeting in 1839, did not.[16] Church of God writers have said next to nothing about the affair, but apparently Winebrenner lost his house and horses when the silk culture bubble burst.

Winebrenner's interest in silk was actually but a part of a broader interest in agriculture. His home in Harrisburg, with several attached lots, had a farm-like atmosphere of self-sufficiency about it. In addition to the usual extensive garden, he kept cows, raised fruit, and experimented with items like silk worms, sugar beets, and new varieties of corn. Both the *Publisher* and *Advocate* from time to time carry advertisements for his "choice fruit trees," "splendid peaches," or "ripe cherries." In 1856, his patented "harrow and clod cutter" won third prize at the Pennsylvania State Agricultural Society Exhibition. Some idea of Winebrenner the farmer, preacher, small-time entrepreneur, and family man comes through in the following letter from Lancaster, Pennsylvania, to his wife, dated June 1, 1841:

Dear Wife:

I drop you this note to say that we arrived here on Satterday [*sic*] evening in health and Safety, and found the brethren in good spirits and prosperity.

I preached on Satterday evening, and sabbath three times, in the morning, afternoon and at night. Last night, I preached in the country. This afternoon we have a Baptizeing [*sic*]— Some 5 or 6 are to be baptized.

As the wether [*sic*] has got cooler, you will please to tell Ellen to make some fire in the [silk worm] Cocoonery, night and morning, so as to keep up the temperature to 70 and upwards.

Tell the boys to clean the peach trees and to hoe the corn, likewise the Garden and early potatoes, and to go on with the cleaning of the Trees as fast as possible. If the Trees were not ploughed, nor the Sugar beet patch tell Lorenzo [a Negro servant?] to see to have it done immediately. Tell him also to keep up the fences, so that the cows don't get into the Lots.

On Monday next, God willing, I expect to return home. I requested Bro. Ford to get and send me 2 qt. bottles of Lorenzo Dow's Medicine . . . Tell Emma to be good and I will bring her a knife and fork. Tell Ellen if she can sell any books and collect [$] 1.53 from Frankans, the plasterer, she may buy her dress. Tell Mary Jane to be good and help to feed the [silk] worms, and I will bring her something.

Yours affectionately,

John Winebrenner [17]

His wife must have been of the understanding sort.

184

"...be good and help to feed the worms."

Both as churchman and reformer, John Winebrenner was a traveling man. The *Advocate* and his letters to his wife told of trips to Baltimore and Washington on publishing business; to New York to attend a temperance meeting; and to the "far west" to preach, sell books and drugs, visit with friends and relatives, and simply to satisfy his curiosity about his expanding country. He kept a close record of his longer trips, as he did of his finances in general. Winebrenner summed up his trip west in 1850, in the January 1, 1851 *Advocate,* by reference to the following statistics:

> We were absent from home four months and eight days; during which time we travelled about 2500 miles, preached 124 sermons, passed through six states [Pennsylvania, Ohio, Indiana, Illinois, Iowa, and Michigan], and 217 cities and towns.

> Our travelling expenses amounted to $92.65, and our receipts, in the shape of collections, etc., to $120.75—so that by the time we sell off our team, we shall probably be about whole, having, temporally, neither loss nor gain, except that of wear and tear.

Visiting Chicago toward the end of June in 1850, he offered an encouraging evaluation of the city:

> The city of Chicago is a great business place. The lumber bought and sold there annually, amounts to 70 or 80 millions of feet. . . . It is likewise a great place for mechanical business— for machine shops and factories. The city is rapidly improving, and contains at present about thirty thousand inhabitants. Some of the streets are beautifully planked. . . . The Chicago and Galena railroad is finished and in operation as far as Elgin, a distance of forty-two miles.[18]

Winebrenner's biggest concern with Chicago was the "cold, heartless and formal" church services. Part of the problem was the fashion in the churches he attended on Sunday, June 30—the First Presbyterian in the morning, the Baptist in the afternoon, and the Methodist in the evening—to "sing standing, and pray sitting."

To sit down while at prayer he considered "both unreasonable and unscriptural." [19]

Winebrenner's first wife, Charlotte, had died on May 20, 1834. According to Forney, of the six children born to this marriage, four died in childhood.[20] Two daughters, Ellen C. (Colder) and Mary Jane (Cassell) reached maturity. On November 2, 1837, Winebrenner married Mary Hamilton Mitchell of Harrisburg. To this union were born Emma Charlotte (Christman), John Abner, Albert Mitchell, and Marshall Hamilton. The second Mrs. Winebrenner died May 22, 1888. None of Winebrenner's sons entered the ministry and there is some indication that they were none too comfortable with their father's religious views. The only child about whom we know more than the barest details is Winebrenner's oldest daughter, Ellen. Not long after her marriage in 1850 to James Kirkwood Colder, the Colders left for the recently opened Chinese mission field under Methodist sponsorship. When they returned to America in 1854 Mr. Colder joined the Church of God, having expressed doubts about episcopal polity and having been baptized by immersion while yet in China.[21] As we have seen, Winebrenner and Colder were estranged by the time of Ellen's death in 1858. Colder's followers later joined him in forming the First Free Will Baptist Church in Harrisburg.[22]

Winebrenner, after a "lingering illness," died on September 12, 1860. He seemed to have suffered some severe financial reverses in the last couple years of his life, and was almost destitute at his death. The *Advocate*—now edited by a long-time friend of Winebrenner's, E. H. Thomas—in late 1859 and 1860 began to carry numerous urgent appeals for money, "donation visits," and payments of old debts to Winebrenner. This tragedy was compounded by the fact that his funeral had to be held in the Harrisburg Methodist Church. In September of 1860 the Church of God in Harrisburg was still in the possession of James Colder and his followers. A year earlier they had locked Winebrenner out of the church, thus completing for him a very bitter cycle.

There is something symbolic about John Winebrenner's death in 1860. By that year the America Winebrenner had known also was expiring. The country was on the eve of the Civil War, and the pleasant optimism of the first half of the nineteenth century was evaporating as the states chose Mars. With the Harrisburg Church situation on his mind, among Winebrenner's last words were: "Tell the brethren to stay together." Good advice; but it was too late for either his church or his country.

The Churches of God in North America (the name was changed from "Church of God" in 1896) is John Winebrenner's most obvious bequest of reform to the twentieth century. Still occasionally known as "Winebrennerian" to distinguish it from other Churches of God, the church accepts most of Winebrenner's teachings with regard to the nature of the church and its ordinances. Of the church's 35,000 or so members, about half are located in Pennsylvania and about nine-tenths east of the Mississippi. Findlay College and Winebrenner Theological Seminary in Findlay, Ohio, are its educational institutions. Presently, the Churches of God support educational and medical missions programs in India, Bangladesh, and Haiti.

A somewhat less obvious, but nonetheless real, legacy of Winebrenner is the Church of God with headquarters in Anderson, Indiana. Its membership is slightly over 200,000. The Anderson Church of God is the result of a "schismatic" or "reform" movement in the late 1870's led by D. S. Warner, a pastor in the Ohio Eldership of the Church of God. Whatever other factors may have been involved, Warner's acceptance of "holiness" doctrines was the theological rationale given for his final separation from the "Winebrennerians." However, Warner perpetuated Winebrenner's general views of the church and its ordinances. The obvious similarities between the Churches of God in North America and the Church of God, Anderson, based upon their common acceptance of Winebrenner's teachings, have been recognized and reinforced in the course of "flowing together" talks between the two groups.

Winebrenner's other reforming interests have elicited a variety of responses on the part of the Churches of God and American society in general.

The antislavery struggle was concluded in the very way Winebrenner had feared it would be, through a civil war. His pleas for public schools and educational reforms were answered in Pennsylvania prior to the end of the nineteenth century. Medicine has changed drastically since Winebrenner's concern for its reform in the 1830's. His suggested relationship between smoking and lung diseases of which "thousands and tens of thousands die" has been confirmed.

The temperance crusade has had a checkered career from Winebrenner's time to the present. Within the Churches of God the official position long has been one of "total abstinence" from all alcoholic beverages. In using Winebrenner to support its position, however, the church has tended to read into him a little more rigidity than actually was there. As noted, Winebrenner occasionally ran recipes for making wine in the *Advocate* and made it himself at home. His efforts in behalf of temperance were directed primarily against the "rum sellers," or "hard liquor" men.

Winebrenner's tentative sentiments in the direction of pacifism have not found a home in the Churches of God or, generally, in America. Yahn, in his *History of the Churches of God*, could write in 1926 that the people in the Churches of God "have never taken the position of 'non-resistants' or 'conscientious objectors.' They have always done their part in the spirit of heroism." [23] There is no recognition here of Winebrenner's conviction that "between the spirit of war and the spirit of Christianity there is an utter incompatibility." [24] But then, allowing Winebrenner to have the final optimistic words on the matter,

> To take the world is no easy matter. The work of reform is a work of time. Old forms and opinions though wrong, most men are loath to part with.[25]

10

A Postscript

Julia Ward Howe was a nineteenth century author and reformer, perhaps best known to history as writer of the lyrics to the Civil War's "Battle Hymn of the Republic." In the Spring of 1870, during the course of her travels, she stopped off at Harrisburg. Her evaluation of the experience for the periodical, *Old and New,* included some negative comments about both the town and one of its more illustrious, though deceased (about 10 years), citizens, John Winebrenner.

The *New York Standard* for Wednesday, June 29, 1870, reported Mrs. Howe's comments and came to the rescue of Harrisburg and Winebrenner in a lengthy article. The *Standard's* article was in turn commented upon by the *Harrisburg Daily Topic* for Thursday, June 30. Both articles are here reproduced, without comment.

From the *New York Standard,* June 29, 1870:

The Winebrennerians

Mrs. Julia Ward Howe has been to Harrisburg, Pa., in her character of clergywoman, and as that city is "old in geography" but "new in reform," she writes out her notes of travel and prints them "between the blue" of Old and New. Having a call to "come over to Macedonia," she had excellent opportunities to study a people unknown to New England reformers, but she seems not to have studied them, for she tells us nothing about them, and blunders sadly in what she attempts to tell.

The idea that Harrisburg is new in reform took possession of her mind, and made her neither a profitable teacher nor a profound observer. The only point upon which she touched that gave promise of any information in regard to the social and religious life of the Pennsylvanians was in a slight reference to a new sect calling themselves, "for modesty," The Church of God, but which she calls the Winne-brunians. Harrisburg, old in geography but new in reform, will smile, and the clergywoman, if she goes back again, will be an object of interest because of her wonderful orthography. Clergywomen ought know how to spell. A slight knowledge of ecclesiastical history would not hurt even a New England clergywoman. John Winebrenner was no obscure preacher, and the sect which takes its name from him—Winebrennerians—is not so new as that which Theodore Parker founded. In many things, among them a fervent eloquence, John Winebrenner was not inferior even to the great apostle of Boston Reform. But their work was performed among different peoples. Parker and his admirers had a certain kind of culture; they had skill in composition as well as platform eloquence; they had access to the newspapers; they made themselves felt in many ways. Winebrenner and his disciples, on the other hand, cared little for these things. Theodore Parker and John Winebrenner were anti-podes in religious thought. The one sought an ideal excellence in this life; the other looked for it beyond the grave. The one addressed a chosen few in historic halls; the other spoke to the multitude in the woods. The one was inspired by a poetic, the other by a religious fervor. Both were great in their way, but Winebrenner was not the smaller of the two heroes.

John Winebrenner was educated for the ministry in the German Reformed Church. He was a man of great zeal. His longings after a spiritual life has something in them that impelled him as Bunyan and Wesley were impelled before him. He left the church in which he had been ordained, but continued to preach, though without any design of founding a new denomination. Other preachers joined hands with him and an organization, now numbering 25,000 souls, were gradually formed. At first his own immediate followers were called Winebrennerians, while those who listened to the preaching of "Father" Mackey, his earliest and most successful associate, took the name of Mackeyites. When numbers gave them strength, they chose as a name "The Church of God," as the most scriptural designation for a church. Their distinctive tenets are few, and are comprised in what they esteem the three sacraments: 1, baptism by immersion; 2, the Lord's Supper; 3, feet-washing. They differ in nothing essential from the New England Baptists, whose organ, the Morning Star, is among the best known religious journals in the country. Indeed, we believe that, except in the practice of washing each other's feet, which they find inculcated in the scriptures a matter of duty to be performed as a mark of humility, there is no difference between them; and nearly twenty years ago Winebrenner went to Providence to a yearly meeting held in that city to assist in perfecting a bond of Christian Union. The project failed only because they clung tenaciously to the name which Mrs. Howe says was chosen "for modesty," but which came from a deeper motive—their sincere belief that it alone was a fitting title for a body of Christians.

Mrs. Howe is not well informed on a subject of which she presumes to write. Harrisburg is "new in reform" only in her imagination. The people of that city think as seriously on all the important questions of the day as the people of Boston. Ideas may differ and conclusions may diverge, but the same purpose animates the hearts of all. But there can be no reform without knowledge. A physician cannot cure who is ignorant of the disease of his patient. Neither can a clergywoman convert unless she knows something about those whom she would lead. When Mrs. Howe is next asked "to come over to Macedonia," we hope she will go believing there are Greeks even among the Macedonians.

From the *Harrisburg Daily Topic*, June 30, 1870:

John Winebrenner

The New York *Standard*, of yesterday, pays a handsome compliment to the memory of the late Rev. John Winebrenner, a divine and a gentleman so well and so long known in this community. We copy what the *Standard* says, that we may join our own respect and admiration for the illustrious dead whose remains now rest amid the scenes and the people he loved so well while he lived. Only a year ago the members of the Church of God, ordered to be erected at the grave of this great leader, in the Harrisburg Cemetery, a fitting monument, expressive as much of their love, as it is designed to aid in perpetuating grateful thoughts of one who labored so long and so disinterestedly in the service of his God and for the benefit of mankind. Mr. Winebrenner is compared by the *Standard* to the late Theodore Parker. In intellectual power there may be a comparison made which cannot fail to reflect the great merit on the former; but in all other respects, alike in Christian attributes, heart culture, amiable, long suffering and sublime humility, there are few divines living or dead who can be compared to John Winebrenner. With intellectual powers of the most magnificent force, with a cultivation wonderful in its varied attainments, he was yet nothing more than the humble Christian, the bearer of His Master's cross and the faithful messenger of His gospel. For practical uses, he made himself acquainted with all the sciences. He understood the theory of our Government better than nine-tenths of those who administered it in his day; he knew keenly how to discriminate between politics and statesmanship; but never permitted himself to be drawn into a closer connection with such affairs than what was meant by simply rendering unto Caesar the things which are Caesars. As we have already written, outside of his labors as a pastor, Mr. Winebrenner indulged in no fancies—he suffered from no mental frivolities, and could never be allured by abstractions. Fact—truth—practical result—were the purposes on and for which he labored. If he did not succeed in all that he attempted, it was not owing to any defect in his plan of action, to the right of his purpose, or to the clear logic of his views—but simply because the time for his success had not arrived. In many things which he failed in doing, others took up where he left off, and followed his line of policy to success. Hence we may safely assert that Mr. Winebrenner was called into original paths of action too soon for the people among whom he moved. Had he lived to the present no name on the American pulpit could have shone with more splendor than his. He was best fitted to deal with the judgment of the people. He knew little of passion, and cared less for art. To ponder and feel the form of truth—to cultivate it, joint forms and breathe into life and action ever commanded all his powers. Some day the life of John Winebrenner will be written, after which his name will have its just place among the great servants of Christ who blessed the world by their labors and now live in glory with their Master.

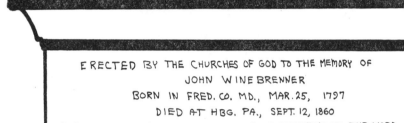

ERECTED BY THE CHURCHES OF GOD TO THE MEMORY OF
JOHN WINEBRENNER
BORN IN FRED. CO. MD., MAR. 25, 1797
DIED AT HBG. PA., SEPT. 12, 1860
A SUCCESSFUL REFORMER AND ABLE MINISTER OF THE WORD,
EARNEST AND SIGNALLY BLEST IN HIS EFFORTS TO SAVE HIS FELLOW
MEN AND BUILD UP THE CHURCH OF GOD, SHE HAVING ONE NAME, ONE
FAITH, ONE BAPTISM, AND ONE MISSION, VIZ. TO GATHER TOGETHER
IN ONE ALL THE CHILDREN OF GOD THAT ARE SCATTERED ABROAD.
HE HAS PERPETUATED HIS OWN MEMORY, NOT ON TABLETS OF STONE
BUT ON FLESHLY TABLETS OF THE HEART.

WINEBRENNER

NOTES

Chapter 1. THE SETTING

1. (Harrisburg, Pa.: Montgomery and Dexter, 1829).

2. *The Writings of Thomas Jefferson, Vol. III,* Ed. Albert Ellery Bergh (Washington, D. C.: The Thomas Jefferson Memorial Association, 1907), p. 383.

3. *Vol. VI* (Washington, D. C.: Langtree and O'Sullivan, 1839), p. 427.

4. Letter: John Adams to Thomas Jefferson, November 15, 1813, *The Writings of Thomas Jefferson, Vol. XIV,* p. 6.

5. (Princeton, New Jersey: D. Van Nostrand, 1960), pp. 7-8. [© 1960 by Henry Steele Commager. Reprinted by permission of Van Nostrand Reinhold Company.]

6. *Vide* Sidney Mead, "Denominationalism," *Church History, XXIII* (December, 1954), pp. 291-320.

7. Pp. ii-iii, *A Brief View . . . of the Church of God.*

8. P. iii.

9. Pp. iv-v.

Chapter 2. EARLY YEARS

1. A good introduction to early German immigration patterns in the United States is found in Albert Bernhardt Faust, *The German Element in the United States* (New York: The Steuben Society of America, 1927).

2. *Ibid.,* p. 170.

3. For general information regarding Winebrenner's life, *cf.*: John Winebrenner, "Experience of J. Winebrenner, V. D. M.," in *The Testimony of a Hundred Witnesses: or, The Instrumentalities, by which Sinners Are Brought to Embrace the Religion of Jesus Christ,* Comp. Elder J. F. Weishampel, Sr. (Baltimore: John F. Weishampel, Jr., 1858), pp. 29-32; Dr. George Ross, *Biography of Elder John Winebrenner—Semi-Centennial Sketch* (Harrisburg, Pa.: George Ross, 1880), pp. 1-22; and C. H. Forney, *History of the Churches of God in the United States of North America* (Harrisburg, Pa.: Publishing House of the Churches of God, 1914), pp. 3 ff. Some new material covering Winebrenner's earlier years is found in James H. Booser, "A Youth Advancing—John Winebrenner," *Church Advocate* (Harrisburg, Pa.), March 1968, pp. 32-33.

Genealogical material is found in Arthur G. Gibbony, "Winebrenner Genealogy" (Mimeographed: Library of Winebrenner Theological Seminary, 1942), pp. 5, Ph 1, Ph 32. Also, our thanks to Mary Winebrenner of Hastings, Michigan, who has supplied more recent information incorporated in this chapter.
We have record of only five of the six Philip and Eve (Eva) Winebrenner children: Catherine (b. ?), Jacob (b. 1790), Mary (b. 1792), John (1797), and Christian (b. 1799).

4. Ross, p. 3, states that German was spoken in the Philip Winebrenner home. Forney, p. 6, claims that the language spoken was English. According to Mrs. Emma Christman, Winebrenner's daughter, "My uncle [probably Uncle Christian] tole [*sic*] me German was not spoken at home. Tho [*sic*] his parents could talk it among themselves. The conclusion is, father got all his German by hard study. . . . ." Unpublished letter, Christman to S. G. Yahn [Editor of *Church Advocate*], March 30, 1925 (Library of Winebrenner Theological Seminary).

5. *Vide* unpublished letter, Samuel Helffenstein, Jr., to Winebrenner, September 5, 1822 (Library of Winebrenner Theological Seminary).

6. Winebrenner, "Experience of J. Winebrenner, V. D. M.," p. 29.

7. *Ibid.,* p. 31.

8. *Ibid.*

9. *Catalogue of the Union Philosophical Society of Dickinson College, Pennsylvania* . . . (Carlisle, Pa.: Elliott's Book and Job Office, 1867). *Vide* also Booser.

10. For general information on the period when Winebrenner was at Dickinson, *vide:* James Henry Morgan, *Dickinson College, The History of One Hundred and Fifty Years, 1783-1933* (Carlisle, Pa.: Dickinson College, 1933), pp. 180-206; *Early Dickinsoniana—The Boyd Lee Spahr Lectures in Americana, 1957-1961* (Carlisle, Pa.: The Library of Dickinson College, 1961), pp. 167-211; and Whitfield J. Bell, Jr., "Thomas Cooper as Professor of Chemistry at Dickinson College, 1811-1815," *Journal of the History of Medicine and Allied Sciences, VIII* (Reprint: n.d.), 70-87.

11. Morgan, p. 184.

12. *Ibid.,* p. 187 and Bell, p. 72.

13. Prof. James I. Good, *History of the Reformed Church in the U. S. in the Nineteenth Century* (New York: Board of Publication of the Reformed Church in America, 1911), p. 19.

14. Quoted *ibid.*

15. *Ibid.,* p. 10.

16. S. G. Yahn, *History of the Churches of God* (Harrisburg, Pa.: Central Publishing House, 1926), p. 23.

17. Winebrenner, "Experience of J. Winebrenner, V. D. M.," pp. 29-30.

18. Cf. Charles E. Schaeffer, "The Helffenstein Family" (Typescript: Library of Lancaster Theological Seminary, 1955).

19. (Philadelphia: James Kay, Jun., and Brother).

20. Cf. James Hastings Nichols, *Romanticism in American Theology* (Chicago: University of Chicago Press, 1961), p. 45.

21. Nichols, *ibid.,* represents Helffenstein, Sr., as maintaining "the older orthodoxy" in the American German Reformed theological spectrum of the time.

22. P. 362.

23. Cf. Nichols, pp. 47, 87, 93, 94.

24. This is somewhat surprising in the light of Finney's extended services at Helffenstein's church in 1828, and the "new measure" inclinations of at least two of Helffenstein's sons, Albert and (especially) Jacob. Cf. Schaeffer. Possibly, by 1842, Helffenstein had "toned down" earlier views on the nature of revivalism.

25. George W. Richards, *History of the Theological Seminary of the Reformed Church in the United States 1825-1934: Evangelical and Reformed Church 1934-1952* (Lancaster, Pa.: Rudisill and Company, Inc., 1952), pp. 102-104.

26. In the Library of Winebrenner Theological Seminary.

27. From a Race Street Church record on file at The Historical Society of Pennsylvania, Philadelphia.

28. E.g., unpublished letter, J[acob] Helffenstein to Winebrenner, August 29, 1823 (Library of Winebrenner Theological Seminary). Jacob tells Winebrenner that he could not get his father's permission to visit him. However, he reminds Winebrenner in closing that he, Jacob, is "still" his "sincere friend and Brother in Christ."

29. *Supra*, p. 10.

30. The dates for the Rev. Frederick Rahauser, Winebrenner's predecessor at Harrisburg, are given as April 3, 1816 to April 5, 1819 in J. N. LeVan, *Anniversary Brochure: A Brief History of the Salem Reformed Church, Harrisburg, Pennsylvania—Compiled On the Occasion of the Sesqui-Centennial Observance, October Third to Tenth, Nineteen Hundred And Thirty Seven* (n.p., n.d.). The pamphlet is located in *Reformed Church Records—Dauphin County* (Library of Lancaster Theological Seminary).

31. Ross, pp. 5-6. *Vide* also, unpublished letter of Harrisburg Church Vestry to the 1820 Synod of the German Reformed Church at Hagerstown, Maryland (Library of Lancaster Theological Seminary).

32. *Verhandlungen der General-Synode der Hochdeutschen Reformirten Kirche in den Vereinigten Staaten von Nord-Amerika, Gehalten in Hagersstadt, Maryland, September, 1820* (Hagersstadt: Johann Gruber, 1820), p. 12.

Chapter 3. THE NEW MEASURES

1. Harrisburg or Dauphin County newspapers consulted were *The Chronicle, the Pennsylvania Intelligencer,* and the *Oracle of Dauphin County.* They are available at the Pennsylvania State Library at Harrisburg.

2. Unpublished journal (Library of Winebrenner Theological Seminary).

3. E.g., *Oracle of Dauphin County,* November 18, 1820; December 2, 1820; and September 13, 1823.

4. Unpublished endorsement letter, December 10 and December 23, 1821 (Library of Winebrenner Theological Seminary).

5. (Harrisburg, Pa.: John S. Wiestling, 1822). The only copy I have been able to find is at Lancaster Theological Seminary, Lancaster, Pennsylvania. It is an imperfect copy, having only thirty-two pages. According to Forney's bibliography, p. 913, the original had forty-seven pages.

6. *Supra*, p. 16.

7. Winebrenner, *A Compendium*, p. [3].

8. (Harrisburg, Pa.: Michael W. McKinley). This thirty-six page pamphlet, probably written in March of 1824, is mentioned by neither German Reformed or Churches of God writers. Ross seems to have been familiar with at least a part of it. Forney, who uses Ross, does not indicate an independent knowledge of the pamphlet.
Winebrenner gives as his reason for writing, to "prevent any further mischief, and to counteract as far as possible, the prejudicial effects that may have been produced by means of misrepresentations." *The Truth Made Known* gives every evidence of being hurriedly written. Several of its dates are in error.

9. *Ibid.*, p. 5.

10. *Vide* H. M. J. Klein, *The History of the Eastern Synod of the Reformed Church in the United States* (Lancaster, Pa.: The Eastern Synod, 1943), pp. 40-41. Winebrenner apparently was referring to this or a similar statute.

11. Winebrenner, *The Truth Made Known*, p. 5.

12. *Ibid.*

13. Ross, p. 7. While Ross follows *The Truth Made Known* up to a point, he adds considerable information not found in Winebrenner's account. One of Ross's primary sources is a letter from Daniel Markley to C. H. Forney [editor] in the *Church Advocate,* September 4, 1872. Elder Markley was a personal acquaintance of Winebrenner's during the period of the latter's dispute with the Harrisburg Reformed Church.

14. Winebrenner, *The Truth Made Known,* p. 10.

15. *Oracle of Dauphin County,* April 7, 1821, and November 17, 1821.

16. *The Truth Made Known,* p. 14.

17. *Ibid.*

18. *Ibid.,* pp. 15-16.

19. *Ibid.,* p. 17.

20. *Ibid.,* p. 18.

21. *Ibid.,* pp. 18-19.

22. Unpublished Winebrenner journal, October 8-31, 1822 (Library of Winebrenner Theological Seminary). Whether the journal continued beyond the thirty-first, when the newlyweds are visiting Winebrenner's parents in Maryland, is unknown.

23. Unpublished letter, John Elliott to Winebrenner, January 14, 1823 (Library of Winebrenner Theological Seminary).

24. Winebrenner, in *The Truth Made Known,* p. 21, gives the date as March 31. However, March 31 fell on a Sunday in 1822, not in 1823. Several wrong dates in *The Truth Made Known* suggest Winebrenner may have had before him a calendar for the wrong year. That March 23 was the correct date can be confirmed by reference to an unpublished letter, Jonas Shartle to Winebrenner, April 21, 1823 (Library of Winebrenner Theological Seminary). *Vide* also Ross, p. 10.

25. Cf. Shartle; *The Truth Made Known,* p. 13; and Ross, p. 10.

26. Cf. Winebrenner, *The Truth Made Known,* pp. 22-25; Ross, pp. 10-13; and Markley. Ross's account and Winebrenner's *The Truth Made Known,* do not always agree on details, although there is a general consensus concerning the direction of events.

27. This meeting with the vestry and the results of the meeting are from Markley, and are later used by Ross, p. 10. Although not mentioned by Winebrenner, Markley's account of the meeting fits in well with Winebrenner's account in *The Truth Made Known* and, in fact, adds to its coherence.
Contemporary newspapers consulted did not deal with the conflict.

28. The locking of the church door is not in *The Truth Made Known.* The first detailed account I could find of the lockout was in Markley (i.e., in 1872, about fifty years after the fact), although passing mention of it is made, independently, by Elder J. Myers in the *Church Advocate,* August 21, 1872. Myers, then a physician, was a parishioner of Winebrenner's while the latter was still with the Reformed Church. Later he became a minister in the Church of God. Neither Markley's or Myers' remembrance of the lockout is challenged, even though there were several people living in 1872 who had some personal recollection of the events surrounding Winebrenner's dismissal.
Disagreements between pastor and church at that time were likely to be settled by a locked door policy. *Vide* Samuel Helffenstein's experience, *supra,* pp. 14-15. Apparently Winebrenner also was locked out of two of his rural charges, Salem and Wenrick's. Cf. Myers, and Markley.

29. Only in Winebrenner, *The Truth Made Known,* pp. 26-28.

30. *Ibid.*, p. 32. The petition is in the Library of Winebrenner Theological Seminary. Winebrenner claims 136 signatures. We count only 134.

31. Pp. 32-33.

32. *Verhandlungen der General Synode der Hochdeutschen Reformirten Kirche in den Vereinigten Staaten von Nord-Amerika Gehalten zu Harrisburg, vom 30sten Sept. bis zum 4ten Oct. 1822* (n.p., n.d.), p. 31.

33. *Supra*, p. 24.

34. *Verhandlungen der Synode der Hochdeutsch Reformirten Kirche in den Vereinigten Staaten von Nord-Amerika, Gehalten zu Baltimore vom 29st September bis zum 4ten October, A. D. 1823* (Easton: Heinrich Held, 1824), p. 22.

35. *Ibid.*

36. *Ibid.*, p. 23.

37. Winebrenner, *The Truth Made Known*, p. 33.

38. For the in-fighting connected with Albert Helffenstein's appointment by the vestry, *vide ibid.*, pp. 21-22.

39. *Vide* unpublished letter, Samuel Helffenstein to Winebrenner, April 30, 1823 (Library of Winebrenner Theological Seminary). Winebrenner's response to the letter is unknown.

40. *Verhandlungen der Allgemeinen Synode der Hochdeutschen Reformirten Kirche in den Vereinigten Staaten von Nord-Amerika Gehalten zu Bedford, in Pennsylvanien, vom 26sten September zu dem 1sten October 1824* (Baltimore: J. I. Hanzche, 1824), p. 11.

41. *Ibid.*, p. 28.

42. Unpublished letter, J. S. Ebaugh to Winebrenner, November 26, 1824; and unpublished letter, Lewis Mayer to Winebrenner, December 3, 1824 (both in Library of Winebrenner Theological Seminary). Both Ebaugh and Mayer are friends of Winebrenner's. Their letters show considerable division in the Synod over the Harrisburg Church affair. Mayer's letter indicates, in addition, that Samuel Helffenstein, Sr. advised the Harrisburg Church not to recognize the election which the Synod had ordered. Winebrenner and his teacher apparently had parted ways.

43. *Auszuege Aus Den Verhandlungen Der Lebanon Classis, 1820-1840* (Typewritten: Library of Lancaster Theological Seminary), p. 12. The synod was a representative body of the entire German Reformed Church. A Classis was made up of ministers and representative elders of a district within the Synod.

44. Good, *History of the Reformed Church in the U. S. in the Nineteenth Century*, p. 59. Good takes a dim view of Winebrenner's appeal to the Susquehanna Classis, suggesting it was merely an evasive tactic. However, it should be noted that the three other churches on Winebrenner's charge, which Winebrenner continued to serve throughout his difficulties with the Harrisburg vestry, and which originally had paid over half his salary, were still a part of the Susquehanna Classis up to the Synod of 1825. Appealing to the Susquehanna Classis would not have been exceptionable.

45. *Synodical Proceedings of the German Reformed Church in the United States of North America, Held at Philadelphia from the 25th to the 30th September, 1825—Translated from the German* (Philadelphia: John George Ritter, 1825), p. 8.

46. *Synodal-Verhandlungen der Hochdeutschen Reformirten Kirche in den Vereinigten Staaten von Nord-Amerika Gehalten in Friedrich City, vom 23sten bis zum 29sten September, A. D. 1826* (Philadelphia: Conrad Zentler, 1827), p. 7.

199

47. *The Proceedings of the Synod of the German Reformed Church in North America at York, Pa., September, 1827* (Hagerstown: Gruber and May, 1828), pp. 9, 11.

48. *Auszuege Aus Den Verhandlungen Der Lebanon Classis, 1820-1840*, pp. 21-22.

49. *Acts and Proceedings of the Synod of the German Reformed Church of the United States of North America, Held at Mifflinburg, Union County, Pennsylvania, September, 1828* (Chambersburg: Henry Ruby, 1828), p. 6.

50. P. 60.

51. P. 58. Cf., Rev. Theodore Appel, *The Beginnings of the Theological Seminary of the Reformed Church in the United States* (Philadelphia: Reformed Church Publication Board, 1886), pp. 39-42; and the anti-Winebrenner letter which appeared in the *Weekly Messenger* (Chambersburg, Pa.), November 15, 1843, signed by "L. S."

52. Richards, pp. 106-107.

53. P. 12.

54. P. 27.

55. "The Heidelberg Catechism," *Weekly Messenger*, August 10, 1842.

56. Quoted in Ross, p. 15.

57. Cf. Good, pp. 124-152; Paul Himmel Eller, *These Evangelical United Brethren* (Dayton: The Otterbein Press, 1950), pp. 21-48; and Prof. James I. Good, *History of the Reformed Church in the United States, 1725-1792* (Reading, Pa.: Daniel Miller, 1899), pp. 592-596.

58. Quoted in Ross, p. 4.

59. H. Harbaugh, *The Fathers of the German Reformed Church in Europe and America, Vol. III*, ed. Rev. D. Y. Heisler (Lancaster, Pa.: J. M. Westhaeffer, 1872), 148.

60. Richards, pp. 537-538, and letter, Mayer to Winebrenner, December 3, 1824.

61. Unpublished letter, J. G. Fritchey to Winebrenner, July 19, 1826 (Library of Winebrenner Theological Seminary).

62. Unpublished letter, Frederick Huber to Winebrenner, November 26, 1825 (Library of Winebrenner Theological Seminary).

63. *Supra*, pp. 21-31.

64. "Dr Beecher and Mr Beman's Convention on Revivals," *The Christian Examiner and Theological Review*, IV (July and August, 1827), p. 359.

65. For the entire report of the "New Lebanon Convention," *vide ibid.*, pp. 357-370.

66. Charles G. Finney, *Lectures on Revivals of Religion* (New York: Leavitt, Lord and Co., 1835), p. 242.

67. Reported in P. H. Fowler, *Historical Sketch of Presbyterianism Within the Bounds of the Synod of Central New York* (Utica, N.Y.: Curtiss and Childs, 1877), p. 275.

68. Unpublished diary in "A memorandum of Levi Merkel of Allen Township." Contained in "Levi Merkel Family Papers, 1818-1912" (Pennsylvania Historical and Museum Commission, Harrisburg, Pa.) We appreciate the assistance of Mr. Robert Crist, Camp Hill, Pa., who called this diary to our attention.

69. *Supra,* p. 23. This may help to explain note #28 for Chapter 2, where Jacob cannot get his father's permission to visit Winebrenner in Harrisburg.

70. *Vide* letter, Mayer to Winebrenner, December 3, 1824. Compare this to note #24 for Chapter 2.

Chapter 4. A NEW CHURCH

1. *Vide infra,* pp. 72-73 for further context.

2. *Gospel Publisher,* December 6, 1843.

3. Klein, p. 125; Richards, p. 101.

4. Richards, pp. 116-124.

5. *Supra,* p. 32.

6. Unpublished letter, Lewis Mayer to James R. Reily, December, 1825 (Library of Lancaster Theological Seminary).

7. Unpublished Letter, Philip Keller *et al* to Winebrenner, January 10, 1826 (Library of Winebrenner Theological Seminary).

8. Unpublished letter, James R. Reily to John Winebrenner, March 21, 1825, and unpublished letter, John Winebrenner to Hagerstown Reformed Church Consistory, April 18, 1825 (Both in Library of Winebrenner Theological Seminary).

9. Unpublished transcript of letter, John Winebrenner to Hagerstown Correspondence Committee, April 27, 1826 (Library of Winebrenner Theological Seminary). The transcript is on the reverse side of the Keller *et al* to Winebrenner letter of January 10, 1826.

10. Unpublished letter, March 18, 1826 (The Historical Society of Pennsylvania, Phila.). Winebrenner wrote Reily that he was "anxiously looking for some account . . . respecting our affairs in Amsterdam and Altenheim." Just what these affairs may have been in Amsterdam is unknown. Winebrenner's wife's father, Michael Reutter, had come from Altenheim.

11. *Ibid.*

12. From a page apparently torn out of a church record (Library of Winebrenner Theological Seminary).

13. *Harrisburg Chronicle,* May 7, 1827.

14. The letter (to one "Bro. Rein") is quoted in full in Rev. S. P. Spreng, *The Life and Labors of John Seybert, First Bishop of the Evangelical Association* (Cleveland: Evangelical Publishing House, 1888), pp. 97-98. Winebrenner and Seybert were friends until the former began to "promulgate some singular notions," *ibid.,* p. 99.

15. Forney, p. 16.

16. John Winebrenner, "History of the Church of God," in I. Daniel Rupp, *He Pasa Ekklesia. An Original History of the Religious Denominations at Present Existing in the United States* (Philadelphia: J. Y. Humphreys, 1844), pp. 173-174.

17. *Ibid.,* p. 172.

18. P. 35.

19. *A Brief View . . . of the Church of God,* p. 41.

20. *Ibid.*

21. Pp. 98-102.

22. "History of the Church of God," pp. 174-176.

23. H. A. Thompson, *Our Bishops: A Sketch of the Origin and Growth of the Church of the United Brethren* (Dayton: U. B. Publishing House, 1906), p. 231. Erb and Winebrenner often worked together.

24. Quoted in Forney, p. 43.

25. Winebrenner, "History of the Church of God," pp. 179-181.

26. Robert Baird, *Religion in America* (New York: Harper and Brothers, 1856), pp. 522-523.

27. Joseph Belcher, *The Religious Denominations in the United States* (Philadelphia: John E. Potter, 1865), p. 785.

28. T. J. V. Bracht, *Der Blutige Schau-Platz oder Martyrer Spiegel* [The Martyr's Mirror] (Ephrata, Pa.: Der Bruderschaft, 1748), pp. 19 ff., and 41 ff. It is a translation from the Dutch.

29. July 24, 1835.

30. Forney, p. 60.

31. In addition to brief references to Elliott in Churches of God sources and in several Lancaster County histories, the only mention of him serving a "Church of God" in Lancaster is in the entry for 1819 in the records of the "Lancaster Bible Society, 1815-1915," *Papers*, 19 (Lancaster, Pa.: Lancaster County Historical Society, 1915), p. 41.

32. Unpublished letter, Elliott to Winebrenner, January 14, 1823.

Chapter 5. THE WINEBRENNER - NEVIN CONTROVERSY

1. *Vide* Dr. Theodore Appel, *The Life and Work of Dr. John Williamson Nevin* (Philadelphia: Reformed Church Publication House, 1889), and Nichols.

2. Reprinted in *Gospel Publisher* (Harrisburg, Pa.), September 14, 1842 and October 18, 1843.

3. "Letter 1," *Gospel Publisher*, October 18, 1843.

4. Winebrenner remained on friendly terms with a number of ministers in the German Reformed Church after his separation from the church. Presumably they were members of the revivalistic "new measure" wing of the church which consistently opposed Nevin and the Mercersburg movement.

5. "Letter 2," *Gospel Publisher*, October 18, 1843.

6. Allowing for some hyperbole, this construction of the differences between the two men is justified by the later correspondence.

7. *Vide supra*, pp. 36-40.

8. "Letter 3," *Gospel Publisher*, November 1, 1843.

9. The letter first appeared as "Winebrenner's Vindication" in the *Weekly Messenger* for July 12, 1843, with an introduction by Nevin. The *Gospel Publisher* reprinted it, as it appeared in the *Messenger* (with Nevin's introduction), on August 9, 1843, with an introduction to Nevin's introduction and a post-script supplied by the editor of the *Publisher*, J. F. Weishampel. It was printed for this second time in the *Publisher*, on November 1, 1843, in order to maintain the continuity of the Winebrenner-Nevin correspondence.

10. Spelling is that of the *Gospel Publisher*. For the original quotation *vide supra*, p. 35.

11. The "similar" refers to Otterbein's United Brethren in Christ. *Weekly Messenger*, August 10, 1842.

12. *Vide* Arthur M. Schlesinger, Jr., *The Age of Jackson* (Boston: Little, Brown and Company, 1945), pp. 291-292.

13. For the complete statement, *vide supra*, p. 57.

14. Nevin was speaking of the situation in the German Reformed Church in the early nineteenth century. The quote was from his series on the Heidelberg Catechism in the *Weekly Messenger*, August 10, 1842.

15. "Letter 4," *Gospel Publisher*, November 1, 1843.

16. "Letter 5," *Gospel Publisher*, November 15, 1843.

17. This was not exactly what Nevin proposed. Winebrenner was obviously trying to extend the discussion into the columns of the *Messenger*. As noted earlier he did have friends in the German Reformed Church. Presumably he felt that these friends could be counted on to give him support against Nevin, who was new to the church. For Nevin's proposition, cf. his letter of October 17, 1842, *supra*, pp. 64-65.

18. From Nevin's point of view, of course, he understood all too well.

19. The "perhaps" is important here. In the correspondence up to this point Winebrenner seemed to feel that if Nevin only understood properly the measures employed by Winebrenner and the Church of God, the charge of fanaticism would be modified. Given Nevin's own negative evaluation of the German Reformed Church in the early nineteenth century, Winebrenner seemed to have assumed that he and Nevin were kindred spirits on most basic issues. Now Winebrenner was not too sure.

20. "Letter 6," *Gospel Publisher*, November 15, 1843.

21. "Letter 7," *ibid.*

22. "Letter 8," *Gospel Publisher*, November 29, 1843.

23. "Letter 9," *ibid.*

24. (Chambersburg, Pa.: n.p., 1843).

25. *Gospel Publisher*, December 6, 1843.

26. In fact, the *Anxious Bench* contains several references to Winebrenner and the Winebrennerians. *Vide* especially pp. 17, 37, 38, and 51.

27. It was written from Harrisburg, and printed in the *Gospel Publisher*, October 11, 1843.

28. Weishampel's actual words were: "The whole matter resolves itself into this. We believed such an intimation had been made to the Professor, but were not told so, in so many words. The fact was, however, that had terms not been acceded to by him, br. W. would have done it. So the only difference in the matter appears to be, that he did not threaten the Professor."

29. *Supra*, p. 41.

30. (New York: J. S. Taylor).

31. Nevin's developing theological position can be seen in a number of his major works published between 1843 and 1848. Cf. *The Anxious Bench; The Mystical Presence* (Philadelphia: J. B. Lippincott and Co., 1846); and *History and Genius of the Heidelberg Catechism* (Chambersburg, Pa.: Publication Office of the German Reformed Church, 1847) — especially Chapter X, "Church Spirit of the Catechism." His theological opinions are further defined by debate in the columns of the *Weekly Messenger* over subjects introduced by the above (and other) works.
  For the influence of Philip Schaff, who arrived in Mercersburg in 1844, upon Nevin *vide* Nichols, pp. 44 ff.

32. P. 6.

33. P. 46.

34. P. 45.

35. Pp. 48 ff.

36. P. 82.

37. The full title is: *History of all the Religious Denominations in the United States: containing authentic accounts of the rise, progress, faith and practice, localities and statistics, of the different persuasions: written expressly for the work, by fifty-three eminent authors belonging to the respective denominations. 2d Improved and Portrait Ed.* (Harrisburg, Pa.: John Winebrenner, 1848). This edition was a revision of the work first published in 1844 as *He Pasa Ekklesia* and edited by Israel Daniel Rupp. Rupp's "Introduction," but not his name, appeared in the second edition. (Winebrenner and Rupp had had some sort of disagreement, but the facts are unknown to me.) Winebrenner published a third (1854) and later editions.

In the second (Winebrenner's) edition, four articles were substituted for ones appearing in the first edition; eight new articles dealing with churches not included in the first edition were added; and several first edition articles were enlarged upon. Winebrenner also added a synopsis of several lesser known church groups primarily, but not exclusively, of German pietistic origin. Among the other filigree, the edition also included twenty-four portraits "of distinguished men of the different denominations."

38. "The Sect System," *Mercersburg Review, I* (Mercersburg, Pa.), 482-507, 521-539.

39. P. 64.

40. "The Sect System," p. 484.

41. Pp. 485-487.

42. P. 489.

43. P. 495.

44. P. 530.

45. P. 529.

46. Pp. 529-530.

47. "Puseyistic" refers to Edward Bouverie Pusey (1800-1882), English Tractarian or "High Church" leader. "Puseyism" was a charge frequently levelled at Nevin.

48. In like manner Winebrenner continued Nevin's commendation for another paragraph. For a comparison of the above with what Nevin actually said, cf. p. 75 *supra,* and "The Sect System," pp. 485-487.

49. It might also be called a display of questionable journalistic practice. In Winebrenner's behalf, it should be mentioned that earlier in the article he had given the source for his comments, *viz., The Mercersburg Review, I,* 482-507. Also, he had explicitly stated that he would "only notice what he [Nevin] has been pleased to say in commendation." However, whatever the mitigating factors, it remains true that in quoting Nevin as he did Winebrenner misrepresented Nevin to his own advantage.

50. The article, entitled "The Church of God," probably is reprinted from a Free Will Baptist publication. Williams has another item in the same article which directly relates to the controversy between Winebrenner and Nevin over the state of education in the Church of God: "Many of the preachers were characterized by a peculiar shrewdness, drawn rather from experience and insight into human nature, than from the discipline of books and profound study."

51. *Anxious Bench,* p. 55.

52. *Ibid.*

53. *Ibid.*, P. 56.

54. *Vide* Nichols, p. 56. This was while Winebrenner and Nevin were corresponding.

55. P. 17.

56. Pp. 37-38.

57. P. 50.

58. P. 51. For the correspondence from which this is quoted, *vide supra*, p. 62.

59. "History of the Church of God," *History of All the Religious Denominations*, p. 171.

60. *Ibid.*, p. 170.

61. *Ibid.*, p. 174.

62. "Terms of Church-membership," *Church Advocate,* June 2, 1851.

63. "History of the Church of God," *History of All the Religious Denominations,* p. 175.

64. "Christian Union," *Doctrinal and Practical Sermons* (Baltimore: John F. Weishampel, Jr., 1860), pp. 227-228.

65. "History of the Church of God," *History of All the Religious Denominations,* p. 172.

66. Recorded in Winebrenner's footnote to "Historical Letters No. 1" by J. Oren, *Church Advocate,* February 1, 1849.

67. "History of the Church of God," *History of All the Religious Denominations,* p. 172.

68. "Vindication of the Church, etc.," *Church Advocate,* October 16, 1848.

69. "Vindication of the Church or Review of Letters on Sectarianism— No. 8," *Church Advocate,* September 15, 1848.

70. "Regeneration, Or the New Birth," *Doctrinal and Practical Sermons,* p. 119.

71. P. 150. The quotation is from Isaac Watts, "The Rational Foundation of a Christian Church," *The Works of . . . Isaac Watts,* 5 [ed. Jennings and Doddridge] (London: John Barfield, 1810), 672.

72. *A Brief View . . . of the Church of God,* p. 152.

73. "The Lord's Supper," *Doctrinal and Practical Sermons,* p. 375.

74. *Supra,* pp. 73-74.

75. P. 4.

76. "Historical Development," *Mercersburg Review, I,* 514.

77. *The Mystical Presence,* p. 127. Although, as Nevin added, "it does not follow immediately from such a concession, that we are at liberty to despise or overlook their authority entirely . . ."

78. *Ibid.*, p. 5.

79. "Historical Development," p. 514.

80. "The Sect System," p. 526.

81. *Supra,* pp. 73-74.

82. "The Classis of Mercersburg," *Mercersburg Review, I,* 385-386. The article was signed simply "N" but was ascribed to Nevin by Theodore Appel, who was both a student and colleague of Nevin's. Appel, *The Life and Work of . . . Nevin,* p. 302.

83. "The Classis of Mercersburg," *Mercersburg Review, I,* 383-384.

84. *Anti-Christ,* p. 46.

85. *Ibid.,* p. 45.

86. *Ibid.*

87. *The Mystical Presence,* p. 148.

88. *Ibid.,* p. 149.

89. "The Sect System," p. 489.

Chapter 6. ANTISLAVERY

1. *J. S. Liber, 29,* 359-360 (Frederick County, Maryland, Courthouse). I am indebted to Mr. James Moss for his valuable research in this area.

2. *G. M. E. Liber, 2,* Folio 649 (Frederick County, Maryland, Courthouse). The will was probated December 27, 1841. Research into the number and length of service of the Winebrenner family slaves is complicated because of the burning of the Frederick County personal property tax records in an 1877 fire.

3. Dwight Lowell Dumond, *Antislavery* (New York: Norton Library, 1966), p. 49.

4. Charles Wagandt, *The Mighty Revolution: Negro Emancipation in Maryland, 1862-1864* (Baltimore: Johns Hopkins Press, 1964), pp. 8-9.

5. January 10, 1849. Quoted by Avery Craven, *The Coming of the Civil War,* 2d ed. revised (Chicago: University of Chicago Press, 1966), p. 303. (Copyright 1942, Charles Scribner's Sons. 2d ed. copyright 1957, Avery Craven.)

6. Quoted by Craven, *ibid.,* p. 406.

7. Louis Filler, *The Crusade Against Slavery, 1830-1860* (New York: Harper and Row, 1960), pp. 160-191.

8. James M. Wright, "The Free Negro in Maryland, 1634-1860," *Studies in History, Economics, and Public Law, XCVII,* No. 3 (New York: Columbia University, 1921), 85 ff.

9. Quoted by Bernard Steiner, *Life of Roger Brooke Taney* (Baltimore: Williams and Wilkins, 1922), p. 76.

10. Ms. in Library of Winebrenner Theological Seminary.

11. *Supra,* p. 20.

12. *Supra,* pp. 44-45.

13. *Gospel Publisher,* December 12, 1845.

14. Ms. in the Library of Winebrenner Theological Seminary.

15. Harn was defending the proposition which was a matter of prolonged debate during the East Pennsylvania Eldership of 1850, *viz.,* "that the bare relation of master to slave should not debar from Christian Fellowship in all cases." The report embodying these sentiments lost on the eldership floor by a nineteen to seventeen vote. In a losing cause, Winebrenner voted with Harn, favoring the proposition. *Church Advocate,* November 15, 1850.

16. *Gospel Publisher,* October 16, 1835.

17. *Gospel Publisher*, October 30, 1835.

18. *Fifth Report of the Executive Committee of the American Anti-Slavery Society* (New York: William S. Dorr, 1838) p. 146.

19. *Emancipator* (New York), February, 1836.

20. Dumond, pp. 184-185, lists Gould as one of the first six of Weld's "70." Although in the *Emancipator* for September 22, 1836, Gould calls himself the "Pennsylvania Agent" for the American Anti-Slavery Society, little seems to be known about him. The *Emancipator* files, in fact, contradict what Dumond says about Gould's whereabouts in the winter of 1835-1836.

21. *Gospel Publisher*, January 29, 1836.

22. *Ibid.*

23. Reprinted in the *Emancipator*, November 15, 1838 (Microfilm at State Historical Society of Wisconsin).

24. *Gospel Publisher*, January 20; February 3, 10; 1837.

25. "Anti-abolition Convention," *Gospel Publisher*, June 2, 1837.

26. Filler, p. 147; and Ralph Korngold, *Thaddeus Stevens* (New York: Harcourt, Brace and Co., 1955), p. 49.

27. *Gospel Publisher*, January 16, 1838.

28. *Gospel Publisher*, February 8, 1838.

29. Richard Nelson Current, *Old Thad Stevens* (Madison: University of Wisconsin Press, 1942), p. 43.

30. According to the *Emancipator* for December 1, 1836, Jonathan Blanchard, one of Weld's outstanding agents, was in Harrisburg by November 8, 1836. His "agency" expired in October, 1837 (*Emancipator*, November 9, 1837.)

31. January 29, 1836.

32. The "Declaration of Sentiments" and Constitution of the American Anti-Slavery Society are found in Charles Elliott, *History of the Great Secession from the Methodist Episcopal Church in the Year 1845* (Cincinnati: Swormstedt and Poe, 1855), pp. 851-858. The quotations are from this source. It was the general practice for affiliate societies, such as Harrisburg, to pattern their "Declarations" and Constitutions after those of the national office.

33. *Gospel Publisher*, June 2, 1837.

34. This is assuming, of course, that Winebrenner generally shared the sentiments of the Harrisburg Anti-Slavery Society. There is no reason to believe this is not the case, given his constant activity in a position of responsibility in the Society. Even if we were to assume that he was somewhat more outspoken than other abolitionists in Harrisburg in, for example, his rigid anticolonization stand, he still did not fit the general Garrisonian mold.

35. *Gospel Publisher*, February 8, 1838. Mackey's letter was almost certainly in response to one sent by Winebrenner urging Mackey to become more involved in the abolitionist movement. In addition to his ministerial duties in Shippensburg, Pennsylvania, he served for at least two terms in the Pennsylvania State Legislature.

36. *Emancipator*, January 26, 1837. Apparently the Union Bethel was the only church in Harrisburg at which Blanchard could speak. Later in life, Blanchard became the first president of Wheaton (Illinois) College.

37. *Gospel Publisher*, May 17, 1838; September 19, and October 24, 1839.

38. Cf. Dumond, pp. 350 ff.; and David Lee Child, *The Culture of the Beet* (Northampton, Mass.: J. H. Butler, 1840), pp. 138 ff. Child was an ardent abolitionist.

I have not found any evidence which would indicate that Winebrenner linked abolitionism with silk culture or with growing the sugar beet. It is true that he did experiment with both silk and sugar beets at a time when abolitionists were extolling the virtues of both as potential economic attacks upon the slavery system. Because of this coincidence I have suggested the possibility of a relationship. However it is equally true that nonabolitionists in the north as well as southern farmers were interested especially in the possibilities of silk raising as a profitable venture. The potential high profits in silk culture remained, for most who became involved in it, potential.

39. In 1839, 54 slaves on the schooner *Amistad* mutinied near Cuba and sailed into Long Island Sound. After a series of legal battles, piracy charges were quashed, and in 1841 the Supreme Court declared the slaves were in fact free.

40. *Gospel Publisher,* March 27, 1844.

41. *Journal of the First General Eldership of the "Church of God," in North America; Held at Pittsburg, Penn'a, from the 26th to the 30th of May, A. D., 1845* (Harrisburg, Pa.: Hickok and Cantine, 1845).

42. *Church Advocate,* January 1, 1847.

43. *Church Advocate,* April 15, 1850.

44. A letter with the same general theme, from lay preacher Henry Scherich to Winebrenner is found in the *Church Advocate* for January 1, 1847. They both indicate problems with slavery in the southwestern Pennsylvania-western Virginia area.

45. The Compromise of 1850 actually incorporated a series of congressional measures. Among other things the Compromise admitted California as a free state; established the boundaries of Texas, New Mexico and Utah; passed a rigid Fugitive Slave bill; and abolished the slave trade in the District of Columbia.

46. *Church Advocate,* October 15, 1850. Harn presented similar qualifications to the Free Will Baptists. They were treated with courtesy but not approbation. The Free Will Baptist Church had a reputation for extremism along antislavery lines.

47. *Church Advocate,* November 15, 1850. The Journal of the East Pennsylvania Eldership in which the debate and vote on Harn's report took place was in the *Advocate* for November 1, 1850.

48. For further details, *vide supra,* p. 97.

49. The letter was dated November 16, 1850. *Church Advocate,* December 2, 1850.

50. John Winebrenner, *Letter on Slavery with an Appendix Containing Various Rejected Articles Addressed to Elder James Colder, Editor of the Church Advocate* (Harrisburg, Pa.: n.p., n.d.). By 1859 Harn had become a strong antislavery advocate, his abolitionism being much more vocal than Winebrenner's during the latter's abolitionist period. Harn, by the way, did not deny the possibility of extenuating circumstances, but he noted, "I'll venture, there never was a case in any one of those congregations of Christ [churches of God], co-operating with the various elderships, whether in Maryland, Virginia, or Texas."

51. Portions of which were included in Winebrenner's editorial, "Our Position on Slavery Re-Defined" in the *Church Advocate,* January 1, 1851.

52. *Supra,* p. 101.

53. *Supra,* p. 110.

54. The question was a continuing source of concern to many denominations throughout the 1840's and 1850's. Cf., for example, W. D. Weatherford, *American Churches and the Negro* (Boston: The Christopher Publishing House, 1957), pp. 102, 182, 202, *et al.*

The United Brethren Church, located in many of the same areas as the Church of God, had similar problems. A comparison of the two churches is instructive. Cf. John Lawrence, *The History of the Church of the United Brethren in Christ, II* (Dayton: Sowers and King, 1861), p. 141; and Eller, pp. 71-72.

55. For a good illustration, *vide* James A. Thome, "Come-outism and Come-outers," *The Oberlin Quarterly Review, II* (1856), pp. 158-187. Thome was an abolitionist in the 1830's, participated in the Lane Seminary Debate, and was one of Weld's "70." Like Winebrenner, he was opposed to "come-outism."

Winebrenner had a high regard for Oberlin and President Finney. He visited Finney and Prof. Fairchild at Oberlin in the 1850's, and advised Church of God students preparing for the ministry to go to Oberlin. He frequently quoted from Oberlin publications in the *Advocate.*

56. E.g., unpublished letters, Winebrenner to Philip Winebrenner: May 23, 1834; April 4, 1835; November 18, 1835; February 4, 1839 (Library of Winebrenner Theological Seminary).

57. "Uncle Tom's Key," *Church Advocate,* June 18, 1853.

58. "Elihu Burrit's Abolition Scheme," July 3, 1856; "Lecture of H. W. Beecher," April 2, 1857.

59. "Questions and Answers," *Church Advocate,* December 27, 1855.

60. E.g., *Church Advocate,* February 15, 1849; May 22, 1852; March 5, 1853; and January 7, 1854.

61. E.g., the East Pennsylvania Eldership, *Church Advocate,* November 16, 1854.

62. Letter of Benjamin Ober to the Editor, *Church Advocate,* May 21, 1857.

63. E.g., the East Pennsylvania Eldership, *Church Advocate,* November 22, 1855.

64. Letter of S. Barnhart to the Editor, *Church Advocate,* August 1, 1849.

65. "The Greene County Church," *Church Advocate,* May 15, 1849.

66. Allan Nevins, *Ordeal of the Union: 1847-1852* (New York: Charles Scribner's Sons, 1947), p. 115. It was this Convention which Horace Greeley immortalized with his observation that after three days of tremendous achievement they had managed to crowd "a woman [Miss Brown] off the platform . . . gagging her . . . and . . . voting that she shall stay gagged." *N. Y. Tribune,* September 9, 1853 (quoted in Nevins).

67. Unpublished letter, Winebrenner to Mrs. Mary Winebrenner, September 8, 1853 (Library of Winebrenner Theological Seminary).

68. "The World's Temperance Convention," *Church Advocate,* September 17, 1853. The Weishampels, father and son, were printers, living most of the time in Baltimore (as far as I can determine). Weishampel, Sr. was something of an anti-Rome man. He was responsible for the pamphlet: *The Pope's Stratagem: "Rome to America!" An Address to the Protestants of the United States, against placing the Pope's block of Marble in the Washington Monument* (Philadelphia: 1852).

69. *Church Advocate,* March 11, 1854.

70. *Church Advocate,* June 15, 1854. This explication became known as "The 1854 Resolution on Slavery." While it was adopted unanimously, Winebrenner, among others, abstained from voting, presumably on the grounds that it did not allow for his "mitigating circumstances." Winebrenner, *Letter on Slavery,* p. 6.

Winebrenner was not altogether unpleased by the results of the 1854 Eldership. A month later he wrote his wife that "the acts and doings of that body are, so far as I know, very generally approved. Anties did not succeed in getting everything their own way. What a comfort it is that God rules in the councils of men!" Unpublished letter, Winebrenner to Mrs. M. H. Winebrenner, June 20, 1854 (Library of Winebrenner Theological Seminary). Winebrenner did not identify the "anties." They probably included the opponents of his position on slavery.

71. Letter of Benjamin Ober to the Editor, *Church Advocate,* April 10, 1901.

72. Letter of Enoch Marple to the Editor, *Church Advocate,* May 21, 1857.

73. Letters of Benjamin Ober to the Editor, *Church Advocate,* August 20 and October 22, 1857.

74. Letter of Benjamin Ober to the Editor, *Church Advocate,* April 10, 1901.

75. The resolution is contained in Winebrenner, *Letter on Slavery,* pp. 5-6. Interestingly enough, the resolution was not journalized and published with the minutes of the General Eldership. It did not appear in the *Church Advocate.* This is probably an indication of its general lack of support.

76. Colder mentioned the correspondence in his editorial review, "The General Eldership on Slavery," *Church Advocate,* June 11, 1857.

77. Unpublished letter, Winebrenner to Ober, August 23, 1857 (Library of Winebrenner Theological Seminary).

78. If we read Colder's innuendo rightly. *Church Advocate,* June 11, 1857.

79. From the General Eldership report on slavery, *ibid.*

80. *Supra,* pp. 125-126.

81. Winebrenner's letter to Colder appeared as "II. The Slavery Question," appended to Winebrenner's *Letter on Slavery,* pp. 23-27.

82. "The Slavery Question," *Church Advocate,* June 18, 1857.

83. Unpublished letter (Library of Winebrenner Theological Seminary).

84. October 22, and November 4, 1857.

85. *Church Advocate,* November 26, 1857.

86. *Church Advocate,* December 3, 1857.

87. *Ibid.*

88. Unpublished letter, E. H. Thomas to Winebrenner, December 21, 1857 (Library of Winebrenner Theological Seminary).

89. P. 5.

90. P. 6.

91. Pp. 6-7.

92. Pp. 11-12.

93. P. 13.

94. P. 15.

95. *Ibid.*

96. *Ibid.*

97. *Ibid.*

98. *Church Advocate,* October 21, 1858.

99. *Church Advocate,* December 2, 1858.

100. April 10, 1901.

101. *Church Advocate,* November 25, 1858.

102. *Church Advocate,* September 16, 1858. See p. 134.

103. *Church Advocate,* October 21, 1858.

104. *Church Advocate,* October 7, 1858.

105. Unpublished letters, Winebrenner to Mrs. M. H. Winebrenner August 27 and September 2, 1858 (Library of Winebrenner Theological Seminary.

106. Forney, p. 334.

107. P. 15.

108. *Vide supra,* p. 128.

109. Unpublished letter, Winebrenner to Mrs. M. H. Winebrenner, October 19, 1858 (Library of Winebrenner Theological Seminary).

110. *Supra,* p. 50.

111. The strength of Union sentiment in the slave state of Maryland is illustrated by comparative statistics in the 1860 presidential election. Breckinridge received 42,482 votes; Bell, 41,760; Douglas, 5,996; and Lincoln, 2,294. Although Breckinridge, the southern Democrat, carried the state, he received a minority of the total votes cast. Bell, Douglas, and Lincoln—all Union men—received 7,538 more votes than Breckinridge. Bell, the Constitutional-Union candidate, lacked but 723 of the votes necessary to carry the state.

Chapter 7. PEACE

1. Alice Felt Tyler, *Freedom's Ferment.* (New York: Harper and Row, 1962), p. 399.

2. *Ibid.,* pp. 400-415.

3. P. 179.

4. "The Battle of Buena Vista," *Church Advocate,* April 15, 1847.

Chapter 8. TEMPERANCE

1. *Autobiography of Peter Cartwright,* ed. W. P. Strickland (New York: Carlton and Porter, 1856), p. 212.

2. *Ibid.,* p. 213.

3. Cf. especially Daniel J. Boorstin, *The Americans—The Colonial Experience.* (New York: Random House, 1958), pp. 82, 91.

4. A good review of the "Temperance Crusade" is presented in Tyler, *Freedom's Ferment,* pp. 308-350.

5. P. 15.

6. *Vide* Chapter 4.

7. *Brief View of the . . . Church of God,* p. 97.

8. *Ibid.,* p. 119.

9. *Church Advocate,* October 1, 1853. Cf. Randall Bistline, "John Winebrenner and the Temperance Movement," *Church Advocate,* November, 1968. Mr. Bistline's research has been of considerable assistance.

10. This unpublished letter, and other materials related to the settlement of the Charlotte Reutter Winebrenner estate, are on file at Winebrenner Theological Seminary. I am deeply indebted to Mr. James Booser for his research in this area.

11. *Gospel Publisher,* November 20, 1835.

12. *Church Advocate,* September 21, 1854.

13. *Gospel Publisher,* November 13, 1835.

14. *Church Advocate,* May 1, 1846.

15. *Gospel Publisher,* September 23, 1836.

16. *Church Advocate,* March 19, 1857.

17. E.g., "Temperance Not a Sectarian Thing," *Gospel Publisher,* September 25, 1835; "License Laws," *Gospel Publisher,* December 11, 1835.

18. *Gospel Publisher,* April 22, 1836.

19. *Ibid.*

20. *Original Church Record—Mechanicsburg Church of God* (Library of Winebrenner Theological Seminary).

21. "Temperance Convention," *Church Advocate,* May 1, 1850.

22. *Church Advocate,* May 1, 1852, p. 2.

23. *Church Advocate,* October 1, 1853.

24. Cf. James Harvey Young, *The Toadstool Millionaires.* (Princeton, N. J.: Princeton University Press, 1961), pp. 68, 125-143.

25. Examples of wine recipes are found in the *Church Advocate* for June 18, 1853; June 25, 1853; July 30, 1853; and, August 2, 1855.

26. Unpublished letter, Winebrenner to Mary H. Winebrenner, August 27, 1858.

27. Cf., for example, *Church Advocate,* May 1, 1852, pp. 2 and 3, where Winebrenner and Weishampel comment on the recent defeat of a liquor law in the Pennsylvania House.

28. E.g., "The Report of the New York State Temperance Committee," *Gospel Publisher,* October 23, 1835.

29. E.g. "Sacramental Wine," *Church Advocate,* January 15, 1857.

30. *Church Advocate,* September 24, 1853.

31. *Supra,* p. 165.

32. P. 180.

33. Cf. Louis B. Wright, *The Cultural Life of the American Colonies* (New York: Harper and Row Torchbook, 1962), pp. 217, 223.

34. *Church Advocate,* May 31, 1855.

Chapter 9. LATER YEARS

1. *Supra,* p. 113.

2. E.g., "Constitution of the Academy of Homoeopathic Medicine," *Gospel Publisher,* January 20, 1837.

3. "Massachusetts, A Pattern State," *Church Advocate,* January 15, 1849.

4. *Church Advocate,* September 21, 1854.

5. P. vi.

6. *Vide supra,* Chapter 5, footnote #37.

7. *Das Neue Testament unsers Herrn und Heilandes Jesu Christi,* ubersezt von Dr. Martin Luther (Harrisburg, Pa.: J. Weinbrenner, 1831).

8. The full title is *Reference and Pronouncing Testament. The New Testament of Our Lord and Saviour Jesus Christ: in the Common Authorized English Version, According to the Standard of the American Bible Society; with a Copious and Judicious Selection of References, to Parallel and Illustrative Passages, Translated from the German and Interspersed with the Text; and a Classical Pronunciation of the Proper Names and Other Difficult Words; Together with a Short Dictionary and Gazetteer, of the New Testament,* seventh edition (Harrisburg, Pa.: J. Winebrenner, V.D.M., 1861).

9. (Baltimore: John F. Weishampel, Jr.).

10. For a partial bibliography of Winebrenner's works, *vide* Forney, p. 913.

11. The full title is *A Prayer Meeting and Revival Hymn Book, or a Selection of the Best "Psalms & Hymns & Spiritual Songs," from Various Authors, for the Use of Social Prayer Meetings, and Revivals of Religion* (Harrisburg, Pa.: J. & M. W. M'Kinley, 1825). Winebrenner relied heavily upon Watts. The hymn book was published while Winebrenner was still a member of the Reformed Church. However, it appears that the book was not popular in that church, even among his revivalistically inclined friends. *Vide* unpublished letter, Lewis Mayer to Winebrenner, December 3, 1824 (Library of Winebrenner Theological Seminary). Mayer, who had been asked to secure subcriptions, wrote to Winebrenner: "For your hymn book no subscriptions have been procured . . . and, dear brother, I tell you plainly, I do not affirm your object."

12. *Supra,* p. 107.

13. *Church Advocate,* April 23, 1857.

14. E.g., unpublished letter, Winebrenner to Mary H. Winebrenner, February 16, 1846 (Library of Winebrenner Theological Seminary). Winebrenner wrote his wife as follows: "I drop you a line or two to say that I shall not be home before Thursday or Friday next. They want preaching at so many places that I cannot get round before that time. . . . You will please save the vaccine virus from the children if the pock is full and the matter clear. I have vaccinated some twenty odd, since I left home."

15. *Supra,* pp. 105-106.

16. *Proceedings of the Pennsylvania Silk Convention Held at Harrisburg on the Twenty-Second and Twenty-Third Days of February, 1839* (Harrisburg, Pa.: E. Guyer, 1839), p. 33. Some indication of the importance attached to sericulture at the time is the fact that the above *Proceedings* were printed by order of the Pennsylvania State Senate.

17. Unpublished letter (Library of Winebrenner Theological Seminary). "The boys" referred to were not Winebrenner's sons. The only surviving son of his first marriage, John Reutter Winebrenner, had died in 1836 at the age of 10. The first son of the second marriage, John Abner Winebrenner, was not born until the year following this letter.

18. *Church Advocate,* August 1, 1850.

19. *Ibid.*

20. We have record of only three of the children who died: John Reutter, August 31, 1826-October 26, 1836; Louisa, September 30, 1833-September 20, 1834; and Harriet, born at an unknown date, died at 8 months. In a letter written to his second wife, Mary, in 1841, Winebrenner mentions two other children in the household, Hannah and Andrew. Sources available to us tend to suggest that these were not Winebrenner children.

21. *Vide* the chapter entitled "Mrs. Ellen C. Colder," *The Mission Cemetery and the Fallen Missionaries of Fuh Chau, China*, ed. Rev. I. W. Wiley (New York: Carlton and Porter, 1858), pp. 337-374.

22. *Supra,* p. 124.

23. P. 116.

24. *Supra,* p. 147.

25. *Supra,* p. 6.

Selected Bibliography

Books

Appel, Theodore. The Beginnings of the Theological Seminary of the Reformed Church in the United States. Philadelphia: Reformed Church Publication Board, 1886.

.... The Life and Work of Dr. John Williamson Nevin. Philadelphia: Reformed Church Publication House, 1889.

Baird, Robert. Religion in America. New York: Harper and Brothers, 1856.

Belcher, Joseph. The Religious Denominations in the United States. Philadelphia: John E. Potter, 1865.

[**Bergh, Albert Ellery (ed.)**]. The Writings of Thomas Jefferson, Vols. III and XIV. Washington, D. C.: The Thomas Jefferson Memorial Association, 1907.

Boorstin, Daniel. The Americans—The Colonial Experience. New York: Random House, 1958.

Bracht, T. J. V. Der Blutige Schau-Platz oder Martyrer Spiegel. Ephrata, Pa.: Der Bruderschaft, 1748.

Catalogue of the Union Philosophical Society of Dickinson College, Pennsylvania, Instituted August 31, 1789. Carlisle, Pa.: Elliott's Book and Job Office, 1867.

Child, David Lee. The Culture of the Beet. Northampton, Mass.: J. H. Butler, 1840.

Commager, Henry Steele. The Era of Reform, 1830-1860. Princeton, N. J.: D. Van Nostrand, 1960.

Craven, Avery. The Coming of the Civil War. 2d ed. revised. Chicago: University of Chicago Press, 1966. (Copyright 1942, Charles Scribner's Sons. 2d ed. copyright 1957, Avery Craven).

Current, Richard Nelson. Old Thad Stevens. Madison: University of Wisconsin Press, 1942.

Das Neue Testament unsers Herrn und Heilandes Jesu Christi. Ubersezt von Dr. Martin Luther. Harrisburg, Pa.: J. Weinbrenner, 1831.

Dumond, Dwight Lowell. Antislavery. New York: Norton Library, 1966.

Eller, Paul Himmel. These Evangelical United Brethren. Dayton: The Otterbein Press, 1950.

Elliott, Charles. History of the Great Secession from the Methodist Episcopal Church in the Year 1845. Cincinnati: Swormstedt and Poe, 1855.

Faust, Albert Bernhardt. The German Element in the United States. New York: The Steuben Society of America, 1927.

Fifth Report of the Executive Committee of the American Anti-Slavery Society. New York: William S. Dorr, 1838.

Filler, Louis. The Crusade Against Slavery, 1830-1860. New York: Harper and Row, 1960.

Finney, Charles G. Lectures on Revivals of Religion. New York: Leavitt, Lord and Co., 1835.

Forney, C. H. History of the Churches of God in the United States of North America. Harrisburg, Pa.: Publishing House of the Churches of God, 1914.

Fowler, P. H. Historical Sketch of Presbyterianism Within the Bounds of the Synod of Central New York. Utica, N. Y.: Curtiss and Childs, 1877.

Good, James I. History of the Reformed Church in the United States, 1725-1792. Reading, Pa.: Daniel Miller, 1899.

.... History of the Reformed Church in the U. S. in the Nineteenth Century. New York: Board of Publication of the Reformed Church in America, 1911.

Harbaugh, H. The Fathers of the German Reformed Church in Europe and America. Vol. III. Edited by D. Y. Heisler. Lancaster, Pa.: J. M. Westhaeffer, 1872.

Helffenstein, Samuel. The Doctrines of Divine Revelation as Taught in the Holy Scriptures—Exhibited, Illustrated, and Vindicated. Philadelphia: James Kay, Jun., and Brother, 1842.

Klein, H. M. J. The History of the Eastern Synod of the Reformed Church in the United States. Lancaster, Pa.: The Eastern Synod, 1943.

Korngold, Ralph. Thaddeus Stevens. New York: Harcourt, Brace and Co., 1955.

Lawrence, John. The History of the Church of the United Brethren in Christ. Vol. II. Dayton: Sowers and King, 1861.

LeVan, J. N. Anniversary Brochure: A Brief History of the Salem Reformed Church, Harrisburg, Pennsylvania—Compiled on the Occasion of the Sesqui-Centennial Observance, October Third to Tenth, Nineteen Hundred and Thirty Seven. n.p.: n.d. (Reformed Church Records—Dauphin County.) Library, Lancaster Theological Seminary.

Morgan, James Henry. Dickinson College, The History of One Hundred and Fifty Years, 1783-1933. Carlisle, Pa.: Dickinson College, 1933.

Nevin, John Williamson. Anti-Christ; Or the Spirit of Sect and Schism. New York: J. S. Taylor, 1848.

.... The Anxious Bench. Chambersburg, Pa.: n.p., 1843.

.... The History and Genius of the Heidelberg Catechism. Chambersburg, Pa.: Publication Office of the German Reformed Church, 1847.

.... The Mystical Presence. Philadelphia: J. B. Lippincott and Co., 1846.

Nevins, Allan. Ordeal of the Union: 1847-1852. New York: Charles Scribner's Sons, 1947.

Nichols, James Hastings. Romanticism in American Theology. Chicago: University of Chicago Press, 1961.

Papers, Vol. 19. Lancaster Bible Society, 1815-1915. Lancaster, Pa.: Lancaster County Historical Society, 1915.

Proceedings of the Pennsylvania Silk Convention Held at Harrisburg on the Twenty-Second and Twenty-Third Days of February, 1839. Harrisburg, Pa.: E. Guyer, 1839.

216

Reference and Pronouncing Testament. The New Testament of Our Lord and Saviour Jesus Christ: in the Common Authorized English Version, According to the Standard of the American Bible Society; with a Copious and Judicious Selection of References, to Parallel and Illustrative Passages, Translated from the German and Interspersed with the Text; and a Classical Pronunciation of the Proper Names and Other Difficult Words; Together with a Short Dictionary and Gazetteer, of the New Testament. 7th ed. Harrisburg, Pa.: J. Winebrenner, 1861.

Richards, George W. History of the Theological Seminary of the Reformed Church in the United States 1825-1934: Evangelical and Reformed Church 1934-1952. Lancaster, Pa.: Rudisill and Company, Inc., 1952.

Ross, George. Biography of Elder John Winebrenner—Semi-Centennial Sketch. Harrisburg, Pa.: George Ross, 1880.

Rupp, I. Daniel. He Pasa Ekklesia. An Original History of the Religious Denominations at Present Existing in the United States. Philadelphia: J. Y. Humphreys, 1844.

[Rupp, I. D. and Winebrenner, John]. History of all the Religious Denominations in the United States: containing authentic accounts of the rise, progress, faith and practice, localities and statistics, of the different persuasions: written expressly for the work, by fifty-three eminent authors belonging to the respective denominations. 2d Improved and Portrait ed. Harrisburg, Pa.: John Winebrenner, 1848.

Schlesinger, Arthur M., Jr. The Age of Jackson. Boston: Little, Brown and Company, 1945.

[Sellers, Charles Coleman (ed.)]. Early Dickinsoniana—The Boyd Lee Spahr Lectures in Americana, 1957-1961. Carlisle, Pa.: The Library of Dickinson College, 1961.

Spreng, S. P. The Life and Labors of John Seybert, First Bishop of the Evangelical Association. Cleveland: Evangelical Publishing House, 1888.

Steiner, Bernard. Life of Roger Brooke Taney. Baltimore: Williams and Wilkins, 1922.

[Strickland, W. P., (ed.)]. Autobiography of Peter Cartwright. New York: Carlton and Porter, 1856.

Thompson, H. A. Our Bishops: A Sketch of the Origin and Growth of the Church of the United Brethren. Dayton: U. B. Publishing House, 1906.

Tyler, Alice Felt. Freedom's Ferment. New York: Harper and Row, 1962.

Wagandt, Charles. The Mighty Revolution: Negro Emancipation in Maryland, 1862-1864. Baltimore: John Hopkins Press, 1964.

Watts, Isaac. The Works of Isaac Watts, Vol. 5 (ed. Jennings and Doddridge). London: John Barfield, 1810.

Weatherford, W. D. American Churches and the Negro. Boston: The Christopher Publishing House, 1957.

Weinberg, Albert. Manifest Destiny. Chicago: Quadrangle Books, 1963.

[Weishampel, J. F., Sr. (ed.)]. The Testimony of a Hundred Witnesses: or, the Instrumentalities by which Sinners Are Brought to Embrace the Religion of Jesus Christ. Baltimore: John F. Weishampel, Jr., 1858.

White, Leonard. The Jacksonians. New York: The Free Press, 1965.

[Wiley, I. W. (ed.)]. The Mission Cemetery and the Fallen Missionaries of Fuh Chau, China. New York: Carlton and Porter, 1858.

Winebrenner, John. A Brief View of the Formation, Government, and Discipline of the Church of God. Harrisburg, Pa.: Montgomery and Dexter, 1829.

.... A Compendium of the Heidelberg Catechism: or, Method of Instruction in the Christian Religion, as the Same Is Taught in the German Reformed Church and Schools in North America. Harrisburg, Pa.: John S. Wiestling, 1822.

.... Doctrinal and Practical Sermons. Baltimore: John F. Weishampel, Jr., 1860.

.... Letter on Slavery with an Appendix Containing Various Rejected Articles Addressed to Elder James Colder, Editor of the Church Advocate. Harrisburg, Pa.: n.p., n.d.

.... A Prayer Meeting and Revival Hymn Book, or a Selection of the Best "Psalms & Hymns & Spiritual Songs," from Various Authors, for the Use of Social Prayer Meetings, and Revivals of Religion. Harrisburg, Pa.: J. & M. W. M'Kinley, 1825.

.... The Truth Made Known; or, A Fair and Correct Account of Facts, which Have Transpired in the German Reformed Congregation of Harrisburg, since the Fall of 1822. Harrisburg, Pa.: Michael W. McKinley, 1824.

Wright, Louis B. The Cultural Life of the American Colonies. New York: Harper and Row Torchbook, 1962.

Yahn, S. G. History of the Churches of God. Harrisburg, Pa.: Central Publishing House, 1926.

Young, James Harvey. The Toadstool Millionaires. Princeton, N. J.: Princeton University Press, 1961.

Articles

"Adelphus." Letter to Winebrenner, Church Advocate (Harrisburg, Pa.) March 15, 1848.

Barnhart, S. Letter to the Editor, Church Advocate (Harrisburg, Pa.), August 1, 1849.

Bell, Whitfield J., Jr. "Thomas Cooper as Professor of Chemistry at Dickinson College, 1811-1815," Journal of the History of Medicine, and Allied Sciences, VIII (n.d.), 70-87. (Reprint.)

Bistline, Randall. "John Winebrenner and the Temperance Movement," Church Advocate (Harrisburg, Pa.) November, 1968.

Blanchard, Jonathan. Letter to the Editor, Gospel Publisher (Harrisburg, Pa.), December 2, 1837.

.... Report, Emancipator (New York), January 26, 1837.

Booser, James H. "A Youth Advancing—John Winebrenner," Church Advocate (Harrisburg, Pa.), March, 1968, 32-33.

Colder, James. "Abusive Language," Church Advocate (Harrisburg, Pa.), June 15, 1854.

.... "The General Eldership on Slavery," Church Advocate (Harrisburg, Pa.), June 11, 1857.

.... "A Hope That Will Be Realized," Church Advocate (Harrisburg, Pa.), December 17, 1857.

.... "Should Slave-Holders Be Received Into Church Fellowship?," Church Advocate (Harrisburg, Pa.), May 27, 1858.

.... "The Slavery Question," Church Advocate (Harrisburg, Pa.), June 18, 1857.

"Dr Beecher and Mr Beman's Convention on Revivals," The Christian Examiner and Theological Review, IV (July and August, 1827), 357–370.

Fasig, Samuel. Letter to the Editor, Church Advocate (Harrisburg, Pa.), October 15, 1853.

.... Letter to the Editor, Church Advocate (Harrisburg, Pa.), November 24, 1853.

Flake, Jacob. "The World in 1846—War," Church Advocate (Harrisburg, Pa.) December 15, 1846.

.... "Transitions of the Church," Church Advocate (Lancaster, Pa.) April 18, 1867.

"A Friend to the German Reformed Church." Letter to the Editor, Weekly Messenger (Chambersburg, Pa.), August 2, 1843.

"A Friend to Truth." Letter to the Editor, Gospel Publisher (Shiremanstown, Pa.), October 18, 1843.

Harn, G. U. Letter to the Editor, Church Advocate (Harrisburg, Pa.), November 15, 1850.

.... "Politics, Religion and Slavery," Church Advocate (Harrisburg, Pa.), December 30, 1858.

.... "Politics, Religion and Slavery," Church Advocate (Lancaster, Pa.), December 8, 1859.

.... "Visit to the General Conference," Church Advocate (Harrisburg, Pa.), October 15, 1850.

Harrisburg Anti-Slavery Society. Constitution and "Declaration of Sentiments," Gospel Publisher (Harrisburg, Pa.), January 29, 1836.

Hickernell, John. Letter to the Editor, Church Advocate (Harrisburg, Pa.), December 15, 1846.

"John Winebrenner," Harrisburg Daily Topic (Harrisburg, Pa.), June 30, 1870.

Kerr, John W. Letter to the Editor, Church Advocate (Harrisburg, Pa.), February 4, 1854.

.... Letter to the Editor, Church Advocate (Harrisburg, Pa.), April 8, 1854.

Loveland, William. Letter to the Editor, Church Advocate (Harrisburg, Pa.), June 19, 1852.

"L. S." Letter to the Editor, Weekly Messenger (Chambersburg, Pa.), November 15, 1843.

McCartney, George. "Legal Murder," Gospel Publisher (Harrisburg, Pa.), March 27, 1844.

Mackey, James. Letter to the Editor, Gospel Publisher (Harrisburg, Pa.), February 8, 1838.

.... "Sermon on Patriotism," Church Advocate (Harrisburg, Pa.), February 15, 1847.

Markley, Daniel. Letter to the Editor, Church Advocate (Harrisburg, Pa.), September 4, 1872.

Marple, Enoch. Letter to the Editor, Church Advocate (Harrisburg, Pa.), May 21, 1857.

Mead, Sidney. "Denominationalism," Church History, XXIII (December, 1954), 291–320.

Myers, J. Letter to the Editor, Church Advocate (Harrisburg, Pa.), August 21, 1872.

Nevin, John Williamson. "The Classis of Mercersburg," Mercersburg Review, I (1849), 385-386.

.... "The Heidelberg Catechism," Weekly Messenger (Chambersburg, Pa.), August 10, 1842.

.... "Historical Development," Mercersburg Review, I (September, 1849), 514.

.... Introduction to "Winebrenner's Vindication," Weekly Messenger (Chambersburg, Pa.), July 12, 1843.

.... "Letter 2," Gospel Publisher (Shiremanstown, Pa.), October 18, 1843.

.... "Letter 4," Gospel Publisher (Shiremanstown, Pa.), November 1, 1843.

.... "Letter 7," Gospel Publisher (Shiremanstown, Pa.), November 15, 1843.

.... "Letter 9," Gospel Publisher (Shiremanstown, Pa.), November 29, 1843.

.... "The Sect System," Mercersburg Review, I (September and November, 1849), 482-507, 521-539.

.... "Winebrenner Again," Weekly Messenger (Chambersburg, Pa.), September 13, 1843.

Ober, Benjamin. Letter to the Editor, Church Advocate (Harrisburg, Pa.), May 21, 1857.

.... Letter to the Editor, Church Advocate (Harrisburg, Pa.), August 20, 1857.

.... Letter to the Editor, Church Advocate (Harrisburg, Pa.), October 22, 1857.

.... Letter to the Editor, Church Advocate (Harrisburg, Pa.), April 10, 1901.

"Republican." Letter to the Editor, Church Advocate (Harrisburg, Pa.), February 22, 1855.

"Resignation of Professor Nevin," New York Observer, quoted in Church Advocate (Harrisburg, Pa.), November 15, 1851.

Rockafellow, D. R. Letter to the Editor, Church Advocate (Mt. Joy, Pa.), April 7, 1859.

Scherich, Henry. Letter to the Editor, Church Advocate (Harrisburg, Pa.), January 1, 1847.

Slyter, A. B. Letter to the Editor, Church Advocate (Harrisburg, Pa.), September 16, 1858.

"The Winebrennerians," New York Standard (New York), June 29, 1870.

Thome, James A. "Come-outism and Come-outers," Oberlin Quarterly Review, II (1856), 158-187.

Weishampel, J. F., Jr. Letter to the Editor, Church Advocate (Harrisburg, Pa.), October 22, 1853.

.... "The World's Temperance Convention," Church Advocate (Harrisburg, Pa.), September 17, 1853.

Weishampel, J. F., [Sr.]. Editorial Comment on Winebrenner-Nevin correspondence, Gospel Publisher (Shiremanstown, Pa.), August 9, 1843.

.... Editorial comment on Winebrenner-Nevin correspondence, Gospel Publisher (Shiremanstown, Pa.), October 11, 1843.

.... "Elihu Burrit's Abolition Scheme," Church Advocate (Harrisburg, Pa.), July 3, 1856.

Williams, A. D. "The Church of God," Church Advocate (Harrisburg, Pa.), March 1, 1849.

.... Letter to the Editor, Church Advocate (Harrisburg, Pa.), December 2, 1850.

.... "Moral and Legal Suasion," Church Advocate (Harrisburg, Pa.), June 15, 1850.

Winebrenner, John. "The Battle of Buena Vista," Church Advocate (Harrisburg, Pa.), April 15, 1847.

.... "Brother H. B.'s Second Letter," Church Advocate (Harrisburg, Pa.), July 1, 1848.

.... "Constitution of the Academy of Homoeopathic Medicine," Gospel Publisher (Harrisburg, Pa.), January 20, 1837.

.... Editorial comment on "Emigration to Liberia," Gospel Publisher (Harrisburg, Pa.), October 16, 1835.

.... Editorial comment on "Immediate Abolition," Gospel Publisher (Harrisburg, Pa.), October 30, 1835.

.... Editorial comment on resolutions passed by Congregational Association of Central Ohio, Gospel Publisher (Harrisburg, Pa.), January 31, 1840.

.... Editorial footnote to "Historical Letters No. 1," Church Advocate (Harrisburg, Pa.), February 1, 1849.

.... "Fourth of July," Church Advocate (Harrisburg, Pa.), July 15, 1847.

.... "The Greene County Church," Church Advocate (Harrisburg, Pa.), May 15, 1849.

.... "Lecture of H. W. Beecher," Church Advocate (Harrisburg, Pa.), April 2, 1857.

.... Letter to the Editor, Gospel Publisher (Shiremanstown, Pa.), October 11, 1843.

.... Letter to the Editor, Church Advocate (Lancaster, Pa.), March 8, 1860.

.... Letter to the Editors of the Weekly Messenger, Gospel Publisher (Shiremanstown, Pa.), December 6, 1843.

.... "Letter 1," Gospel Publisher (Shiremanstown, Pa.), October 18, 1843.

.... "Letter 3," Gospel Publisher (Shiremanstown, Pa.), November 1, 1843.

.... "Letter 5," Gospel Publisher (Shiremanstown, Pa.), November 15, 1843.

.... "Letter 6," Gospel Publisher (Shiremanstown, Pa.), November 15, 1843.

.... "Letter 8," Gospel Publisher (Shiremanstown, Pa.), November 29, 1843.

.... [Letter 10], Gospel Publisher (Shiremanstown, Pa.), December 6, 1843.

.... "Massachusetts, a Pattern State," Church Advocate (Harrisburg, Pa.), January 15, 1849.

.... "Nevin on the Sect Spirit," Church Advocate (Harrisburg, Pa.), October 15, 1849.

.... "News from Mexico," Church Advocate (Harrisburg, Pa.), June 15, 1846.

.... "Our Position on Slavery Re-Defined," Church Advocate (Harrisburg, Pa.), January 1, 1851.

.... "Peace Congress," Church Advocate (Harrisburg, Pa.), November 15, 1848.

.... "Position of the Eldership on the Subject of Slavery," Church Advocate (Harrisburg, Pa.), December 2, 1850.

.... "Prof. Nevin's Sermon on the Name Christian," Church Advocate (Harrisburg, Pa.), April 1, 1850.

.... "Questions and Answers," Church Advocate (Harrisburg, Pa.), December 27, 1855.

.... "Resignation of Professor Nevin," quoted in Church Advocate (Harrisburg, Pa.), November 15, 1851.

.... "The Slavery Question," Church Advocate (Harrisburg, Pa.), June 5, 1856.

.... "Smoking," Gospel Publisher (Harrisburg, Pa.), June 5, 1835.

.... "Spirit of Anti-Abolitionism," Gospel Publisher (Harrisburg, Pa.), April 19, 1838.

.... "Spontaneous Combustion of a Drunkard," Church Advocate (Harrisburg, Pa.), September 3, 1853.

.... "Terms of Church-membership," Church Advocate (Harrisburg, Pa.), June 2, 1851.

.... "Uncle Tom's Key," Church Advocate (Harrisburg, Pa.), June 18, 1853.

.... "Vindication of the Church or Review of Letters on Sectarianism— No. 8," Church Advocate (Harrisburg, Pa.), September 15, 1848.

.... "Vindication of the Church, etc.," Church Advocate (Harrisburg, Pa.), October 16, 1848.

Winebrenner, John et. al. "Anti-abolition Convention," Gospel Publisher (Harrisburg, Pa.), June 2, 1837.

Wright, James M. "The Free Negro in Maryland, 1634-1860," Studies in History, Economics and Public Law, XCVII (New York: Columbia University, 1921), 85 ff.

Newspapers and Periodicals

Chronicle. Harrisburg, Pa. 1820-1840.

Church Advocate. Harrisburg, Mt. Joy, and Lancaster, Pa. 1846-1968.

Emancipator. New York. 1836-1838. Microfilm at State Historical Society of Wisconsin.

Gospel Publisher. Harrisburg and Shiremanstown, Pa. 1835-1845.

Monthly Preacher. Baltimore: John F. Weishampel, Jr., 1859.

Oracle of Dauphin County. Harrisburg, Pa. 1819-1825.

Pennsylvania Intelligencer. Harrisburg, Pa. 1820-1831.

United States Magazine and Democratic Review. Washington, D. C.: Langtree and O'Sullivan, 1839.

Weekly Messenger. Chambersburg, Pa. 1842-1843.

Church Minutes

Auszuege aus den Verhandlungen der Lebanon Classis, 1820-1840. Library, Lancaster Theological Seminary. (Typewritten.)

Verhandlungen der General-Synode der Hochdeutschen Reformirten Kirche in den Vereinigten Staaten von Nord-Amerika, Gehalten in Hagersstadt, Maryland, September, 1820. Hagersstadt: Johann Gruber, 1820.

Verhandlungen der General Synode der Hochdeutschen Reformirten Kirche in den Vereinigten Staaten von Nord-Amerika Gehalten zu Harrisburg, vom 30sten Sept. bis zum 4ten Oct. 1822. n.p., n.d. Library, Lancaster Theological Seminary.

Verhandlungen der Synode der Hochdeutsch Reformirten Kirche in den Vereinigten Staaten von Nord-Amerika, Gehalten zu Baltimore vom 29st September bis zum 4ten October, A. D. 1823. Easton: Heinrich Held, 1824.

Verhandlungen der Allgemeinen Synode der Hochdeutschen Reformirten Kirche in den Vereinigten Staaten von Nord-Amerika Gehalten zu Bedford, in Pennsylvanien, vom 26sten September zu dem 1sten October 1824. Baltimore: J. I. Hanzche, 1824.

Synodical Proceedings of the German Reformed Church in the United States of North America, Held at Philadelphia from the 25th to the 30th September, 1825—Translated from the German. Philadelphia: John George Ritter, 1825.

Synodal-Verhandlungen der Hochdeutschen Reformirten Kirche in den Vereinigten Staaten von Nord-Amerika Gehalten in Friedrich City, vom 23sten bis zum 29sten September, A. D. 1826. Philadelphia: Conrad Zentler, 1827.

The Proceedings of the Synod of the German Reformed Church in North America at York, Pa., September, 1827. Hagerstown: Gruber and May, 1828.

Acts and Proceedings of the Synod of the German Reformed Church of the United States of North America, Held at Mifflinburg, Union County, Pennsylvania, September, 1828. Chambersburg, Pa.: Henry Ruby, 1828.

Journal of the First General Eldership of the "Church of God," in North America; Held at Pittsburg, Penn'a, from the 26th to the 30th of May, A. D., 1845. Harrisburg, Pa.: Hickok and Cantine, 1845.

Journal of the Sixteenth Annual Eldership of the "Church of God," in East Pennsylvania [November, 1845]. Church Advocate (Harrisburg, Pa.), December 12, 1845.

Journal of the First Annual Eldership of the "Church of God" in the State of Indiana [November, 1846]. Church Advocate (Harrisburg, Pa.), January 1, 1847.

Journal of the First Eldership of the Church of God in Michigan [March, 1850]. Church Advocate (Harrisburg, Pa.), April 15, 1850.

Journal of the Twenty-first East Penn'a. Eldership [October, 1850]. Church Advocate (Harrisburg, Pa.), November 1, 1850.

West Pennsylvania Eldership of the Church of God, Standing Committee Report [March 4, 1854]. Church Advocate (Harrisburg, Pa.), March 11, 1854.

Journal of the Fourth General Eldership of the "Church of God" in North America [May-June, 1854]. Church Advocate (Harrisburg, Pa.), June 15, 1854.

Journal of the 25th East Penn'a, Eldership of the Church of God [October, 1854]. Church Advocate (Harrisburg, Pa.), November 9 and 16, 1854.

Journal of the 26th East Penn'a Eldership of the Church of God [November, 1855]. Church Advocate (Harrisburg, Pa.), November 22 and 29, 1855.

Journal of the Fifth General Eldership of the Church of God in North America [June, 1857]. Church Advocate (Harrisburg, Pa.), June 11, 1857.

Journal of the Fifteenth Annual Eldership of the Church of God in West Pennsylvania [October, 1857]. Church Advocate (Harrisburg, Pa.), December 3, 1857.

Journal of the Twenty-eighth Annual Meeting of the East Pennsylvania Eldership [November, 1857]. Church Advocate (Harrisburg, Pa.), November 26, 1857.

Journal of the Second Annual Meeting of the West Ohio Eldership [September, 1858]. Church Advocate (Harrisburg, Pa.), October 7, 1858.

Journal of the Twenty-Second Annual Meeting of the East Ohio Eldership [October, 1858]. Church Advocate (Harrisburg, Pa.), October 21, 1858.

Journal of the 29th Annual Meeting of the East Pa. Eldership of the Church of God November, [1858]. Church Advocate (Harrisburg, Pa.), November 25, 1858.

Journal of the Sixth Annual Meeting of the Illinois Eldership [November, 1858]. Church Advocate (Harrisburg, Pa.), December 2, 1858.

Journal of the Sixth Triennial Meeting of the General Eldership of the Church of God in North America [May, 1860]. Church Advocate (Lancaster, Pa.), June 21, 1860.

Unpublished Material

Christman, Emma. Letter to S. G. Yahn, March 30, 1925. Library, Winebrenner Theological Seminary.

.... Biographical information relating to John Winebrenner prepared for centennial anniversary of Winebrenner's birth at Harrisburg Church of God in 1897. Library, Winebrenner Theological Seminary.

Ebaugh, J. S. Letter to John Winebrenner, November 26, 1824. Library, Winebrenner Theological Seminary.

Elliott, John. Letter to John Winebrenner, January 14, 1823. Library, Winebrenner Theological Seminary.

Frederick County, Maryland. G. M. E. Liber, 2, Folio 649. Courthouse.

Frederick County, Maryland. J. S. Liber 29, 359-360. Courthouse.

Fritchey, J. G. Letter to John Winebrenner, July 19, 1826. Library, Winebrenner Theological Seminary.

Gibbony, Arthur G. Winebrenner Genealogy. October, 1942. Library, Winebrenner Theological Seminary. (Mimeographed.)

Harrisburg Church of God. Church Record, May 9, 1826. Library, Winebrenner Theological Seminary.

Harrisburg Reformed Church Congregation. Petition to retain John Winebrenner as pastor, late 1823-early 1824. Library, Winebrenner Theological Seminary.

Harrisburg Reformed Church Vestry. Letter to 1820 Synod of the German
Reformed Church at Hagerstown, Maryland, [September] 1820. Library, Lancaster Theological Seminary.

Harrisburg Reformed Church Vestry and Helffenstein, Samuel, Sr. Endorsement letter to churches, December 10 and December 23, 1821.
Library, Winebrenner Theological Seminary.

Helffenstein, J[acob]. Letter to John Winebrenner, August 29, 1823.
Library, Winebrenner Theological Seminary.

Helffenstein, Samuel. Letter to John Winebrenner, April 30, 1823. Library, Winebrenner Theological Seminary.

Helffenstein, Samuel, Jr. Letter to John Winebrenner, September 5, 1822.
Library, Winebrenner Theological Seminary.

Huber, Frederick. Letter to John Winebrenner, November 26, 1825. Library, Winebrenner Theological Seminary.

Keller, Philip, et al. Letter to John Winebrenner, January 10, 1826. Library, Winebrenner Theological Seminary.

Mayer, Lewis. Letter to James R. Reily, December, 1825. Library,
Lancaster Theological Seminary.

.... Letter to John Winebrenner, December 3, 1824. Library, Winebrenner Theological Seminary.

Merkel, Levi. A Memorandum of Levi Merkel of Allen Township. Contained in "Levi Merkel Family Papers, 1818-1912." Pennsylvania
Historical and Museum Commission, Harrisburg, Pa.

Original Church Record—Mechanicsburg Church of God. Library, Winebrenner Theological Seminary.

Race Street German Reformed Church, Philadelphia. Church Record (Helffenstein family births). Historical Society of Pennsylvania, Philadelphia.

Reily, James R. Letter to John Winebrenner, March 21, 1825. Library,
Winebrenner Theological Seminary.

Schaeffer, Charles E. The Helffenstein Family. 1955. Library, Lancaster
Theological Seminary. (Typewritten.)

Shartle, Jonas. Letter to John Winebrenner, April 21, 1823. Library,
Winebrenner Theological Seminary.

Thomas, E. H. Letter to John Winebrenner, December 21, 1857. Library,
Winebrenner Theological Seminary.

Winebrenner, John. German Copy Book. 1817-1820. Library, Winebrenner
Theological Seminary.

.... Journal, October 8-31, 1822. Library, Winebrenner Theological
Seminary.

.... Journal, January 1-18, 1826. Library, Winebrenner Theological
Seminary.

.... Letter to Hagerstown Reformed Church Consistory, April 18,
1825. Library, Winebrenner Theological Seminary.

.... Letter to Hagerstown Reformed Church correspondence committee, April 27, 1826. Library, Winebrenner Theological Seminary.
(Transcript.)

.... Letter to Benjamin Ober, August 23, 1857. Library, Winebrenner Theological Seminary.

.... Letter to James R. Reily, March 18, 1826. Historical Society of Pennsylvania, Philadelphia.

.... Letter to unknown, March 26, 1849. Library, Winebrenner Theological Seminary.

.... Letter to Mary H. Winebrenner, June 1, 1841. Library, Winebrenner Theological Seminary.

.... Letter to Mary H. Winebrenner, February 16, 1846. Library, Winebrenner Theological Seminary.

.... Letter to Mrs. Mary Winebrenner, September 8, 1853. Library, Winebrenner Theological Seminary.

.... Letter to Mrs. M. H. Winebrenner, June 20, 1854. Library, Winebrenner Theological Seminary.

.... Letter to Mrs. M. H. Winebrenner, August 27, 1858. Library, Winebrenner Theological Seminary.

.... Letter to Mrs. M. H. Winebrenner. September 2, 1858. Library, Winebrenner Theological Seminary.

.... Letter to Mrs. M. H. Winebrenner, October 19, 1858. Library, Winebrenner Theological Seminary.

.... Letter to Philip Winebrenner, May 23, 1834. Library, Winebrenner Theological Seminary.

.... Letter to Philip Winebrenner, April 4, 1835. Library, Winebrenner Theological Seminary.

.... Letter to Philip Winebrenner, November 18, 1835. Library, Winebrenner Theological Seminary.

.... Letter to Philip Winebrenner, February 4, 1839. Library, Winebrenner Theological Seminary.

.... Manuscript Sermons in German. 1817-1820. Library, Winebrenner Theological Seminary.